REBELS WITH A CAUSE

The Failure of the Left in Iran

Maziar Behrooz

I.B.TAURIS
LONDON · NEW YORK · OXFORD · NEW DELHI · SYDNEY

To the memory of

Bizhan Jazani

(1937–75)

I.B. TAURIS

Bloomsbury Publishing Plc

50 Bedford Square, London, WC1B 3DP, UK

1385 Broadway, New York, NY 10018, USA

29 Earlsfort Terrace, Dublin 2, Ireland

BLOOMSBURY, I.B. TAURIS and the I.B. Tauris logo

are trademarks of Bloomsbury Publishing Plc

First published in Great Britain 2000

This paperback edition published 2024

Copyright © Maziar Behrooz, 1999, 2000

Maziar Behrooz has asserted their right under the Copyright,

Designs and Patents Act, 1988, to be identified as Author of this work.

For legal purposes the Acknowledgements on p. ix constitute

an extension of this copyright page.

All rights reserved. No part of this publication may be reproduced or

transmitted in any form or by any means, electronic or mechanical,

including photocopying, recording, or any information storage or retrieval

system, without prior permission in writing from the publishers.

Bloomsbury Publishing Plc does not have any control over, or responsibility for,

any third-party websites referred to or in this book. All internet addresses given

in this book were correct at the time of going to press. The author and publisher

regret any inconvenience caused if addresses have changed or sites have

ceased to exist, but can accept no responsibility for any such changes.

A catalogue record for this book is available from the British Library.

A catalog record for this book is available from the Library of Congress.

ISBN: HB: 978-1-8606-4381-1
PB: 978-0-7556-5201-3
ePDF: 978-0-7556-1604-6
eBook: 978-0-7556-1209-3

Typeset in Palatino by Dexter Haven, London

To find out more about our authors and books visit

www.bloomsbury.com and sign up for our newsletters.

CONTENTS

List of Illustrations	*iv*
Preface to the Second Edition	*v*
Preface	*vii*
Acknowledgements	*ix*
Introduction	*xi*
1 DEFEAT AND REVIVAL: THE GREAT DEFEAT OF THE LEFT (1953–70)	1
The Communist Tudeh in the 1950s	3
The Communist Tudeh and Factionalism	16
The Communist Tudeh and the Soviet Union	22
The Azarbaijan Democratic Party: the Other Communists	26
The Third Force: Khalil Maliki and the Independent Leftists	31
Transition and Revival: the Third World Call (1960–70)	34
The Communist Tudeh in a Decade of Transition	37
Marxist Cells: the Move to Violence	43
2 OFFENSIVE AND STALEMATE (1971–9): VIOLENCE AND SUPPRESSION	48
The Fadaiyan Guerillas	51
The Mojahedin (Marxist-Leninist): the Birth of the Paykar	70
The Tudeh and Communist Splinter Groups	74
Marxist Cells Abroad	91
3 REVOLUTION: THE DANCE OF DEATH (1979–83)	95
Revolution	95
The Fadaiyan and Revolution	105
The Paykar and Revolution	121
The Tudeh and Revolution	124
Kurdish Groups and Revolution	130
The Marginal Marxists and Revolution	132
4 WHY THE FAILURE?	135
Communists and General Factors of Failure	136
Communists and Particular Factors of Failure	144
Communists and Structural Factors of Failure	147
Appendix: Chronology of Events (1941–83)	*167*
Notes on the Text	*185*
Bibliography	*217*
Index	*233*

LIST OF ILLUSTRATIONS

1 Bizhan Jazani (1937–75): major Marxist theorist and Fadaiyan founder, assassinated in prison.

2 Hamid Ashraf (1946–76): founder of Fadaiyan and a main organiser of guerilla activity in the 1970s, killed in shootout with police.

3 Mas'ud Ahmadzadeh-Heravi (1947–72): founder and theorist of Fadaiyan, executed.

4 Amir Parviz Puyan (1947–71): founder and theorist of Fadaiyan, killed in shootout with police.

5 Khosrow Roozbeh (1915–58): leading member of Tudeh Party's Military and Intelligence Organisation, executed.

6 Mostafa Shoa'ian (1936–75): independent Marxist theorist and guerilla, killed in shootout with police.

7 Nur al-Din Kianuri (b 1915): a leading member of the Tudeh Party and its former first secretary (1979–83).

8 Bizhan Jazani's painting 'Siyahkal' was produced while he was in prison. What the painting lacks in artistry it makes up in zeal.

PREFACE TO THE SECOND EDITION

Since the publication of the hardcover edition of this book, Iran's political dynamics have changed rapidly. With a new parliament elected in spring 2000, the reform movement among Islamists in Iran has been given a new lease of life likely to lead to more open political space and room for participation. This development is creating the possibility, even the probability, of secular-leftist politics once again finding the opportunity to express themselves openly at some point in the future. Yet, political developments in Iran since 1997 show that secularist forces in general, and the secular left in particular, have played a marginal role in the on-going developments. Most of the 'organised' Iranian Marxist groups, all of them living in exile and none of them with any apparent popular base inside the country, boycotted both the May 1997 presidential election and the 2000 parliamentary election, this at a time when an overwhelming majority of Iranian voters participated in both elections and pushed forward the movement for reform in Iran. The left's apparent failure to comprehend the political dynamics of Iran bolsters the perspective provided in this book that the organised Marxist left persists in its failure to recognise the realities of the very society it intends to change. The root cause of this failure remains an outdated, dogmatic and ideological world view tied, for so long, to the Bolshevik experience of the Russian Revolution. The organised left's apparent irrelevance in early twenty-first century Iran makes it more important than ever to understand the movement's past performance and to appreciate the dilemmas it faces in a post-Cold War world where ideological role models no longer exist.

It must be added, however, that some former Marxist activists, almost all acting individually, have woken up to the realities of a different age. Many, both in Iran and abroad, have shed their ideological skin, have come to terms with the new post-Soviet world, and seem to have accepted the failure of the Bolshevik experience. It is from among this group, if at all, that any future secular-leftist movement will arise in Iran.

Maziar Behrooz

PREFACE

The Persian term 'chap', meaning left, has had a dual use in Iran's political culture. First, it has been broadly used to refer to any group with a tendency to Marxism. These groups cover a broad political range, from the Social Democrats who participated in the Constitutional Revolution of 1905–9 to left-wing democrats of later years. It would also include left-wing religious parties (eg the People's Mojahedin Organisation) which freely borrowed from Marxism in order to modernise and bring up to date its own notion of revolutionary Islam. Second, and more precisely, it has been more commonly used to refer to the Marxist-Leninist, or communist, groups which advocated the violent revolutionary overthrow of the socio-political establishment, and its replacement with a socialist state on the Soviet, or other, model. The use of the term 'left' in the subtitle of this book is meant to convey the second notion, not either to neglect the first or inaccurately mix the two.

As a history of the left in Iran, this work covers the activities of the communist movement from 1941, when the movement re-established itself following the collapse of Reza Shah's authoritarian regime, to 1983, when the last communist organisation was dismantled by the Islamic regime. As such, this is a study of an important, complex and volatile period in Iranian history, with often contradictory trends of thought competing to define and put into practice their visions of progress and justice. In this venture, Iranian communists (those I also refer to as Marxists throughout the book) played a significant role. This book, therefore, is an attempt to document, analyse and sum up the history of this movement as Iran prepares itself to meet the challenges of the twenty-first century. One of the book's main conclusions is that after its shattering defeat in the 1980s and the collapse of the Soviet system as model, the meaning of the left, in its second definition, is rapidly changing, and coming to mean something more like social democracy. At the same time, the meaning of Marxism is changing worldwide, and this is inevitably influencing perceptions of social democracy. On the threshold of a new century, as the world moves to find a new, perhaps more flexible, definition for what it is to be on the left, Iran seems to be moving in the same direction.

This book covers the history of three generations of Iranian Marxists. In a cultural environment such as Iran's, where thoughts and political beliefs are deemed in absolute terms, where accepting mistakes and shortcomings is difficult, and where historical memory is short, it is hard, if not impossible, to produce a historical work of this scale and expect, even in a very general way, to satisfy those passionate about the subject, particularly those who participated in the events. But then perhaps the historian should put in perspective the judgements of passionate participants of any period when dealing with the past, and hope for the best. It will not be surprising if this work is unsatisfactory to many. It is a humble attempt to reconstruct the history of three generation of Iranians who were, in one way or another, associated with Marxism in Iran, and who were indeed rebels with a cause. It is directed at the future, the new century, and the new generation of Iranians who have not seen the past but so desperately need to know about it in order to be able to meet the challenges of the future.

Maziar Behrooz,
Spring 1999,
San Francisco

ACKNOWLEDGEMENTS

One's work rarely seems to be the result of one person's labour alone. Added to this is the old tradition of giving recognition to those who have contributed to the work. In this case there are a number of people who I need to thank. My gratitude goes to Professor Nikki R. Keddie, who supervised the original draft of this book when it was in the form of a dissertation, to Professor Ervand Abrahamian for his comments and insight, to Dr Afshin Matin-asgari for his comments on the final chapter, and to the anonymous reader appointed by I.B. Tauris for her or his insight; to Roshanak for editing the entire manuscript and to Layli Arbab-shirani for editing parts of it; to a promising photo-journalist and former student, Frederico 'Pico' van Houtryve, for helping me with the book photo; to Robert Hastings for his copy editing of the manuscript.

I should thank my parents, Sara and Jahangir, and my brother Karan for their lifetime investment, support and belief in me. They have my eternal gratitude. My thanks go also to my many friends in Tehran, London, Los Angeles and Berkeley whose names would take a few pages but without whose friendship I could not have reached this point. Needless to say, the shortcomings in this work are my responsibility alone.

INTRODUCTION

The history of communism in Iran has two inter-related dimensions which make its study an important venture. First, as part of the international communist movement, Iranian Marxists struggled to bring about a new world order in one of the most important geo-political regions of the world. In this context, communism in Iran has been affected and given new directions by such important global events as revolutions – especially the October revolution in Russia – liberation movements and the Cold War. Second, as part of twentieth-century Iranian history, Iranian communism has played a notable, sometimes determining, role in the country's history. Indeed, while Iranian Marxists ultimately failed to secure state power or survive as a viable force, they have left their mark on every major event in the twentieth century history of Iran. This is to suggest that while Iranian Marxists ultimately failed politically, they succeeded in bringing many new ideas to the social arena and even into the Islamic movement.

During the twentieth century, Iran has witnessed a competition for political power among three socio-political trends. Religion, nationalism and communism have struggled against the state and competed against each other in order to provide direction to the nation by defining such issues as progress, modernisation, westernisation, social justice, national independence and people's sovereignty. Each has presented its own solution, but only two, religious forces and nationalists, have had the opportunity to control the state, and therefore, to attempt to realise their ideal. Thus, among the three, Iranian Marxists were the most repressed, and overall had the smallest popular base.

Nationalists, both enlightened individuals and parties affiliated with the land-owning classes and bourgeoisie, have at times controlled the state. Some, who wholeheartedly participated in the

Constitutional Revolution of 1906 and the civil war that followed, saw in the regime of Reza Shah Pahlavi (1926–41) a chance to bring about many of those changes which they sought when in opposition to the Qajar court. In this context, personalities such as Hasan Taqizadeh and Ali Akbar Davar joined the new regime in order to reform the system from within. Many others, however, remained in opposition to Reza Shah, and chose exclusion over collaboration with a regime they saw as lacking national independence. Dr Mohammad Mosaddeq, prime minister 1951–53, was among the former. The Oil Nationalisation Movement under Mosaddeq's leadership was the manifestation of this group's political aspirations.

The religious forces, led mostly by the clergy, have always been present on Iran's twentieth-century political scene. During the Constitutional Revolution the clergy was divided between those who opposed the revolution, favouring a shari'a-based monarchy, and those who favoured supporting a more secular constitution. In the 1920s, led by Ayatollah Hasan Modarres, some religious forces opposed Reza Shah and his reforms. In the 1940s and early 1950s, a minority of religious forces under Ayatollah Abol Qasem Kashani and the Islamic Fadaiyan, and again in the 1960s, mostly under Ayatollah Khomeini and the Liberation Movement, proved to be a serious political force. Since 1979 religious activists have been in charge of the state, creating the Islamic Republic of Iran.

Iranian Marxists, always denied the luxury of state power by adversaries who often proved both brutal and effective in containing the communist movement, have been active in Iran's socio-political arena since the Constitutional Revolution of 1906. The term 'communism' is used in this study to refer to all those who advocated Marxism and the creation of a socialist state, based on the Third Communist International (Comintern) model, by violent means if necessary. Highly affected by the experience of the Russian revolution of 1917, the Marxists in Iran created the Iranian Communist Party (ICP) in 1920, modeled on the Bolshevik Party. As a result, most Iranian Marxists rejected socialism based on the Second Socialist International – which advocated social democracy on a Western European model for working class organisation – opting instead for the October-Revolution mode, based on a professional revolutionary party. The spectre of Bolshevism would continue to play a determining role in Iranian Marxism from this point until the end of the 1980s.

The ICP was active in Iran's political upheaval throughout the 1920s, even as a junior partner to the Jangal movement in Gilan.[1] The movement produced such well-known Marxist personalities as

INTRODUCTION

Avetis Sultanzadeh, known for his theoretical contributions to the Comintern, and Haydar Khan Amuoghlu.[2] The ICP, however, was effectively suppressed by the emerging power of Reza Shah Pahlavi, which forced many of its cadres to seek refuge in the Soviet Union as Stalinist rule was taking root in that country. Such ICP members as Ja'far Pishehvari and Ardeshir Avanessian were arrested and put in jail, while others, such as Sultanzadeh, Abdol Hosein Hesabi and Morteza Alavi, perished during the Stalinist terror of the 1930s. The ICP, for all practical purposes, was removed as an effective political force after 1930. Some of its adherents, however, were to re-emerge and play a role in re-establishing the movement in the 1940s.

During the 1930s, the communist cause in Iran was picked up by a small intellectual group, led by Dr Taqi Arani, which came to be called the Group of Fifty Three. The Group was composed of educated intellectuals who had converted to Marxism, either while studying abroad or within Iran. In the early 1930s, the Group was more a study group gathered around Arani's journal *Donya*, which published mostly scientific and philosophical essays on current issues.[3]

The exact relations between the Group and the ICP are not clear at this point. The basic uncertainty is that the affiliation of the Group of Fifty Three has yet to be clarified. Was the Group an independent gathering of Marxist intellectuals, or was it affiliated with the Comintern, making it an extension of the ICP?[4] Furthermore, some historians have argued that the group was social democratic and not a pro-Soviet communist group, regardless of any Soviet connection.[5] Others, while accepting the notion that the group's Marxism was not similar to the Soviet (Stalinist) version, still argue that it was not social democratic.[6] What is clear, however, is that the group was in touch with some members of the ICP, notably Morteza Alavi, Abdol Samad Kambakhsh and Col. Ezatollah Siyamak. Alavi, as a student in Germany in the 1920s, had befriended Arani, and was already a member of the ICP when he moved to the Soviet Union, never to be heard from again.[7] Siyamak and Kambakhsh were among the very few communist activists who had managed to escape arrest in the 1920s and were active in the 1930s. As will be seen later, it is now clear that the group was exposed and its members arrested because of its contacts with the underground ICP cell, especially after the arrest of Kambakhsh in the mid-1930s. While Arani died during his imprisonment, the remnants of the group joined forces with activists from the ICP and other groups to form the Tudeh Party of Iran in 1941 after the collapse of Reza Shah's rule.

xiii

The Tudeh was the main political party associated with Marxism between 1941 and 1953. Soon after its establishment it became the largest and most effective political force in the country, until its up-rooting after the 1953 coup. It managed to establish a strong popular base among the working class, and was attractive to much of the young modern intelligentsia. The 1953 coup, among other things, dealt a crushing blow to communist activities in Iran. That the Tudeh met its demise without putting up much resistance became a major topic of discussion and polemics among a younger generation of Marxist activists who were getting ready to enter the scene in the late 1960s. The guerrilla groups of the late 1960s and early 1970s were both a way to confront the imperial regime of the Shah and the result of years of evaluation and experience in the political field. The main aim of the guerrilla groups was to secure state power by rallying the masses in a popular, armed revolution. In this, the movement failed as the 1979 revolution developed into a movement led by the Islamists. But, as a result of a period of armed struggle against the Shah's regime (1971–1979), and the ability of some guer-rilla groups to play a significant role in the final downfall of the imperial regime, the movement as a whole, and the guerrilla groups in particular, found prestige and popular support after the revolution. This development made the communist movement a force to be reckoned with during the two years after the 1979 revolution as the new Islamic leadership moved to neutralise the appeal of Marxism amid mounting social and political problems.

The popularity and prestige of the movement was not enough, however, for it to survive in the 1980s. Due to a number of factors, Marxism in Iran was decisively defeated by the mid-1980s. It should be noted, however, that the movement died before the age of Gorbachev's reforms in the Soviet Union, and therefore did not have much to do with the downfall of the USSR. This is important because Marxism in Iran was defeated not through ideological crisis engulfing international communism, but due to its inability to understand and cope with the internal dynamics of the 1979 revolution in Iran.

Since Iranian Marxists have never been able to gain power, and because due to the Iranian revolution of 1979 much attention has been devoted to the other two main political trends, communism in Iran remains an under-studied subject. What little attention it has received often concentrates on the period before and immediately after the 1953 coup.

There are three major studies of post-Second-World-War com-munism in Iran. Sepehr Zabih's work (based on his dissertation) on

INTRODUCTION

the history of the Tudeh Party of Iran is a good study of the subject. It is, however, limited to the Tudeh and one of its splinter-groups in the 1940s, and ends in the early 1960s. The study, however, does not include the memoirs and other material which have come to light since.[8] Ervand Abrahamian has written on the subject (also based on his dissertation) as part of a much larger work covering the history of Iran between the Constitutional revolution of 1906 and the 1979 revolution. Abrahamian's work is a good study of the Tudeh Party up to the 1953 coup and immediately after. It also includes sections on the guerrilla movement of the 1970s,[9] but does not cover the history of the movement after the revolution or newer material. Sepehr Zabih's second major work on communism in Iran is an attempt by the author to study major, non-Tudeh, trends in the movement, and is the latest study on the subject.[10] It was, however, conducted at a time when the author had been away from the subject for a long time, and thus reveals an incomplete grasp of the material and subject.

The scholarly neglect of the Iranian communist movement has left a void in the field of Iranian studies. A lack of comprehensive research of the subject, especially the role Marxists played in the period before the 1979 revolution and the circumstances that led to the movement's demise after it, has highlighted the need for a full study. This work intends to fill that void by covering the period from the 1953 coup (which led to the virtual demise of the Tudeh) to 1983, when the last legal communist organisations were banned. The study's goal is twofold: first, to document the history of communism in Iran during these 30 years, filling gaps left by the previous studies; and second, to provide an analysis of how and why the movement disintegrated in the 1980s. The first three chapters include careful documentation and analysis of the major players in the movement and their interaction with the state and the socio-political problems of the period. The minor players are briefly mentioned but not analysed in depth due to limitations of space.

The sources used in this study are divided into three categories, the first of which is publications and analyses provided by the major players themselves. Mostly in Persian, this category includes documents, the history of various communist organisations, journals and publications, and interviews with individual activists. The second is material and documents on the movement produced by those opposed to them, the third, secondary sources, including books on Iran's contemporary history and the history of communism written by other scholars.

xv

1

Defeat and Revival: the Great Defeat of the Left (1953–70)

> At the time I was arrested there were no remaining secrets. The Bahramis, Qoreishis... had told everything... The volume of the regime's information was truly ten times that of mine.
>
> Khosrow Roozbeh, Tudeh member, in his last defence in military court (1958)

19 August 1953 is a fateful day in Iranian history. On this date, the united front of the imperial court and its allies, the CIA and MI-6, managed to topple the Government of Dr Muhammad Mosaddeq, do away with Iran's constitutional processes and impose on the country what the opposition came to call the Shah's dictatorship, but what Shah Muhammad Reza Pahlavi's Government liked to call the imperial system (*nezam-e shahanshahi*).[1] From 1953 to the period 1960–3 (when the Shah was forced to lessen repression of the opposition and allow some political activity) the coup leaders were mostly engaged in consolidating power and suppressing opposition. The height of this process came in 1957 with the creation of the Shah's secret police, SAVAK (*Sazman-e Ettela'at va Amniyat-e Keshvar*) with the help of the CIA and Israel's MOSAD.[2] Internationally, the oil dispute with the British was settled in August

1954, and Iran came out the loser, despite the fact that the nationalised Anglo-Iranian Oil Company remained in Iranian hands. While Iran had nominal nationalisation, received a 50 percent share of the profits, and was to be in control of domestic oil distribution, it had no other say in how things should run on its own soil.[3] International sales remained in the hands of a consortium in which Britain had 40 percent of the shares, US companies had 40 percent, Dutch and French companies the rest. This was a sign of growing American power in Iran at the expense of the British.[4] As the Cold War intensified, Iran moved to the Western camp by officially joining the Baghdad Pact, later called CENTO, in 1955. As a result of this and the signing of a bilateral agreement with the United States in 1959, giving Iran military protection in the event of aggression, Iran's relations with the Soviet Union, its powerful northern neighbour, deteriorated. The Soviets failed to convince the Shah to strive for neutrality in the East-West rivalry. From 1959 until the Shah's implementation of his reform programme in 1963, Iran-Soviet relations remained hostile. The Soviet media started to bombard the Shah's regime with negative propaganda.

Little else changed in the country. Iran remained a basically backward pre-industrial society with the majority of the population in rural areas living their lives in illiteracy and ignorance. The Shah's Government was more concerned with getting military aid from the West, particularly the United States, than with initiating any kind of reform. The new deal with the international oil consortium, plus America's $1 billion in economic and military aid in the 1950s, put more money in the Government's hands. But the lack of any meaningful strategy for reform and widespread corruption failed to result in any long-term recovery. With the economic outlook grim, the Shah's political tactics only added fuel to the already strained social situation. Suppression of all independent political parties, rigged parliamentary elections, and incompetent cabinets were the order of the day in the 1950s. The *Majles* (parliament) elections showed that the Shah's main power-base, those who supported him in the 1953 coup, remained the land-owning class and a large segment of the commercial bourgeoisie which benefited from increased trade with the West. A combination of the above factors exacerbated the inability of the pre-industrial and agrarian infrastructure to cope with the new socio-economic problems, and culminated in growing political and social unrest in early 1960. As a result, the number of major strikes jumped from only three between 1955 and 1957 to over 20 between 1957 and 1961.[5] Hence, seven

2

years after the coup, while the Shah's regime enjoyed both international support and internal confidence, it was faced with a major social crisis. Perhaps the only difference this time, compared to the immediate pre-1953 period, was that the communist and nationalist opposition to the Shah was suppressed so completely that no nation-wide organisation existed which could take advantage of the political situation.

The very fact that AJAX (the name CIA chose for the 1953 coup) was victorious with minimal expenditure and not much resistance proves that forces loyal to the constitutional Government were not able to put up much of a struggle. Iranian communists were both the most significant and the most organised of the forces opposed to the coup.[6] The insignificance of communist resistance and the fact that the coup led to the decimation of communist networks throughout Iran and the loss of many lives reveals major shortcomings on their part. The effects of these shortcomings and the attempt to overcome them would haunt the movement for the next three decades.

In August 1953, the parties and organisations associated with Marxism consisted of two groups active inside Iran and one active as a party in exile. The two groups active inside Iran were the Tudeh Party of Iran (*hezb-e Tudeh-ye Iran*), founded in 1941, and a much smaller group of Marxists who had split from the Tudeh in 1948, known as the Third Force (*niru-ye sevvom*). The group active outside Iran was the remnant of the Azarbaijan Democratic Party (*ferqeh-ye demokrat-e Azarbaijan*) which had been crushed by the Government in 1946, but maintained a symbolic presence in Baku, capital city of Soviet Azarbaijan.

THE COMMUNIST TUDEH IN THE 1950s

During the period under study, the history of communism in Iran was synonymous with the Tudeh Party of Iran, the major Marxist party in the country. The Tudeh was established only a month after allied forces had put an end to Reza Shah Pahlavi's despotic rule. In the beginning, the party's constitution bore little resemblance that of parties which were members of the Comintern.[7] Therefore, while the Tudeh would depict itself as the rightful heir to the old Iranian Communist Party (1920–30) and the Group of Fifty-three (1930s), the facts suggest that initially the party was not founded as a communist party, that is with the ultimate goal of establishing a socialist state. Rather, it was created as a united front for anti-fascist activities and constitutional rule; indeed, the name Tudeh (mass) was a reflection of this. The secretary of the party for its first two years, Soleiman Mirza Eskandari, was a Qajar prince turned social democrat, who had sympathies for the Soviet Union but was certainly not a communist.

The fact that at the time of the party's establishment Iran was under allied occupation meant that the occupying powers could directly influence events. The Soviets, who occupied roughly the northern and central parts of Iran, influenced the founding of the Tudeh in line with their own global policies. These policies, until the end of World War II, were directed at maintaining the coalition with the United States and Britain, so bolstering the Soviet Union's war effort. In Iran, these policies meant the maintenance of the status quo in an anti-fascist coalition of all forces.[8] Hence, according to some accounts, the Soviets exerted influence on the Tudeh not to establish a communist party, but rather a more general democratic party including all social strata.[9] The extent of the Tudeh's Soviet links, which became a major characteristic of the party throughout its life, will be discussed later; at this point suffice it to say that the Soviets had an important role in founding and giving the Tudeh direction.

From 1941 to 1953, the Tudeh changed from a relatively inexperienced collection of intellectuals to a mass party and a political force taken seriously abroad.[10] The party successfully managed two crises that nearly destroyed it. First, in the aftermath of Soviet withdrawal from Iran in 1946, the Tudeh's ally, the Azarbaijan Democratic Party (ADP), was attacked by central government forces, and its autonomous government in Azarbaijan overthrown. The demise of the ADP was a disaster for the Tudeh not only because a close ally was removed from the political scene, but also because in 1945 the Tudeh network in Azarbaijan had been dissolved into the ADP and was now lost. Moreover, a dissident group split from the Tudeh in early 1948 and threatened to take a sizeable part of the party with it. These constituted the future Third Force, led by Khalil Maleki, whose departure, as it turned out, failed to attract many defectors. The second crisis came in 1949 in the aftermath of an attempt on the Shah's life, when the Tudeh was accused of complicity and declared illegal.[11] Many Tudeh leaders were arrested, and activities throughout the country came to a halt.

In spite of these pressures and setbacks, the party recuperated, arranged a jail-break to free its leaders, and reorganised itself on a semi-legal basis. Hence by 1951, when the oil nationalisation movement under the National Front acquired momentum, the Tudeh had become an experienced mass party (according to some, the only real party in Iran) based in urban areas and especially strong among the working class, experienced in underground and semi-legal activity, and with an extensive military organisation which had even penetrated the intelligence network of the army and could mobilise tens of thousands of people for mass demonstrations in Tehran. The party's performance among the working class was impressive. According to one analysis, 'The Tudeh was like an iceberg, with the party organisation corresponding to the visible tip, and the much larger labour movement to the hidden mass below'.[12] The party played a leadership role in the major trade union organisation, the Central Council of the United Trade Unions of Iranian Workers and Toilers (*shora-ye mottahed-e markazi-ye kargaran va zahmatkeshan-e Iran*), which had unionised some 75 percent of the industrial labour-force.[13] The party's popularity with the intellectual community was also impressive. Despite the departure of the Third Force, which had the support of many prominent intellectuals, the Tudeh was still supported by many writers, journalists and artists.[14] The party had also gained experience through participation in parliamentary processes, and even had, for a brief period, three ministers in Ahmad Qavam's cabinet in 1946.

The Tudeh reaction to the oil nationalisation movement, led by the National Front and Premier Mosaddeq, was at best contradictory, and the party's decisions were made with the interests of the Soviet Union in mind. The roots of the problem went back to the Second World War, when Iran was under allied occupation. In late 1943, the cabinet of Premier Sa'ed opened talks with British and American oil companies over a contract for the exploration of oil-fields in the south which were not being explored under existing terms. This was at a time when both the Tudeh and the nationalists had a minority presence in the fourteenth Majles. The negotiations were conducted secretly for a time, until they were exposed by a Majles member. Both the Tudeh members of the Majles and the nationalists attacked the idea of new concessions to foreigners.[15] But the situation changed drastically when in September 1944 a Soviet mission, headed by Sergei Kavtaradze,[16] arrived in Tehran and asked for negotiations on possible Soviet exploration of Iran's northern oil fields. The pro-British Sa'ed cabinet rejected the Soviet offer, prompting the Soviet mission to resort to threats.[17]

From this point until one year before the coup, the nationalists and the Tudeh went their separate ways on the oil question. The nationalists, under Mosaddeq, were against any concessions to the Soviets if Iran did not have full control over its resources. Furthermore, in 1944 Mosaddeq rushed a bill through the Majles prohibiting any ministry from discussing any issues related to the oil industry with foreigners without the full knowledge and participation of the Majles.[18] During the Majles discussions on the issue, Mosaddeq further developed his 'negative equilibrium' thesis which would become the cornerstone of his foreign policy . He suggested:

> What I said is in the interest of the country and the government that seeks 'political equilibrium'. If we pursue the 'positive policy' we must give out the northern oil concession, for the next 92 years, in order to bring about political equilibrium. Not mentioning the fact that the people of Iran are for ever against this and the Majles is opposed to it today, to give concessions is like a man without one arm agreeing to have his other arm amputated in order to reach an equilibrium.[19]

Mosaddeq's strategy, it became apparent in subsequent years, was to stop any new concessions on Iranian oil and buy time in order to plan for nationalisation of southern oil under the British.

The Tudeh policy ran counter, being for 'positive equilibrium'. As soon as the Soviet offer and the Sa'ed rejection became known, the Tudeh turned 180 degrees. On 28 October 1944, under the protection of Soviet troops, the party staged a demonstration in Tehran against the Sa'ed cabinet and in favour of the Soviet position.[20] Later that year, Ehsanollah Tabari published a notorious article in the party journal, *Mardom Barai-e Roshanfekran*, suggesting that all governments had a sphere of influence in Iran, including the Soviets. He continued, 'If the American government, as we mentioned, is after spheres of influence, and is interested in being strongly engaged in the post-war politics and wants its companies to explore the Baluchestan oil fields, then it is quite natural that our northern neighbour, in its international interests, do the same'.[21] Tabari went on to attack Mosaddeq's 'negative equilibrium' as being one-sided, allowing the old powers and foreign interests to maintain their position in Iran while denying the Soviets access. This blunt support for Soviet interests, at the expense of Iran's own, exposed the Tudeh to criticism from both the centre and right of the political spectrum. It showed overtly, for the first time since the founding of the party, the close links between Tudeh and Soviet interests, even when the national interest was at stake. Furthermore, it put the party alongside the right-of-centre and pro-Western politicians who argued for 'positive equilibrium'. The two accounts of the party's history, supposedly the party's official view on the period, either ignore this issue or manoeuvre around it.[22] Subsequent to these developments the Sa'ed cabinet declared that any negotiation of oil rights would be postponed until after the allied withdrawal. After this, the cabinet was forced to resign and other crises, notably the Azarbaijan affair, overshadowed the oil issue for the time being.

Oil nationalisation resurfaced in 1949, and once again the Tudeh proved unprepared for the challenge. In July 1949, Sa'ed, once again premier, tried to rush a supplementary bill through the fifteenth Majles (which was about to adjourn for elections). The bill, nick-named Gass-Golsha'ian (after the British and Iranian negotiators), would have confirmed and legitimised the renegotiated Anglo-Iranian oil agreement of 1933, which extended British oil rights, due to end 1962, to 1993. But since the 1933 negotiations were conducted during Reza Shah's autocratic rule and confirmed by his hand-picked Majles, the agreement's legitimacy was not accepted by the Iranian side. Even Hasan Taqi-zadeh, the Iranian signatory to the agreement, denied the validity of his own deed, and suggested that the Shah had forced him into signing the agreement.[23] The fact that the 1933 agreement was being seriously contested by Iranians was common knowledge, and the British, via Sa'ed, were trying to get a confirmation from a supposedly more legitimate Majles. The attempt failed when the Majles ran out of time without passing a bill in this regard. During elections for the sixteenth Majles, in the summer and autumn, the National Front was created by Mosaddeq and his colleagues, and managed to send a few members to the new Majles despite rigged elections. Soon Mosaddeq became the head of the Majles's sub-committee on oil, and the stage was set for the nationalisation struggle. The sub-committee opened its discussion on the Gass-Golsha'ian Bill in July 1950, and rejected it. Mosaddeq asked for two months to review the possibility and the implications of nationalising the oil industry. By April 1951, the industry was nationalised and Mosaddeq was appointed Prime Minister at one of the nation's most critical and historic points. The Tudeh entered this new round of crisis by, once again, miscalculating the internal balance of power, misunderstanding the new wave of nationalism and patriotism unleashed by the oil nationalisation act and, again, maintaining a close link with Soviet interests.

At this point the Cold War was well underway and the United States and Soviet Union were engaged in competition on a world-wide scale. The victory of the Chinese revolution in October 1949 and the start of the Korean War in July 1950 only added fuel and intensity to the superpower struggle for control and hegemony. But the situation in Iran was very different to that in the rest of the world. Here, a nation under indirect rule by foreign powers for the previous 150 years was engaged in a life-and-death struggle with the oldest colonial power in its history – Britain – for control of its national resources. The oil nationalisation act was a 50-year dream come true for many Iranians, the natural continuation of goals set by the constitutional revolution of 1906 for others. At any rate, the mass support in urban areas which followed the nationalisation showed the act's popularity. Nationalisation put the Mosaddeq cabinet on a collision course with the British empire, but not necessarily with US interests, or at least not yet. Initially, the Americans, under a Democratic administration, had their differences with the British, both on the way the situation was handled and on the issue of greater profit-sharing with US oil companies. One observer of Iran-US relations commented: 'The Truman administration's policy as developed by Secretary of State Acheson was to attempt to placate the British while trying to convince Musaddiq to agree on a compromise'.[24] Mosaddeq was well aware of these differences, and tried to exploit them to Iran's benefit. The presence of such pro-American figures as Gen. Fazlollah Zahedi (the future coup leader and Mosaddeq's successor) and Ali Amini in Mosaddeq's first cabinet, and the support of such figures as Mozaffar Baqa'i attest to this fact. These were the people who supported Mosaddeq while he was on good terms with the Americans but who deserted him when he fell out with them. The National Front was in fact a coalition of elements, consisting of the pro-American, nationalist and religious right. The religious forces at this point were, for the most part, only indirectly involved in politics. This was because of the apolitical nature of Grand Ayatollah Muhammad Hosein Borujerdi, the leading Shi'i cleric who prevented his followers from direct political participation. A small group under Ayatollah Abol Qasem Kashani, speaker of the sixteenth Majles, was the exception. This group, in association with the Islamic Fadaiyan, founded by Navvab Safavi in 1946, were highly active in the movement. Holding together the National Front had become a delicate balancing act which demanded equally delicate policies from other parties. It was the break-up of this coalition which, in the end, helped the coup leaders overthrow the Government. The Tudeh's analysis of the nationalisation movement was based not on internal Iranian realities but on the international situation, and Soviet interests. Hence, while the National Front was engaging the British and its internal supporters, the

DEFEAT AND REVIVAL: THE GREAT DEFEAT OF THE LEFT (1953–70)

Tudeh viewed the situation in terms of US-Soviet rivalry. For example, after the start of hostilities in the Korean peninsula, the Tudeh established the Iranian Society For Peace (*jam'iyat-e Irani-ye havadar-e solh*) and started to attack the United States. This was at a time when Iran was not at war with any country, or close to it. The society was formed with the sole purpose of dealing with international issues related to East-West rivalry in Iran, and clearly showed a lack of comprehension on the part of party leaders.[25] From the very beginning, when oil nationalisation became a household term in Iran, the Tudeh denounced it as imperialist, and suggested that only the nationalisation of the southern oil was appropriate.[26] In analysing the sixteenth Majles, where the National Front had a minority presence and eventually managed to pass the nationalisation bill, in *Besui-ye Ayandeh*, September 1950, the Tudeh divided the members into three categories: first, the opportunists, who had no position of their own and would follow the most powerful; second, those who depended on foreigners, and so carried out their wishes; third, the deceivers, who had all the characteristics of the first two but pretended to care for the people, whom they had never really understood.[27] Of course, this third group was the National Front. The daily, *Mardom*, described the oil nationalisation effort in the following terms in June 1950: 'Already we can be sure that revisions in the southern oil contract will not be in favour of our people and will only result in the consolidation of England's position in our country. The only time our people may realise their rights in the southern oil resources is when they can determine their destiny. Hence, the solution of the oil question is related to the victory of our party, ie the people of Iran.'[28] When the Majles sub-committee on oil rejected the Gass-Golsha'ian Bill, the Tudeh attributed it not to the efforts of the National Front but to the people of Iran: '[the Gass-Golsha'ian bill] was rejected by the people of Iran and not by the disgraced National Front...'[29] Even Mosaddeq's rejection of the American offer of compromise, put forward by Averell Harriman in July 1951, failed to convince the party of the genuinely patriotic nature of the movement. To sum up, the Tudeh's position between the start of the second round of the oil debate in the summer of 1950 and mid-1952 was one of antagonism toward the authors of the movement.

Ironically, while the party's policy on the oil nationalisation question was implemented with Soviet interests in mind, this did not mean that it mirrored Soviet policy on the subject. The Soviets, while not doing much to help Iran at a time when it was under a British embargo, did recognise the importance of the nationalisation act. The Soviet media supported nationalisation and gave positive coverage to Mosaddeq and the National Front.[30] The Tudeh was acting on its own perception of what its international duties (ie Soviet interests) were.

The party's antagonism toward the Mosaddeq cabinet continued well into the second year of his term in office. In July 1952, Mosaddeq resigned his post over a dispute with the Shah. A bloody uprising followed on 21 July, forcing the Shah to reinstate Mosaddeq and grant him more power. From this point until the day Mosaddeq was overthrown, the Tudeh's policy changed to support for Mosaddeq at the expense of maintaining the party's independence.

This support was qualified at the beginning but included support for his main theme of oil industry nationalisation. But as time went by, and the coup approached, Tudeh support for the Mosaddeq cabinet grew.[31] Under the new policy, the party gradually fell behind the nationalists to the extent that when asked to clear the streets, in the period between the two coup attempts, it complied.

Despite its organisational network and popular base, the Tudeh performed rather inadequately against the forces of the 1953 coup. Perhaps the best way to describe the party's reaction to the coup is ineffectual. Through its intelligence network in the armed forces, especially the Imperial Guard Division, the prime mover behind the coup, the Tudeh had advance warning, and even told Mosaddeq.[32] Between 16 August, when the first coup attempt failed, and 19 August 1953, the party was alert and in touch with the Premier. Between the two coup attempts the party was engaged in bringing down the Shah's statues around the country, publishing articles condemning the coup and demanding the abolition of the monarchy and the establishment of a people's democratic republic. On 18 August, Mosaddeq asked the party to stop the demonstrations, with the intention of bringing the situation under control.[33] The Tudeh complied, but this meant that on the day of the coup it had demobilised its supporters, leaving the streets to the army and its hired thugs. Hence, on the day of the coup the party remained indoors and passive. Subsequent attempts to organise armed resistance were haphazard, and proved no match for the organisation of the coup leaders. Despite the hawkish and aggressive policies of the preceding years, the party took Mosaddeq's word at face value and failed to organise resistance at the most critical moment. The party's initial explanation for its inactivity came a few months later: 'If we had taken general armed action, the repression would have been more severe and, without overall readiness, we would have lost the position of the vanguard in this unequal battle. The repression may have been more severe than the one which followed the 19 August repression if we had opted for general mass demonstrations.'[34]

Between 1953 and 1958, when the last organised Tudeh resistance vanished inside the country, the party lost its social base, its organisation and its military network as well as many of its leaders and adherents. During the year following the coup, the Tudeh printing house was shut down and its military network exposed. During 1955, top Tudeh leaders were arrested. These included Muhammad Bahrami, the acting first secretary of the party and executive committee member; Nader Sharmini, central committee member and at this point the *de facto* head of the Tudeh's Youth Organisation; Amanollah Qoreishi, central committee member in charge of the Tehran organisation, nerve-centre of the party's network; Morteza Yazdi and Ali Olovvi, both members of the party's executive committee. During the same year the remains of the military network, ie its intelligence branch, was discovered and decimated. The head of the network, ex-captain Khosrow Roozbeh, perhaps the most daring middle-ranking Tudeh member, was arrested the next year.

Overall, the Tudeh rank-and-file and middle-ranking members resisted the coup while the leadership either fled the country or co-operated with the coup leaders in order to save themselves. While repression of the party was much more severe than it was of other parties (eg the National Front), and much more harsh and concentrated than anything the party had witnessed or experienced before, it seems that the rank-and-file were more resistant to its effects than the leaders. The increased use of modern torture after the coup made heroes of some ordinary members, but collaborators of some of the leaders, who provided sufficient information for the state to uproot the party. A good example of this resistance was the case of Vartan Salakhanian (mentioned as Balakhian in some sources), a Tudeh activist arrested in 1954. Vartan was arrested while, with his comrade Mahmud Kuchak-shushtari, he was distributing Tudeh publications in Tehran. Both men were subjected to heavy torture by the organisation of the Military Governor of Tehran, which was central to the coup and the forerunner of SAVAK. Although both men were low-ranking members, and could not provide much important information, they both resisted until death. This act of heroism and resistance prompted Ahmad Shamlu, the prominent Iranian poet, to write the poem 'Marg-e Vartan' ('Vartan's Death').[35] The Tudeh leadership behaved very differently. Almost all arrested leaders co-operated with the Military Governor of Tehran. Of the five-man executive committee of the party – Bahrami, Yazdi, Ali Olovvi, Kianuri and Hosein Joudat – the first three were arrested. Bahrami and Yazdi, alongside Sharmini and Qoreishi, co-operated with the regime and managed to save their lives, while Olovvi was executed despite alleged co-operation.[36] Yazdi went as far as claiming to be proud of having been able to help to prevent the party from overthrowing the monarchy, and that for this he deserved an imperial pardon.[37] The other two escaped from Iran and returned after the 1979 revolution to lead the party until its disastrous end in 1983. Roozbeh suggested in 1958, in his final defence in court, that by the time he was arrested the coup leaders knew everything there was to know about the Tudeh, and blamed the arrested party leaders for this.[38] Some leaders went as far as giving detailed accounts of the party organisation and network. These accounts, *Seyr-e komonizm dar Iran (The Development of Communism in Iran)* and *Komonizm dar Iran (Communism in Iran)*, became the outward manifestation of the effectiveness with which the repression of the party was carried out.[39]

One of the major blunders of the leadership, during the initial post-coup years, was the signing of 'regret letters'. Following the mass arrests of activists, the Military Governor asked the prisoners to sign documents attesting to their association with the party. The Tudeh leadership forbade its members to sign. The members' compliance became an easy way for coup organisers to distinguish Tudeh members from those arrested wrongly or belonging to other parties. After the decimation and arrest of the Tudeh's Military Organisation, the leadership changed its policy, and ordered its jailed members to sign, as a way of freeing themselves. This resulted in the daily publications of letters not only by military members, but also members, and especially leaders, condemning the party. The demoralising effect of this on activists who still wanted to resist the coup was tremendous.

If the Tudeh was to put up a meaningful and organised resistance against the coup, its Military Organisation had to play an important and leading role. Created in 1944, the Military Organisation of the Tudeh Party of Iran (*sazman-e nezami-ye hezb-e Tudeh-ye Iran*), sometimes called the Officers' Organisation (*sazman-e afsaran*), was a network of military officers supporting the party. The military personnel who came to create the Military Organisation had established their cells in the defeated Iranian armed forces a year after the allied occupation of Iran in 1941.[40] Prominent among these officers were Col. Ezatollah Siyamak, one of the few communist officers not exposed to the police during Reza Shah's rule, Col. Muhammad Ali Azar, Maj. Ali Akbar Eskandani and Capt. Khosrow Roozbeh. Between 1942 and 1944 these officers operated without direct contact with the Tudeh. In 1944, through Siyamak's contacts with Abdol Samad Kambakhsh, the cells were put in touch with the party and the Military Organisation created, with Kambakhsh as its party liaison officer. Between 1944 and 1946, the Military Organisation was involved in two episodes which led to an attempt to disband it and to sever ties with the Tudeh. In the first, in August 1944, around 20 army personnel in the Khorasan division of the army rebelled and attempted to reach the Turkman areas of West Khorasan and East Mazandaran in order to wage war against the central Government. The rebellion was led by Eskandani and Azar. Many of the personnel involved in this venture, including Eskandani, were killed before they reached their destination, and others, such as Azar, fled to the Soviet Union.[41] In the second, the Military Organisation sent aid and officers to Azarbaijan at a time when the province was rebelling against the Tehran Government. The defeat of the Azarbaijan movement (see below) caused the party's leadership to attempt to disband the organisation or at any rate cut all contacts with it. It was not disbanded, however, as the party wanted, and officers such as Roozbeh resigned their party membership in order to keep the Military Organisation alive.[42] The party asked the organisation back into its ranks in 1948, as a result of active Soviet pressure, and the reunion was finalised the following year.[43]

The Military Organisation has generally been considered the party's strongest card in the years preceding the coup. Estimates on the number of officers involved vary from 466 to 700.[44] All the estimates on the number of the Organisation's personnel were provided by the coup organisers, as the party did not have clear estimates of its own.[45] The official Tudeh estimate of 466 members suggests that after 429 people were arrested following the coup, 37 managed to flee the country. On 19 August 1953, 243 officers were stationed in Tehran, and only three or four were serving in the Imperial Guard Division. Most of these were in non-combat positions. The low estimate provided by the Tudeh has been used by the party to argue that the party could not have made any meaningful use of the Military Organisation, but is contradicted by the fact that 466 military personnel had been brought to trial by 1958.[46]

There are different assessments as to what the Military Organisation could have done and what kind of threat it posed to the imperial regime. One historian has suggested, 'With army doctors, air force cadets, and bridge-building engineers, the Tudeh could influence rank-and-file troops and even distribute weapons to party members, but could not possibly pull off a successful coup d'etat'.[47] Although it may not have been possible for the Military Organisation to stage a coup against the imperial regime or the coup plotters, the fact remains that it did not make any move. The leaders of the Military Organisation had notified party leaders that they would be ready to take immediate military action against the coup.[48] During 1952 and 1953, through an intelligence network in the armed forces, it helped uncover plots against the nationalist Government. It was well aware of the coup plot, and had warned party leaders. Fereidun Azarnur, a high-ranking officer in the Military Organisation, has described the important military posts Tudeh officers occupied during the coup, and suggests that his estimate of 491 Tudeh military personnel could have helped the party defeat the coup.[49] According to Kianuri, an officer in charge of a battalion from Hamadan brought to Tehran to take part in the coup, and another in charge of a company in Chalus, were both party members and were in a position to distribute weapons to the party.[50] According to one prominent member of the Military Organisation, besides the opportunity to take out the radio station and distribute weapons, some members were in key positions, and could have assasinated important members of the coup leadership, including Gen. Zahedi.[51]

While the bulk of the Military Organisation was decimated in 1954, a remnant survived under Roozbeh, who headed its intelligence branch. He attempted to revive the party, but his arrest and execution in 1958 put an end to organised Tudeh activity. Roozbeh had embraced Marxism-Leninism and joined the Tudeh in 1943. By the time of his execution in 1958, he had 36 books and pamphlets to his name, written on a variety of subjects from mathematics to artillery ballistics to literature and philosophy, politics and chess. Some of his military writings were used in the army's officer academy for years. He had been considered as having a bright future in the imperial forces. Roozbeh had the chance to leave the country after the coup but chose not to do so. Instead, just before his arrest, he conveyed a message to the leadership in exile, sharply criticising them for their performance, and for fleeing the country, and stating that he would not do the same.[52] He behaved similarly during his last defence, attacking the leadership for not showing courage, while underlining his loyalty to the party.

The fact that the Military Organisation could not have pulled off a coup, and the Tudeh assertion that the organisation's abilities were limited, still does not answer the question of why it took no action at all. It seems that the answer to this question is rooted in the state of paralysis that had overtaken the Tudeh leadership. Under the new repressive circumstances the Military Organisation would not have acted without the consent of the party leadership, and the party was simply unable to make a move. Future Marxists would blame the party for inaction, using the Military Organisation as an example. They would point out that even if the organisation and the party had been defeated in action resisting the coup, this would have been preferable to the party's destruction through inaction. The Military Organisation afforded the party protection during the year after the coup. But the Government's uncovering and decimation of the organisation in 1954 cleared the path to the uprooting of the Tudeh itself.[53]

The retreat of the Tudeh was so hasty – and the victory of the imperial regime so complete – that by 1958 the regime could discount any threat from the Tudeh. The question of how and why the Tudeh's strategic defeat came about would haunt the communist movement for many years, and communist activists of the next generation would look into the lessons of the 1953 coup and of the Tudeh's demise before proceeding. The official Tudeh reaction to the party's failure came during the historic fourth plenum, held in Moscow in July 1957.[54] Approximately 80 leaders and members from all over Europe and Iran participated.[55] The plenum criticised the party for its policy towards the National Front:

> ... the mistaken position on the problem of nationalisation of the oil industry (in the beginning of the movement) and the mistaken and leftist policies toward the National Front and Dr Mosaddeq's government, were the most important mistakes of our party in the period before the August 19 coup. The party's slogans on the oil issue were based on the mistaken analysis that perceived the oil industry's nationalisation as the result of a contradiction between the two imperialist powers of America and England.[56]

Calling its policies toward the nationalist Government sectarian and leftist, the party also suggested that its policy between 16 and 19 August 1953 – pulling down statues and demanding a people's democratic republic – had been misguided.[57] The party admitted to its state of paralysis, blaming it on the leadership inside Iran while suggesting that the leadership abroad had failed to provide help and guidelines. The party blamed the leadership's weakness on its own lack of internal democracy, an absence of connection between the leadership and party members, the low level of theoretical knowledge among the leadership, and the existence of deep differences among party leaders. On differences within the central committee, the plenum identified two factions – one dominant and centred around Eskandari and Radmanesh, the other in opposition around Kianuri and Qasemi – but suggested that the differences were mostly personal and due to character flaws. Nevertheless, the plenum put the general responsibility for the party's failure collectively on the executive committee of the time. The party blamed Hosein Joudat, the party's liaison officer in charge of the Military Organisation at the time of the coup, for his poor performance in protecting the organisation. The plenum limited its criticism of party leaders present at the meeting to those mentioned, and made the party's Youth Organisation and its *de facto* head, Nader Sharmini, a scapegoat, blaming him for leftism and for creating a faction within the party.

Hence the plenum's criticism was mostly directed at the party's shortcomings *vis-à-vis* the National Front and Mosaddeq, with some criticism of party leadership; certain arrested collaborators, such as Sharmini, received the bulk of the criticism. Yet even here the Tudeh failed to explain, and therefore rectify, why the party vacillated between confronting the nationalists on the one hand and supporting them to the point of paralysing the party on the other. The plenum failed to address the party's failure to respond to the coup, except by blaming everything on the imperialists, coup leaders' viciousness and some party shortcomings. Issues such as factionalism within the party and Soviet influence were not touched on officially, although the former issue was discussed.

THE COMMUNIST TUDEH AND FACTIONALISM

Factional infighting had existed in the Tudeh from its inception, and continued to play an important role in the party's paralysis in the face of the coup. According to one of the party's former leaders, 'The existence of two factions in the leadership of the Tudeh Party of Iran can be seen like a red line in the 38-year history of the Tudeh Party in Iran and in exile'.[58] Avanessian, another party leader, wrote about his disappointment when he learned that instead of a communist party his comrades had established the Tudeh, although he came to accept the idea when he learned that an undercover communist centre had been created to guide the Tudeh and its central committee.[59] Avanessian did not explain what happened to this centre, but it seems that its members were instrumental in transforming the party to an overtly pro-Soviet stance.

Many factors helped fuel factional and personal differences within the Tudeh, and jealousy of individual leadership figures was among the most significant of these. Indeed, some former Tudeh leaders have claimed that the existence of factions owed more to personal and organisational differences than to ideological ones.[60] In general, personal animosity played an important role in the Iranian politics of this period, and continues to do so to this day, although to a much lesser extent. Nevertheless, the existence of two sets of approaches in many Tudeh decision-making processes throughout the period under study suggests that the issue went beyond that of differences among individual party leaders. This subject will be examined more thoroughly in the final chapter as one of the causes for the movement's eventual demise.

Different names could be applied to the two factions: extremist and conservative, left and right, or radical and moderate. Both factions shared an admiration for the Soviet Union, adhered to the Soviet version of Marxism-Leninism as the party gradually changed to a pro-Moscow communist party, and were united against the splinter group led by Khalil Maleki (the Third Force). The party's second congress gave more definite shape to the factions. The oil nationalisation movement brought the two factions further into conflict.

The radical faction's principal members were such young activists as Nur al-Din Kianuri, Ehsanollah Tabari, Amanollah Qoreishi, Ahmad Qasemi and Gholam Hosein Forutan, as well as older members such as Avanessian and Abdol Samad Kambakhsh.[61] Of these, Kambakhsh (1903–71) was the most controversial figure. An air force officer during Reza Shah's rule, Kambakhsh was active in the Iranian Communist Party and the Group of Fifty-three. He was arrested in the mid-1930s and co-operated with police against the Group of Fifty-three.[62] After the collapse of Reza Shah's regime, it took Kambakhsh two years to become a member of the Tudeh, and then only after considerable pressure from the Soviets.[63] Many Tudeh leaders did not want him in their ranks, and some went so far as to accuse him of association with the Soviet secret service (regarded as very different to the official association with the Soviet leadership).

The left-wing, or radical, faction presented a more dogmatic perception of Marxism, and was more insistent on the leadership of the working class and on party rules. The radicals were generally against the nationalist Government. The policy of confronting the Mosaddeq cabinet was largely a result of this faction gaining the upper hand. The radical faction considered Mosaddeq and the National Front part of the Iranian bourgeoisie, with its close ties with the Americans, in opposition to the imperial court and the land-owning class, which maintained close ties with the British. Because of this two-sided understanding of international and domestic alliances, the radical faction viewed the dispute between the National Front and the British as being in reality one between British and US policy in Iran. When the party proposed the united front policy, the radicals insisted that any such front with non-communist forces should come under party leadership. The radicals considered the Tudeh to be the working-class party, and this perception became a major point of dispute with the moderate faction. The radicals used their considerable organisational might within the party to win converts to their cause, and leftist and extremist policies of opposition to the nationalist Government were the result, and these changing only when tide began to turn following the July 1952 uprising.

The right, or moderate, faction's principal members were Morteza Yazdi, Iraj Eskandari (both veterans of the Group of Fifty-three), Reza Radmanesh, Freidun Keshavarz, Hosein Joudat and Nader Sharmini. This faction, although initially against Mosaddeq, gradually came to accept his leadership. The moderates de-emphasised the leadership role of the working class and the party, and believed that a united front with non-communist forces could be undertaken without the party being the dominant partner. They had a more populist view of Marxism, and considered the Tudeh not as the party of the working class, but as a toilers' party which represented other deprived classes. The policy of supporting the nationalists to the point of Tudeh subordination to nationalist policies after July 1952 was the result of this faction gaining the upper hand.[64] The two factions took firmer shape after the coup as the party moved into exile. Before the coup, although the factions existed, individual members held a variety of views on policies. Here, the dynamism of personal rivalry and differences played a significant role. Among the above-mentioned names, the case of Sharmini and Kianuri has baffled some scholars. Sharmini, whose power-base was the Youth Organisation, and who was its head until 1952 proposed the most radical stances while siding with the moderate faction on most issues. Under him the Youth Organisation became a vehicle for undermining the authority of key personalities of the radical faction and their appointees, as this faction was attacked as being reformist and Menshevik. Throughout his memoirs Kianuri claims he was a proponent of Mosaddeq after the July 1952 uprising, although he does admit that he, along with the other members of the leadership, opposed the oil nationalisation movement before July 1952. Indeed he suggests that through his wife's connection with Mosaddeq's family he was the one who warned the Prime Minister of the impending coup. Kianuri's claim is only partially true. Among the key radical faction personalities he was number three, after Kambakhsh and Qasemi. Kambakhsh was no theorist, but a party functionary with strong personal Soviet connections. Qasemi was a staunch Stalinist and dogmatic theorist who was the main force behind the party's anti-Mosaddeq policies during 1951 and 1952. These two had to leave the country by mid-1952. Hence, during the year before the coup Kianuri was the only member of the radical faction left on the party's five-man executive committee. Kianuri believed in the hegemony of the proletariat in any coalition with non-proletarian forces, while Qasemi did not envision any coalition with a bourgeoisie which he deemed to have betrayed the anti-imperialist movement. Qasemi's view was closer to Stalin's, while Kianuri's was more moderate and closer to Mao's, but both were at odds with the moderates, who proposed closer co-operation with Mosaddeq after July 1952. This doctrinal difference only added to factional differences within the party.[65]

The factional competition sometimes led to factions accusing each other of operating outside the Tudeh framework. One directly-related controversy was the creation of a Tudeh hit-squad. The squad was designed to physically eliminate the party's real and imaginary enemies. Although there are differing accounts from Tudeh leaders, there is no doubt either that it existed and functioned under the Military Organisation, or that it assassinated a number of people. According to Tabari, the whole leadership, both factions, was aware of the squad, but not of all operations. According to Keshavarz, only the radical faction was aware of the squad, so that all assassinations were in line with radical, rather than moderate, aims.[66] The Military Organisation, which ran the hit-squad, answered to Kambakhsh, while he was in Iran, as the party's liaison officer in charge. Kianuri and Forutan took over after Kambakhsh left the country, and Joudat was the last party liaison officer. This puts the squad under the radical faction between 1948 and 1950, but does not rule out the possibility that the entire leadership may have known about its existence. What is clear in both sources is that the entire party leadership was aware of some of the most notorious cases in which it was involved. These included the assassination of five party members who were seen as a threat to party security, the most famous of which was of Hesam Lankarani.[67]

Other infamous acts attributed to the radical faction by Keshavarz were the assassination of Ahmad Dehqan, the anti-Tudeh and pro-imperial journalist in May 1950, the assassination of a popular anti-Shah journalist and publisher of the daily *Marde-e Emrooz*, Muhammad Mas'ud, in 1947, the attempt on the Shah's life in 1949, and the Khorasan officers rebellion.[68] Keshavarz never substantiated his accusations regarding Tudeh involvement in the Dehqan case, and the accusation was rejected by Eskandari. Roozbeh, who would have been in charge of the Dehqan assassination, makes no mention of it in his confessions, while leaving little else hidden. Kianuri's explanation leaves little doubt that his faction, and the party as a whole, was not involved in the assassination.[69] In the Mas'ud case, Keshavarz and Tabari allege that a hit-squad commanded by Roozbeh, and with links to the radical faction, assassinated Mas'ud in order to put the blame on the Shah.[70] Indeed, this policy seemed to work for a while, as the national media blamed the imperial court. But according to the confessions of Roozbeh and his right-hand-man Capt. Abol Hasan Abbasi, the assassination was carried out by a squad they and others had created, at the time when the Military Organisation had been disbanded by the Tudeh, and its members not party members, so the party was probably not aware of it. Kianuri agreed with this in his account of the events.[71] Kianuri denied any role in the 1949 attempted assassination of the Shah which cost the party dearly, but the evidence of his knowledge of it is overwhelming and undermines his claim of innocence. In any event, it is still not clear whether the radical faction, acting on its own or on behalf of the party, was solely behind it or whether there were non-Tudeh interests involved. Kambakhsh was the party member who gave the go-ahead to the Military Organisation for the Khorasan rebellion. At this point he was also the liaison between the party and the Soviets. Kianuri, Kambakhsh's closest ally in the party, has suggested that the whole party was aware of the operation, although this is disputed by Eskandari.[72] Hence, while two members of the moderate faction have claimed no knowledge of the rebellion, there is little doubt that Kambakhsh, a member of the radical faction, approved the venture.

Perhaps the most revealing document to date on the issue of factionalism and its role in hampering party activity during and immediately after the coup is the correspondence between the party leadership abroad and the executive committee inside Iran.[73] The letters, four in all, were written immediately after the coup and were in effect an evaluation of factional differences and a request for mediation by the leadership abroad. They show the extent of factional in-fighting and the state of paralysis of the party. The first letter, written by Bahrami, Yazdi and Joudat, blames the party's failures on Kianuri and his faction, accusing him of opportunism and sectarianism. It reveals that on the day of the coup in an executive committee meeting Olovvi had proposed that the party call a general strike, but that this measure was opposed by Kianuri. Furthermore, the letter disputes Kianuri's attempt to portray only his opponents as having incorrectly analysed the nationalist Government, accusing him of similar failure. The second letter, written by Olovvi, who generally sympathised with the moderate faction but had independent views on some issues, suggests that the party was paralysed by internal factionalism. The third letter, written by Kianuri, at this point the only radical faction member in the executive committee, confirms the scope of disagreement and suggests that the party could not continue as it had done without serious changes.

The party's fourth plenum started with a confrontation between the two factions, but ended in compromise. According to Tabari, Keshavarz did his best to expose Kianuri and Kambakhsh throughout the proceedings.[74] Indeed the moderates concentrated their criticism on these two radical members and the policies associated with them. The radicals in turn blamed the moderates for their populism, and for losing party independence through blind allegiance to the nationalists. At any rate, the two factions reached a compromise by the end of the meeting. According to Keshavarz, the Soviets had a representative at the meeting and were very much against any split.[75] Eskandari and Radmanesh played a leading role in forging the compromise[76] by which the two factions agreed to limit criticism and not to attempt any removal of each other. The radicals accepted leadership by the moderates by electing Radmanesh as the party's first secretary. Keshavarz, shocked by the betrayal of his factional comrades, left the party in 1959. And so the factionalism which had so paralysed the party in the face of the coup persisted, despite its damaging impact.

THE COMMUNIST TUDEH AND THE SOVIET UNION

The relationship between the Tudeh and the Soviet Union has always been a major point of controversy in the history of the Iranian communist movement, and a part of any evaluation of the Tudeh. The party has always explained its relationship with the Soviets as that of internationalist duty between fraternal communist parties. The party's foes have criticised the Tudeh from three perspectives. First, the party's opponents on the right and centre, religious and secular, have always argued that the party was a spy network for the Soviets rather than an independent national political party. Second, some Tudeh leaders who split from the party prior to its demise in the mid-1980s have argued that some within a certain faction had close ties to the KGB, and that this faction always carried out Soviet wishes. Third, independent Marxist groups usually argued that the Tudeh dependency on the Soviet Union forced the party to put Soviet interests ahead of the interests of Iranian workers, and therefore accused it of betraying the revolutionary movement at every important juncture. The Tudeh's relationship with the Soviet Union will be examined here from the early stages until the end of the 1950s.

The Soviets exerted considerable influence in Iran while occupying the country during the Second World War. As noted, they had some influence on the Tudeh at its inception. During the 1940s, Rostam Aliev, a Soviet diplomat, had many contacts with the party and influenced its development. He was instrumental in forcing the party leadership to accept Kambakhsh as a member. Aliev was a close ally of Ja'far Baqerov, chief of the Soviet Azarbaijan Communist Party, who in turn was close to Lavrenti P. Beria, the head of GPU under Stalin.[7] Baqerov played an important role during the Iranian Azarbaijan crisis of 1945–6, and met his death alongside Beria after Stalin's death.

The Tudeh was established as a mass party, but without the common constitution of parties which were members of the Comintern. While the war was still being waged outside Iran, the Tudeh followed a policy close to that of the Soviet Union. This policy was designed to strengthen the allied coalition by putting forward anti-fascist slogans and trying not to antagonise the Soviet Union's principal allies in Iran, the British and Americans. Avanessian talks about a letter sent to the Tudeh by the Comintern which outlined the polices the party should follow. These were: to fight against fascism through propaganda and other means; to fight for the establishment of democracy; and to make the Iranian people understand that the Soviet Government only wanted their well-being and freedom.[78]

The Soviets did their best to strengthen the party while occupying Iran. As noted, the Soviet army protected the Tudeh while the party staged demonstrations against the Sa'ed cabinet, and most of the eight Tudeh members elected to the fourteenth Majles came from the Soviet zone of occupation. The party's support for the Soviet cause in Iran was more than coincidental, and followed a pattern throughout the Tudeh's activity in Iran. The party's support for the northern oil concession in 1944 and the creation of peace groups in support of Soviet international policy in the late 1940s has also been mentioned. Even the party's anti-Mosaddeq policy – promoted mainly by its radical faction, but initially supported by some moderates – although not aligned with Soviet policy, was partially based on misinterpretation of Soviet policy. This policy, which manifested itself in the resolutions of the nineteenth congress of the Communist Party of the Soviet Union (CPSU), of October 1952, suggested that the bourgeoisie had let down the cause of democracy on the international scale, and that now it was the duty of the international proletariat to pick up the banner of democracy.[79] The radicals took this observation too literally and attacked the Iranian nationalists as the manifestation of the Iranian bourgeoisie.

The Tudeh's relationship with the Soviet Union becomes more complex when it is studied against the background of factionalism. It is clear that both the radicals and the moderates had great admiration for the October Revolution and the Soviet Union as the bastion of victorious proletarian revolution. Members of both factions submitted to Soviet policy throughout the 1940s. Both factions believed that the party had to observe and respect its internationalist duties by co-ordinating the party's policies with those of the Soviet Union. It should also be noted that as long as Stalin was alive the CPSU demanded discipline and obedience from fraternal parties around the world.[80]

Within the context of general support for Soviet policies in Iran and around the world, the two Tudeh factions had different perceptions and relations with the Soviets. Members of the moderate faction have accused the radicals, especially Kambakhsh and Kianuri, of being outright KGB associates or operatives. Keshavarz has accused the Soviets of misusing the trust and admiration the Tudeh had for the October Revolution and the Soviet Union. According to him, '... by misusing the belief we and the majority of party members honestly had in internationalism, the CPSU forced its operatives and spies on its "fraternal party"'. Keshavarz suggested that through Soviet support these operatives rose in party ranks 'until they reached high party posts and gradually changed the Tudeh party of Iran into a tool of the Soviet Union's policy in Iran'.[81] Here, Keshavarz was criticising Soviet conduct in promoting Kambakhsh and Kianuri in the Tudeh. He suggested that both men had ties to the GPU and were closely supported by Beria and Baqerov as long as Stalin was alive.[82] Keshavarz recalled that during one meeting of the leadership in exile, Kianuri defined his perception of the party's relations with the Soviet Union in these words: 'I believe that if the Soviet comrades ask one of us to do something but not to let the rest of the [Tudeh] central committee know about it, we must obey'.[83] Keshavarz suggested that the radical faction continued to operate even after de-Stalinisation and the removal of Baqerov and Beria. According to him, the compromise of the fourth plenum maintained their position in the party and the union with the Azarbaijan Democratic Party boosted their position.

Keshavarz wrote his accounts of the Tudeh when he was no longer a party member and felt no sympathy for it. But Eskandari wrote for the next generation of the party, and while he still felt some connection with it. Hence, Eskandari's accounts are more cautious but no less revealing. While confirming the existence of factions and Soviet influence, Eskandari viewed Tudeh-Soviet relations as more complex and less conspiratorial. He suggested that the Soviets had different departments in their Government which sometimes pursued contradictory policies. This meant that uniform policies toward a certain issue were not always possible. Eskandari agreed with the suggestion that the Soviets tried to exert influence on the fraternal parties, but believed that their success depended on how receptive the fraternal party was to that influence.[84] He suggested that as long as the Tudeh was operating inside Iran and had a mass following, the Soviet influence was less, but that after exile between 1960 and 1979, first in the Soviet Union and then in the German Democratic Republic (GDR), the influence increased. As far as the factions are concerned, Eskandari suggested that his faction, the moderates, were in favour of independence from the Soviets, while the radicals under Kambakhsh and Kianuri were dependent on the CPSU and always carried out its commands.[85] He suggested that both Kianuri and Kambakhsh, not to mention Kianuri's wife, Mariam Firouz, had direct connections to Soviet intelligence.[86] In one case, Eskandari recalled asking Tabari, the party ideologue, why he agreed with him (Eskandari) on every issue, but voted with Kianuri. Tabari's startling answer was, 'Because the Soviet comrades have approved him'.[87] Kianuri denied that he, his wife and Kambakhsh had a connection with the Soviet intelligence, but suggested – interestingly enough – that Kambakhsh indeed had a special relationship with the Soviets, enjoyed their trust, and that he was a member of the CPSU.[88]

The Tudeh dependence on the Soviet Union, both in public policy and direct Soviet influence in the party's central committee, a fact that went beyond the party's perception of internationalist fraternal relations. It may also help to explain the paralysis of the party leadership in confronting the 1953 coup. Joseph Stalin died in March 1953, about five months before the coup. During this period the CPSU was engaged in a struggle for power between two groups, one around Beria, the other around Georgy M. Malenkov and Khrushchev, which forced the Soviet leadership to spend more time and energy on its domestic affairs and less on international ones. That situation provided an excellent opportunity for the proponents of the coup in Iran, both Iranian and foreign, and allowed them to take advantage of the Soviet Union's temporary preoccupation. It may have been equally disadvantageous to the Tudeh in its dependence on and expectation of Soviet leadership and support at this historical point.

Of the many reasons behind the Tudeh's inability to effectively respond to the 1953 coup, factionalism, Soviet interest and negligence have been discussed. Another important factor, which cannot be substantiated and documented at this point, but remains a strong possibility, is CIA, MI-6 or Iranian security force infiltration. The allegation of such infiltration has been made on two occasions by Mark Gasiorowski, who has done extensive interviews with CIA officers involved in the 1953 coup. According to Gasiorowski, the CIA had infiltrated the Tudeh at a very high level during the coup period, and the Lankarani brothers were in fact MI-6 agents.[89] None of the former Tudeh leaders who have written their memoirs know anything about this. While Kianuri has been accused by some of his former foes in the party as being an agent not only of the KGB but also of MI-6, these charges cannot be substantiated from available material.[90] The question must be left open until there is of more information.

THE AZARBAIJAN DEMOCRATIC PARTY:
THE OTHER COMMUNISTS

The continued presence of the Tudeh in Iranian politics since the early 1940s sometimes overshadows the existence of the second pro-Soviet Iranian party, the Azarbaijan Democratic Party(ADP), or *fer-qeh-ye demokrat-e Azarbaijan*. As one historian has put it: 'Iran has experienced the rare phenomenon of having two pro-Soviet Communist parties simultaneously'.[91] The ADP's brief period of activity inside Iran, in 1945 and 1946, and its eventual merger with the Tudeh in 1960 has led to less attention being paid to it. Yet, as we shall see, the ADP's role in the factionalism within the Tudeh after merger makes the study of the ADP an important part of any understanding of the Tudeh and the pro-Soviet wing of Iranian communism.

The ADP was established in September 1945, principally on the efforts of Ja'far Pishehvari, alias Javadzadeh (1893–1947) and his Azarbaijani comrades. Born in Azarbaijan, Pishehvari was a leading member of the old Iranian Communist Party, and had spent 10 years in jail during Reza Shah's rule, released only after the allied invasion.[92] The ADP was established while Azarbaijan was under Soviet occupation. Pishehvari established the party after consulting with Ja'far Baqerov in Baku, and with direct material and moral aid from Soviet forces in Azarbaijan.[93] Therefore, the reliance of the ADP on the Soviet Union, and more specifically the Soviet Azarbaijan Communist Party, was evident from the start, and increased over time.

Today, Azarbaijan is defined as the north-west provinces of Iran, south of the River Aras, and the former Soviet republic of Azarbaijan, north of it. The entire area was part of Qajar Iran until the Russo-Iranian wars of the early nineteenth century, when the northern part was ceded to the Russians in two phases in 1813 and 1828 by the Treaties of Golestan and Turkmanchai respectively.[94] The name Azarbaijan is an Iranian name for a pre-Islamic province south of the River Aras, and was not used in any definite or clear manner for the area north of it; nor was it mentioned in either the Golestan or Turkmanchai treaties. Use of the name Azarbaijan to include the Aran region immediately to the north of the river was the exception.[95] The adoption of this name for the northern area was initiated by the nationalist, Baku-based, Mosavat Government (1918–20) and later retained by the Soviet Union. Nevertheless, the seven million Azari-speaking people of the Republic of Azarbaijan share many historical and cultural similarities with the 12 million Iranian Azaris.

Iranian Azarbaijan took a leading role in the constitutional revolution and remained a bastion of opposition to despotism until 1925, when Reza Shah established the Pahlavi dynasty. Azarbaijan's historical stand against despotism, the region's proximity to the Soviet Union, and Reza Shah's official state ideology of Persian cultural superiority over Iranian minorities all led to repression and neglect of the region during Reza Shah's rule. The Azarbaijani population was divided into three provinces, Zanjan and West and East Azarbaijan, the latter including a substantial part of northern Iranian Kurdestan. Official state policy during this period was the eradication of Azari culture through the prohibition of the Azari language as much as possible and by systematic Persianisation. The region's industrial development was neglected as both Iran and the Soviet Union centralised trade. By the time Reza Shah's regime collapsed, Azarbaijan therefore had many grievances against the centre, so that once the strong hand of central Government was removed, spontaneous and organised activities began.

During the World War II Soviet occupation of Azarbaijan, political activists and agitators from Soviet Azarbaijan began to arrive with the Red Army. These included both Iranians who had been living in Soviet Azarbaijan, and Soviet Azarbaijanis themselves. The activists were under the Soviet Azarbaijan Communist Party, headed by Baqerov, and their principal task was to co-ordinate their efforts with the army command and to establish links with the local population.[96] The activists were organised under The Azarbaijan Toiler's Organisation (*jam'iyyat-e zahmatkeshan-e Azarbaijan*), but it seems they were not very successful as far as mass mobilisation was concerned.[97]

A second organisation which sprang up immediately after the allied invasion was the Azarbaijan Province Committee of the Tudeh Party of Iran (APC), and this started its work in Tabriz in late March 1942.[98] Under the leadership of Ali Amirkhizi, the strategy of the APC from 1942 to its dissolution in the wider ADP in 1945 was active participation in the spontaneous movement against the central Government, with the goal of giving it direction. In doing so, the APC got involved in the Azarbaijani peasant movement which had challenged the land rights of the local landowners, the only time the Tudeh became involved in this activity in any significant way. Yet by 1945, the Tudeh had failed to organise mass support in Azarbaijan, and its emphasis on class struggle to the neglect of communal issues was an important factor in this.[99]

The ADP was the third group in the region, and eventually incorporated both of the others. Beside Pishehvari, its principal members were Azarbaijani activists from pre-Pahlavi politics such as Ali Shabestari, Sadeq Padegan, Amir Ali Lahroudi, Qasem Cheshm-azar and Gholam Yahya Daneshian. Some of these had become Tudeh members and were active in the APC. Pishehvari had also become a member of the Tudeh, but had serious political differences with the Tudeh leadership on communal issues, and personal differences with such figures as Avanessian. These differences were a source of tension between Azarbaijani Tudeh activists and the main Tudeh throughout this period, and led to the resignation of Amirkhizi and his replacement by Padegan one year prior to the ADP's creation. The ADP was established without prior notice to the Tudeh leadership, which was shocked when the APC merged with it the next day.[100] The Tudeh leadership wanted to publicly condemn the act, but the Soviets and the Soviet Azarbaijan Communist party, which had a direct hand in this venture, prevented the Tudeh from showing any public discontent, even forcing it to congratulate publicly the ADP.[101] After complying, the Tudeh leadership wrote a letter of complaint to the CPSU, but never received an answer.[102]

The ADP's programme between September and December 1945 defended Iran's constitution and was mild in tone and substance. It included the re-establishment of the Azari language in Azarbaijani schools and bureaucracy, and the creation of provincial councils, which were part of the constitution of Iran, although never implemented. Because the ADP did not emphasise class differences, and instead concentrated on communal issues, the party consisted of activists from different social strata, with different political and social programmes but united on those communal issues under communist leadership. Under the protection of the Red army, the ADP managed to expel the imperial army from Azarbaijan and convene its first national congress.[103] By December 1945, the ADP was strong enough to convene a parliament, form a cabinet and appoint Pishehvari head of state, and create a national militia, the Fadaiyan 'devotees' numbering around 20,000. The Azarbaijan Government in Tabriz still claimed to be an autonomous region within Iran, but its actions sounded alarms all over the country. The fact that the ADP was created under Soviet protection, had named a head of state, created a national parliament, and was at odds with its only potential ally – the Tudeh – in the national political arena only added to the party's isolation.

When the Azarbaijan crisis is put in a national perspective, its dimensions become even clearer. By the end of the Second World War, the Soviets had failed to evacuate Iran, as agreed in the 1943

Tehran conference, and demanded the northern oil concession. The Red Army not only aided the establishment of the autonomous Government, but also prevented the Iranian imperial army from entering a region which was legally part of Iran. The Azarbaijan crisis ended just as quickly as it had started. Premier Ahmad Qavam was the architect of the ADP's demise, the United States the international force behind it. Once the Soviet Union failed to evacuate Iran, as Britain and the United States had done, the United States put pressure on the Soviets to comply. In May 1946, a cabinet formed under Qavam asked the Tudeh to participate by naming three ministers. Qavam then signed an agreement with the Soviets regarding the northern oil concession, pending Majles approval and evacuation of Iran. In June, the Soviet army evacuated Iran, and in December 1946, one year after its creation, the autonomous Government of Azarbaijan was crushed by the imperial army. Pishehvari and most of the ADP leadership fled to Soviet Azarbaijan, and those who remained were massacred alongside thousands of ADP supporters and sympathisers.[104] Qavam resigned in late 1947 when he failed to get Majles approval for his agreement on the oil concession.

The ADP's conduct and defeat had great repercussions for Iranian communists. The party's overt dependency on the Soviets, its failure to fight back against the imperial army, despite its propaganda that it would not be easily moved, the fleeing of its leadership, and its failure to co-ordinate its actions with that of the Tudeh all resembled a dress-rehearsal for the 1953 coup. The most immediate result of the ADP's defeat, beside the reign of terror in Azarbaijan, was government attacks against the Tudeh and a crisis and split in that party.

Between its defeat in 1946 and merger with the Tudeh in 1960, the ADP did not have any significant independent presence inside Iran. The party moved its headquarters to Baku, and as long as the Stalinist regime was functioning, the ADP was under the thumb of Baqerov and the Soviet Azarbaijan Communist Party. The leadership of the party passed to Qasem Chashm-azar after the mysterious death of Pishehvari in 1947.[105] In 1953, the situation began to change in the Soviet Union, which in turn signaled change both in the ADP and the Tudeh. Stalin's death in March 1953 was followed by the arrest and imprisonment of Baqerov in June of that year. The de-Stalinisation of the Soviet Union had started.

Once the Tudeh leadership moved to its place of exile, first in the Soviet Union and later in the GDR, objections were raised about the need for two communist parties in a single country. Members of both factions began to raise objections based on the Leninist notion of a single national working-class party.[106] In 1955, the Tudeh wrote an official letter to the CPSU asking it to intervene and settle the issue. The ADP under Chashm-azar, supported by the Soviet Azarbaijan Communist Party, resisted the idea well into 1957, but the weight of the CPSU eventually cleared the way. In 1957, Chashm-azar was replaced by Gholam Yahya Daneshian, and the ADP and the Tudeh started talks about unity. It soon became clear that although the ADP had agreed to the idea of unity in principal, under Daneshian's leadership, and with the Soviet Azarbaijan Communist Party's support, the ADP was manoeuvring to maintain its autonomy even after joining the Tudeh. Therefore, three years of manoeuvring and negotiations were accompanied by the four principal players (the ADP, Tudeh, CPSU and Soviet Azarbaijan Communist Party) each jockeying for position. In the end, the CPSU decided to accommodate the Azarbaijan Communist Party, and asked the Tudeh to accept whatever it could get. This meant accepting the ADP as the Tudeh organisation in Azarbaijan, the ADP retaining its name, its central committee and chairman, and appointing members to the Tudeh central and executive committees. The Tudeh approved the deal in its seventh plenum in June 1960, and the union was completed in August of that year.[107]

The merger was in reality neither union nor accomodation. The Tudeh, with two factions co-existing in an uneasy truce, was already ill-prepared to meet the challenges of the 1960s and 1970s, and the addition of the ADP only added to fragmentation and factionalism in the party. The ADP entered the Tudeh with its own set of connections in the Soviet Union, and became another faction. The Tudeh leadership soon realised that the ADP was no more under Tudeh authority than it was before the merger. The only positive element in the merger, however, was the projection of a false sense of unity among the pro-Moscow Iranian communists at a time when Iran was entering a new era of turmoil and crisis, and a new generation of Iranian Marxists were preparing to take up arms and follow their own independent path.

THE THIRD FORCE: KHALIL MALIKI AND
THE INDEPENDENT LEFTISTS

The defeat of the ADP in December 1946 sparked a crisis in the Tudeh which ended only after a major split in 1948. A group of Tudeh members began to speak out about the incompetence of the leadership in handling a number of matters, particularly the Azarbaijan crisis. The complaints of the Reforming Group (*goruh-e eslah talab*), as these dissidents came to be called, centred on the Tudeh's acceptance of Soviet pressure and the party's public defence of the ADP. To accommodate the Reforming Group and other complaints, and to show some move towards reforming the party, a new eleven-member provisional executive committee was selected, from different branches, to replace the central committee until the next party congress. Of the eleven, only Khalil Maleki was with the Reforming Group, and soon became its leader, but others sympathised with some of its grievances. Maleki (1901–69),was born in Tabriz, and was a member of the Group of Fifty-three, a leading member of the Tudeh, and was involved in efforts to reconcile the Tudeh and the ADP, having been sent by the party to Azarbaijan to try to contain the crisis. In the post-ADP period, he emerged as a leading figure in the Tudeh who would spearhead complaints against the party leadership.[108]

The Tudeh provisional executive committee, in response to complaints directed at the party, issued two declarations on 14 January 1947. In these declarations the Tudeh criticised itself for its past dealings with the ADP, promised to punish those responsible for mistakes, underlined its independence and promised a party congress within three months in order to choose a new leadership and set new policies.[109] According to Tabari, the Soviets did not approve the content of the declarations and, through Aliev, asked the party to withdraw some of its positions, which the Tudeh did in a number of articles in party publications.[110] From this point on, struggle between the Reforming Group and the rest of the party intensified. The promised party congress was postponed, adding to the dissatisfaction.

Throughout 1947, heated discussions erupted between the two groups, virtually paralysing the Tudeh. In June 1947, the third Tehran regional conference was held, and the Reforming Group received a majority in the Tehran regional committee. With its power-base in the Tehran committee secured, the Reforming Group pushed for the second party congress, where it hoped to make its case and defeat the party leadership. The leadership, which comprised the future radical and moderate factions, fought back using its overwhelming majority in the executive committee to exert control over party organisation, and started a propaganda campaign, accusing the Reforming Group of factionalism and lack of discipline, and refusing to hold the promised party congress. The crisis came to a head when in January 1948 the Reforming Group issued a communique announcing its split from the Tudeh, and calling itself the Socialist Society of the Tudeh of Iran (*jam'iyat-e sosiyalist-e Tudeh-ye Iran*).[111] In the communique this group claimed to be a continuation of the progressive side of the Tudeh – less past mistakes – and to believe in scientific socialism, but stated that its programme would suit Iran's socio-economic conditions and not simply copy that of other socialist countries.

While the Reforming Group had some grievances regarding the Soviet role in the Tudeh organisation, its members still believed in the Soviet Union and expected its support, or at least its neutrality. But the fate of the Reforming Group was sealed when the Soviets condemned it. Many who had joined the group started to desert once the Soviet position became clear. In all, one hundred joined the group, including such prominent figures as Maleki, Anvar Khameh'i, Jalal Al-e Ahmad, Nader Naderpour, Eshaq Eprime, and Ebrahim Golestan.[112] The split was small-scale numerically, but many of those departing were prominent intellectuals. The group virtually ceased to exist after the Soviet condemnation.

The Reforming Group was not a united force, and consisted of three tendencies united against the Tudeh leadership.[113] While the group stopped all activities as a unified force for a few years, some of its members, under Maleki and his close colleagues, began to reorganise as the oil nationalisation movement began to gain momentum. Maleki and his group joined the populist journalist and publisher of *Shahed* (the *Witness*), Mozaffar Baqa'i, to create the Toilers Party of the People of Iran (*hezb-e zahmatkeshan-e mardom-e Iran*) in May 1951. With Baqa'i's charisma and his publication, the Toilers Party entered the political scene in defence of Mosaddeq as a left-of-centre party. The organisational, educational and ideological duties of the new party were left to Maleki and his comrades, and some publication duties and parliamentary participation was left to Baqa'i and his team. Maleki's group included Al-e Ahmad, Nader-pour, Muhammad Ali Khonji, Naser Vosuqi and others. This group soon started the publication of the weekly *Niru-ye Sevvom* (the *Third Force*), which became the publication of the party's youth organisation, and the monthly *Elm va Zendegi* (*Science and Life*), while Baqa'i kept *Shahed* under his own control.

The two groups around Maleki and Baqa'i actually made up the two wings of the Toilers' Party, with the former Tudeh members constituting the left wing. The union between the two groups came to an end after the July 1952 uprising and Mosaddeq's return to power. The root of differences lay in how to react to Mosaddeq, the left wing proposing complete support, the right wing finding itself increasingly alienated from Mosaddeq. The right wing, a minority on the party central committee, persisted in its opposition to Mosaddeq, and this accentuated the differences. Personal differences and rivalry (a characteristic of Iranian politics of this era) between Maleki and Baqa'i also played a role in splitting the party. The split materialised in late summer 1952 when Maleki's group, under the name The Toilers Party of the People of Iran (Third Force), closed ranks with Mosaddeq and Baqa'i's group joined the anti-Mosaddeq forces under the original party name.[114]

Maleki's group, which came to be called the Third Force from this point on, numbered a few thousand at its peak in 1952–3,[115] continued to support the Mosaddeq cabinet to the end, and was suppressed after the coup. It suffered another split after the coup when a group under Khonji accused Maleki of receiving money from coup leaders.[116] Maleki, in prison, denied everything, but the separation went ahead. Between 1953 and 1960 Maleki and his remaining supporters remained in Iran but could not be active as the Shah's repression did not allow much political activity. The group managed to enter the political scene between 1960 and 1963, when there was a relaxation of repression, but only as a small force in conjunction with the Second National Front, and did not appear as a social force again. The policies of Maleki and his group have been compared to those of Marshal Tito and his independent brand of socialism, but in the 1960s the Third Force resembled a social democratic party more than anything else.

The 1950s was the decade of great defeat for Iranian Marxists. A generation of young, largely well-educated activists saw their ideals crushed by a preventable coup which succeeded with minimum effort. The political parties which many of these activists expected to organise resistance and lead the anti-coup movement proved unable to adapt to the new political environment. Nevertheless, this great defeat did not lead to any solution of Iran's socio-political problems, and the end of the 1950s brought a resurgence of social unrest and turmoil. The imperial regime had managed to create relative political stability by eliminating all other political forces, but had failed to address the social issues which resulted from decadent pre-industrial conditions. These problems remained to be tackled in the new decade, posing new challenges to Iranian Marxists.

TRANSITION AND REVIVAL: THE THIRD WORLD CALL (1960–70)

The 1960s opened with a three-year period of turmoil, a lifting of political repression, and reform, followed by a reinstitution of repression. By 1963 the Shah started a process of reform which helped change Iran from an agrarian-based, pre-industrialised, pre-capitalist society to a semi-industrialised, capitalist one ready for integration into the world economic system. The centrepiece of the reform programme, which he liked to call the 'white revolution' or 'Shah-people revolution', was land reform.

Two elements underlay the need for reform. Firstly, the agrarian-based economy was dying of old age: it was unable to reform in order to become economically viable, and the land-owning class and imperial court alliance of 1953 would not allow any meaningful change. Secondly, internationally the winds of change had manifested themselves in the new Kennedy administration, which was determined to assert US dominance among its allies and to pre-empt any revolutionary movement which might benefit the Soviet Union.[117]

Internally, by the late 1950s, the agrarian economy of Iran was facing crisis, and could not accommodate the changing realities of the world economic system. According to Najmabadi, the economic relations of most under-developed countries generally required change and 'both the gradual build-up of internal markets and changing structure of international economic order made an accelerated expansion of internal markets and commodity production in these countries not only possible but positively desirable'.[118]

In relation to the role played by foreign powers, the competition between the United States and Britain must be noted. Britain played the dominant role in Iran until the end of the Second World War. The 1953 coup was a joint venture by the United States and the Britain, and represented an accommodation of their interests in Iran. By the late 1950s, the understanding between the two was coming to an end. The British power-base in Iran, the land-owning class, was a serious obstacle to the reforms that the Americans had in mind. Hence, when reform was mooted as the solution to Iran's economic crisis, to prevent possible social revolutions, the British-US coalition in Iran began to break up. In this competition, the British relied on their traditional allies, the land-owning class, while the Americans relied on a segment of the bourgeoisie which had sided with them in the 1953 coup.

A combination of internal and external elements resulted in the general political and social crises of 1960–63. In 1958, the Government announced the uncovering of a planned coup by a pro-American army general.[119] The coup sounded alarms for the Shah, the land-owning class and the British. From 1961, as a general policy, the US Government made future loans conditional on a policy of reform, with set criteria.[120] The Shah, initially reluctant to implement major reforms, soon changed sides and began to co-operate. Under US pressure, in May 1961 he named Ali Amini, a well-known pro-American politician, leader of a new government. Amini in turn named Hasan Arsanjani, a reform-minded agrarian expert, Minister of Agriculture. Under Arsanjani's guidance, the cabinet proposed a land reform programme which would do away with Iran's reliance on agriculture. Sensing the inevitable change, the Shah went to Washington and persuaded President Kennedy that he, and not the Amini cabinet, was the right implementor of reform. Thus, upon his return he dismissed Amini, named his long-time confidant, Amir Asadollah Alam, as the new Prime Minister, kept Arsanjani in the cabinet and proclaimed his white revolution on 27 January 1963.

At grass-roots level, the period 1960–3 was one of struggle between the opposition and the Shah, who was forced to relax the repression of the previous decade. The opposition at the beginning of this period was headed by the Second National Front, founded in July 1960 by some former colleagues of Mosaddeq. Its strategy was to demand free elections and call for reforms, and it was joined by university students, professional unions and some Marxist intellectuals. The Shah, once confident of US support, and armed with a reform programme, moved decisively against the front, and had suppressed it by 1963. Other opposition to the Shah came from religious circles. Headed by Shi'i grand ayatollahs, the religious opposition confronted the Shah on a number of issues, including land reform and the proposal for women's suffrage. The most vehement opposition came from Grand Ayatollah Ruhollah al-Musavi al-Khomeini, who opposed the Shah on a number of issues centred on the influence of the United States in Iran.[121] This too came to a bloody end on 5 June 1963, when the Shah ordered the army to suppress all opposition. Under Alam's direct leadership, the repression was effective, and Ayatollah Khomeini was sent into exile the next year.

Once the Shah took charge of the land reform programme, the direction changed away from Arsanjani's plan. The reform was originally supposed to redistribute the land among a large portion of the peasantry, but its second and third phases were quite conservative. As one observer put it, 'the peasants were supposed to be the principal beneficiaries of the reform programme, but due to the methods by which the reform was undertaken, the overwhelming majority of peasants did not benefit in any measurable sense from the redistribution, and within a few years their economic position began to worsen'.[122] While the land reform programme did not attain its original goals, together with the other provisions of the Shah's white revolution, it did extend capitalist relations of production and moved the country towards the Shah's vision of modernity.

For the rest of the 1960s, the Shah ruled as a confident despot, depicting himself as a reform-minded king and close ally of the United States and the West, with normalised relations with the Soviet Union. When he confidently crowned himself, and for the first time his empress, in 1967, he could see no serious opposition to his rule or his design for Iran, and the foreign press seem to have agreed with this, seeing him as a progressive ruler who had wrought a modern miracle.[123]

The Iranian communist movement in the 1960s underwent a generational change, the turbulent events of the 1960s making their mark on the movement as it prepared to meet new challenges. The defeat of 1963, the international competition of the superpowers over Iran, the Sino-Soviet split and the emergence of Maoism as an alternative to the Soviet version of socialism, and most important of all the victory of liberation movements around the globe all affected Iranian Marxists. Some of these issues had historical dimensions, such as why the movement was defeated in 1953, or what kind of relations a communist movement should have with other communist parties around the world. Others were new challenges: for example, an analysis of Iranian society, which was undergoing profound change, became a precondition of further action. In this context, analysis of the Shah's reform programme, the nature of the Shah's rule and the role played by foreign powers in Iran's internal affairs became significant. More practical – but no less challenging – was how to organise the movement, and the task of developing a mass base among the working class under relentless repression. Finally, there were theoretical issues such as whether to build a party strictly communist in nature, and how to deal with the Sino-Soviet dispute which was tearing communist solidarity apart.

While setbacks during the previous decade caused an atmosphere of defeat at the outset of the 1960s, by the end of the decade a large proportion of Marxists would come up with a new agenda, ready for implementation despite great odds. This decade represented a period of transition and revival for the movement. The new generation of Marxists would move away from a Tudeh-like organisation – able only to function under legal and semi-legal conditions, and dependent on foreign powers – to one independent of outside influence and conditioned to operate under extreme repression and a police state. A reverence for the Bolshevik revolution, hallmark of the previous generation, was diluted by the experience of Chinese, Cuban, Algerian and Vietnamese revolutions. From this point on, the Iranian communist movement may be divided into two categories, old and new. Perhaps the two had more in common than they wished to admit; after all, the new had emerged from the bosom of the old. But the main differences cannot be disregarded. The new generation was more self-assured, ready to declare war on the imperial system even when that meant starting from nothing. With sheer courage as their only capital, without expecting aid from the outside, with little or no experience in armed action, this generation challenged the imperial regime at the height of the Shah's power and stunned the old generation, most of whom were outside the country. This was at a time when the old generation's attempts to re-establish a foothold the country were frustrated more than once, its members forced to remain in exile. Mehdi Bazargan, a major opposition figure of the time and the future Islamic Republic provisional Prime Minister, prophetically captured the spirit of the coming age in his military trial in the 1960s: 'We are the last to struggle politically in accordance with the [monarchical] constitution. We expect the head of this court to convey this point to his superiors.'[124]

THE COMMUNIST TUDEH IN A
DECADE OF TRANSITION

Although the Tudeh-ADP union was complete by the time political opportunity arose and the party had declared Marxism-Leninism its official ideology, the party was ill prepared for the new social turmoil and crisis. Unlike nationalist and religious parties, the Tudeh did not have an organised presence in the country during the political turmoil of 1960–3. Marxist cells formerly associated with the Tudeh did participate in the movement, but the Tudeh was only a shadow of its former self. The party had borne the brunt of the Shah's repression in the previous decade, and this left it unable to participate in any meaningful manner, let alone to pose any threat. Moreover, SAVAK infiltration on two occasions in the 1960s greatly compromising its ability to re-establish a foothold inside the country. Under these circumstances, and with three factions manoeuvring against each other, the Tudeh was side-lined, impotent against its opponents.

In the 1960s, the Tudeh was under the leadership of Reza Radmanesh (1905–83), its first secretary (Kambakhsh and Eskandari were the other two secretaries), representing the dominance of the moderate faction in the party. By all accounts, Radmanesh was naive, and during his weak leadership the Tudeh was unable to come up with a unified policy on the imperial regime and the Shah's reforms.[125] Throughout the 1960s the party offered contradictory analyses of the reform programme, at times praising, at others condemning.[126] By this time the Tudeh considered itself the true communist party of Iran, and the New Party of the Working Class (*hezb-e taraz novin-e tabaqeh-ye kargar*), but here there was more propaganda and image-building than truth. There is no evidence that the party at this point had any foothold among the working class, and the contradictory analyses of the reform programme suggest that it did not have a realistic understanding of the social changes going on in Iran. When the SAVAK infiltrations are taken into account, the false nature of the image projected becomes yet clearer.

The first, and less threatening, SAVAK infiltration was discovered in 1962, perpetrated by the Yazdi brothers, Hosein and Fereidun. The sons of Morteza Yazdi, the former Tudeh leader who co-operated with the coup after his arrest, they had contacted the Tudeh leadership in the GDR and offered their co-operation. Because of family relations to Radmanesh (whose wife was Morteza Yazdi's sister), the two brothers soon became Radmanesh's trusted companions, and visited his home on a regular basis. At this point Radmanesh was the first secretary of the party and the person in charge of overseeing operations inside the country. The Yazdi brothers would steal important party documents from Radmanesh's safe and deliver them to SAVAK in West Berlin. Other party members found out about the operation by chance, and with the help of GDR police apprehended the spies. The party's tenth plenum in 1962 was a heated meeting convened around this subject, and an attempt was made on the part of the radicals to remove Radmanesh for his lack of leadership and character. The meeting ended with yet another compromise, and Radmanesh staying on.[127]

The second SAVAK infiltration of the Tudeh was devastating, not only for the party but for those in contact with it inside Iran. Through the 1960s, and while Radmanesh was in charge of the party organisation inside the country, an old rank-and-file Tudeh activist and *agent provocateur*, Abbas Ali Shahriarinezhad (henceforth Shahriari), was in charge of the party's operations in Iran. The organisation Shahriari headed was the Tehran Organisation of the Tudeh Party (*tashkilat-e Tehran-e hezb-e Tudeh*), which acted as the central command for all activities in Iran. Shahriari, who later became notorious as SAVAK's 'man with a thousand faces', had turned collaborator in the late 1950s, and had, according to Tabari, been introduced to Radmanesh and the party by the Soviets.[128] At any rate, Shahriari had Radmanesh's complete confidence, which meant SAVAK was in complete control of Tudeh activities inside Iran throughout the 1960s, until Soviet warnings and indisputable evidence led to a severing of relations with him in the late 1960s.[129] The SAVAK infiltration cost the party dearly. Two attempts to send in activists to help organise party activities inside the country were compromised. In the first Muhammad Hosein Ma'sumzadeh and Hasan Razmi entered Iran, were arrested and never heard from again. In the second, Parviz Hekmatju and Ali Khavari entered Iran and were arrested. Hekmatju died in prison, Khavari lived to head the remnent of the party after 1983.

Radmanesh was warned repeatedly about Shahriari, both by the Soviets and other party members, but refused to listen. Factional conflict and competition within the party can only partially account for Radmanesh's late reaction, and his own character and naivete must be held mainly responsible. This blunder cost Radmanesh dearly, and he was removed from his position and the central committee after the party's thirteenth plenum in 1969. This meant a split in, and a weakening of, the moderate faction, even though Radmanesh was replaced by another moderate, Eskandari.

The 1960s were also disruptive of Tudeh unity. Along the lines of the Sino-Soviet dispute and split, the Tudeh went through two splits, both caused by the departure of those sympathetic to Chinese communism and Maoism, but resulting in two different new organisations.

The first split came in February 1964, as a result of dissatisfaction with party leadership, its inability to evaluate critically its past or to organise resistance in Iran. The group was sympathetic to the Cuban revolution without really having much knowledge of it,[130] but the dispute later developed along Sino-Soviet lines, the dissenters calling the Tudeh a revisionist party and the Soviet Union a social imperialist state in which capitalism had been restored.[131] Naming itself the Revolutionary Organisation of the Tudeh Party of Iran (ROTPI, *sazman-e enqelabi-ye hezb-e Tudeh-ye Iran*), the base of the new party was among young Tudeh students active in the Confederation of Iranian Students in Western Europe. Indeed, according to one source, 'The Maoist split was the largest in the party's history and carried away a significant portion of the party's supporters in the West, perhaps 90 percent'.[132] The majority of these students had become sympathetic to the Tudeh after the 1953 coup, and while studying abroad, but some of the leading members were active in the Tudeh Youth Organisation, as high school students, prior to the coup.[133] Leading activists of ROTPI were young students such as Mehdi Khanbaba-tehrani, Bizhan Hekmat, Kurosh Lasha'i and Mohsen Rezvani. After the initial sympathy for Cuba, the new organisation soon developed solid relations with China and Albania, sent members to China for training and to help with the Persian programme of Radio Beijing, and began publishing *Tudeh* and *Setareh-ye Sorkh* (the *Red Star*) in Western Europe.[134]

ROTPI was a staunch Stalinist group with a dogmatic and strict belief in Maoism and the Chinese experience. The group was adamantly against Khrushchev's de-Stalinisation and the CPSU's proposed peaceful co-existence thesis.[135] Against this background, the ROTPI's analysis of the Shah's reform programme led it to believe that no meaningful change had been brought to Iranian society, and that it remained feudal and pre-capitalist (a semi-feudal semi-colony).[136] Based on these analyses, ROTPI came up with a blueprint of Chinese revolution for Iran, and concluded that to fight the imperial regime the vanguard organisation must work among the peasants, create a people's army and surround the urban areas from rural bases.[137] ROTPI believed that the Tudeh had been a deviant and opportunistic party from its inception, and that therefore the task of creating a proper communist party to spearhead revolution still lay ahead.[138]

Based on the above analyses of the international situation, Iranian society and the communist movement – and with China's backing – ROTPI attempted to organise inside the country, but failed at every turn. First, in 1964, Parviz Nikkhah, a member of ROTPI and a former member of the Tudeh Youth Organisation, returned from Britain to establish revolutionary cells among the peasants. He managed to set up a small group trying to map rural areas, but the venture came to a quick end when one of the group's associates attempted to assassinate the Shah, without the group's knowledge, in April 1965. SAVAK arrested the group, and they were put on trial and given prison sentences.[139] Second, following an uprising by nomadic tribes centred around the Fars province in 1963, ROTPI encouraged Bahman Qashqa'i, a medical student and member of the prominent Qashqa'i tribe, to return to Iran and reorganise the movement. Qashqa'i returned to Iran, joined the uprising in 1964, gathered a few followers around him and managed to harass the security forces for a while, but by 1966 his forces were outnumbered and the uprising was running out of steam. Bahman gave himself up after his family was taken hostage by the regime, and was executed the same year, despite Alam's guarantees that he would not be.[140] Third, ROTPI tried to join an uprising in Iranian Kurdestan between 1967 and 1969, led by Abdollah Mo'ini, Sharifzadeh and Molla Avareh. A team headed by Kurosh Lasha'i was sent to the region, but arrived just as the uprising was crushed, and had to return.[141] ROTPI had its own share of fragmentation in this period. In 1967, a group led by Mehdi Khanbaba-tehrani left it in a dispute over organisational and personal issues. The departing group, which preferred to use the obscure name *Kadrha* (cadres), accused the remaining leadership of lack of direction and organisational discipline, and opportunism.[142] Kadrha soon became a centre for any and all former ROTPI members dissatisfied with its leadership, but never really devised a clear strategy of its own, and only remained active outside Iran.

The second split in the Tudeh came when three high-ranking members of the party were expelled in 1965 for Maoist views. The trio, Hasan Sagha'i, Ahmad Qasemi and Gholam Hosein Forutan, all belonged to the radical faction, and the latter two were central committee members. While close to Kambakhsh and Kianuri, and through them close to Soviet intelligence, the trio had begun to develop differences with the Soviets after the beginnings of de-Stalinisation in 1956. Staunch Stalinists, the trio had no appetite for Khrushchev's peaceful co-existence and attacks on Stalin's 'mistakes'. Furthermore, as the Chinese under Mao started to present a more radical alternative, the trio was attracted to, and began to defend, the Chinese line in the Tudeh. Their presence in the party weakened the radical faction and hampered its efforts to replace Radmanesh after the Yazdi affair. But by 1965 their presence could not be tolerated in the light of younger members leaving the party to form

ROTPI the previous year and worsening Sino-Soviet relations, and the moderate faction, along with the ADP faction, spearheaded a drive to have them expelled which succeeded in 1965 during the party's eleventh plenum.[143]

The trio were in touch with ROTPI during their lonely fight in the Tudeh central committee. But once out of the Tudeh they found it hard to get along with the younger ROTPI members. Their differences centred on a number of personal and political issues. The young ROTPI leadership expected the trio to maintain a low profile and busy themselves with the translation of Mao's works, whereas the trio themselves expected to be able to assume leadership roles immediately. A more important dispute between the two was ROTPI's pro-Cuba sentiments during the early years, which ran counter to the trio's Maoism. But perhaps the most important difference was that the trio considered the Tudeh had gone some way to becoming the working-class party, and wanted to reorganise it, while ROTPI considered the Tudeh revisionist from the start, and wanted to form a new party.[144]

Hence the trio were expelled from ROTPI and left to form the Marxist-Leninist Organisation of Tufan (*sazman-e Marxist-Leninisti-ye Tufan*), publishing pamphlets in Europe in defence of their views. While Sagha'i died shortly after the trio left ROTPI, Qasemi and Forutan developed differences in the 1970s. Tufan (which means tempest) never managed to establish a foothold inside the country, and remained an opposition group abroad until the 1979 revolution.

Despite claiming to be substantially different, the departing Maoist groups were very similar to the Tudeh. They maintained the same party organisation, primarily based on the Stalinist model – only substituting as their inspiration the Chinese and Albanians for the Soviets – and most important of all were as unrealistic about Iranian society and the results and effects of the reforms as the Tudeh. Because of this – like the Tudeh – they tried but failed to start an operation in Iran. The best example of this unrealistic approach can be seen in ROTPI's attempts to form peasant armies among the Iranian peasantry. ROTPI wanted to repeat the Chinese experience in Iran without taking into consideration that Iranian peasantry lacked a revolutionary character, at least in modern times, and that most social movements in twentieth century Iran centred around urban areas.[145]

MARXIST CELLS: THE MOVE TO VIOLENCE

Alongside the failed attempts by the Tudeh-associated groups to return to Iran and organise resistance, the 1960s was an era of disorganised struggle by Marxist cells. These cells were either Tudeh remnants which had turned against it doctrinally, or were newly converted intellectuals looking for a way to organise the communist movement. Besides being disorganised, these Marxist cells lacked a clear theory and, therefore, a strategy, and operated as part of the crowd participating in the spontaneous movement whenever the opportunity presented itself. With their power-base mostly among intellectuals and university students, they participated wholeheartedly in the political activities of 1960–3, alongside the nationalists and the religious opposition. The defeat of 1963 and the consolidation of the Shah's power was a turning-point, however. Faced with repression and subjugation at home, and highly affected by the victory of liberation movements in Cuba and Algeria and the intensification of the Vietnam War, these cells turned to armed struggle and the use of systematic violence as the only way to confront the imperial regime. There were many of them, and not all survived the 1960s. Below, the history and development of some of the most important ones is dealt with, those whose members played a determining role in organising the guerrilla movement in the 1970s.

Two of the most important Marxist cells during this period were the Jazani-Zarifi group and the Ahmadzadeh-Puyan group. The importance of these two groups was twofold: first, both groups were front-runners in formulating and taking the initial steps in implementing guerrilla warfare in Iran; second, they both survived in sufficient numbers to launch guerrilla attacks on the imperial regime in the 1970s. Indeed in 1971 the Fadaiyan Guerrillas was formed from a merger of the two groups.

The Jazani-Zarifi group was named after two of its leading members, Bizhan Jazani (1937–75) and Hasan Zia'-Zarifi (1937–75), and its history goes back to the late 1950s and early 1960s. Members of the group were mostly active in the Tudeh's Youth Organisation before the coup, and had remained active as underground cells throughout the 1950s. The group was active between 1960 and 1963, but the defeat of 1963, the June massacre, and consolidation of the Shah's rule had a profound effect on it, and resulted in a major shift in tactics. Affected by the Cuban and Algerian experiences, the group concluded that armed struggle was the only way to confront the regime. By the beginning of 1967, Jazani and Zarifi had co-authored and distributed a pamphlet which formally announced the group's view on Iranian society and means of struggle.[146] The group spent two years, 1966 and 1967, preparing for this task, and was a leading organiser of demonstrations following the mysterious death of Gholam Reza Takhti, the wrestling medalist, in December 1967.[147] Although the group's members were experienced in open political activity, they had little or no experience in armed struggle or underground organisation, a situation which led them into contact with Abbas Shahriari and the hands of SAVAK before they were able to stage any military operation, the principal members being arrested in February 1968.[148] The remnant of the group managed to escape and continue the task of organisation. Among the remaining members, Ali Akbar Safa'i-farahani (1939–71) and Muhammad Saffari-ashtiani left the country for Lebanon and joined the Palestinian movement to get training and arms. The youngest member of the group, Hamid Ashraf (1946–76), remained in Iran to reorganise and recruit new members in order to keep the group alive,[149] and under Ashraf and Farahani the group continued with preparation for armed struggle in both rural and urban areas. In 1970, Farahani and Ashtiani returned from Lebanon with arms and ammunition,[150] and the first contacts with the Ahmadzadeh-Puyan group were made in August 1970.

Mas'ud Ahmadzadeh-heravi (1947–72) and Amir Parviz Puyan (1947–71) led a group which, unlike the other, was made up of younger activists from religious and National Front backgrounds, less experienced in political activity and less exposed to Marxist theory. In the early 1960s, Ahmadzadeh and Puyan were highly religious, and had established several political-religious cells in their native Mashhad, Khorasan province, in order to participate more actively in the opposition movement. In 1965, Ahmadzadeh moved to Tehran to go to university, and befriended Abbas Meftahi (1945–72), who had already met Farahani in his native town of Sari, Mazandaran province, and was exposed, through him, to Marxism. In 1967, after Puyan had already moved to Tehran, the three activists, and other friends, formed a secret cell to discuss social issues. At this point Puyan had already accepted Marxism, and within a year both Ahmadzadeh and Meftahi joined him. By this time group members had learned foreign languages, such as English and Spanish, and had started to translate political and theoretical articles and books.

The group's history at this stage may be divided into two phases. First, from February 1967 to March 1968, the group was established, accepted Marxism (the group was sympathetic to Mao's interpretation), and managed to expand both its numbers and network. Ahmadzadeh and Puyan, through contacts in Mashhad, managed to establish a cell in March 1968. In the same period, Meftahi managed to establish a cell in Sari, Mazandaran, and through the literary contacts of Puyan, the group managed to contact an already established cell in Tabriz. The Tabriz cell was created by such Azari intellectuals, and future guerrilla fighters, as Behrouz Dehqani (1939–73), and Ali Reza Nabdel (1944–72), and had already accepted armed struggle. In the 1970s, Dehqani became a hero to the guerrilla movement, and a symbol of resistance, when he died under torture without revealing any information. Nabdel was the author of a pamphlet severely criticsing the ADP, the Tudeh and Soviet policy in Iran.[151] But perhaps the most notable personality in the Tabriz cell was Samad Behrangi, whose literary contacts with Puyan connected the Tabriz cell to the Ahmadzadeh-Puyan group. He was a young school-teacher, from a humble background, who had worked among rural Azari children and had come to identify with their suffering and despair. His short stories in defence of armed struggle were addressed to a new generation of Iranians who, he believed, were unwilling to accept the status quo. Indeed, his *Little Black Fish* and *Twenty Four Hours Adrift* inspired a whole new generation and were widely read. Behrangi's tragic accidental death in 1969 was blamed on SAVAK by the guerrilla movement, in the context of a total physical and psychological war on the imperial regime. To the guerrilla movement, Behrangi was the first of their number killed by the enemy before the start of the actual battle, and songs and poems were written inspired by his martyrdom. It is now clear, however, that Behrangi was indeed accidentally drowned in the river Aras, with no SAVAK involvement.[152]

During the second phase, between March 1968 and 1971, the group developed a theory of armed struggle (it essentially believed in urban warfare) and an analysis of the reform programme, rejected the Chinese model of revolution, made contacts and discussed merger with the remnant of the Jazani-Zarifi group.[153]

The two groups that established the Fadaiyan Guerrillas made a number of theoretical contributions which will be examined in the next chapter. But briefly, while the two groups had come to conclude that armed struggle was the only way to confront the imperial regime, there were many differences between the two. Yet it seems that their shared repression and the need for unity held them together more than their differences drove them apart. Before the establishment of the Fadaiyan, each group held up a bank (in the spring and autumn of 1970) in order to raise funds.[154]

Two other groups which had come to see armed struggle as the only way were the Palestine Group (*goruh-e felestin*) and *Arman-e Khalq* (Ideal of the Masses). Notable in the first group were Shokrollah Pak-nezhad, Naser Khaksar and Hosein Tajir-riahi, alias Puya, and its membership consisted mainly of university students who had been nationalists at the beginning of the decade but had turned to Marxism in the mid-1960s. Initially, the group had strong Maoist tendencies, and had come to accept armed struggle on the Chinese model. The Palestine Group was active in the Takhti demonstrations, and was preparing for armed action when it was discovered by SAVAK in 1969. The group's efforts to get assistance from the Chinese were frustrated when those sent to help were discovered while trying to cross the border. The arrested members were put on trial and given long sentences, while the rest fled the country to reorganise. In the 1970s, members of this group joined other groups with different theoretical affiliations.[155] The second group was mostly made up of young workers, and prominent in it were, Homayoun Katira'i, Hushang Tarreh-gol and Naser Karimi. In 1971, the group was ready to join the Fadaiyan, after executing a few armed actions, when it was discovered by SAVAK, and all its members killed.

The 1960s also saw the creation of a number of underground cells which did not survive into the 1970s. The importance of these cells was as a breeding ground for some of those prominent in the movement in the 1970s. However, lack of information makes it almost impossible to identify most of these cells, let alone write their history. One such was called *Proseh* (Process), and was created in the late 1950s and was disbanded before 1970. The cell's members had associations with the Tudeh in the 1950s, but had developed Maoist tendencies and were basically involved in organising group studies of Marxist texts. Prominent members of the cell were Mostafa Madani, Mostafa Shoa'ian and Behrouz Rad. The first two joined the Fadaiyan in the 1970s.[156] Of the three, Shoa'ian was by far the most individual personality, not only in the cell but in the movement generally. An independent and shrewd thinker, Shoa'ian was developing in this period the vehemently anti-Leninist stance which became his trademark in the 1970s.[157]

Finally, a mention should be made of the major Iranian group in Western Europe and the United States. The Confederation of Iranian Students Abroad was a body consisting mainly of Iranian university students who acted against the imperial regime from the 1953 coup to the 1979 revolution. Although the confederation was tolerated by the imperial regime until the end of the 1960s, it was banned with the advent of armed struggle. It acted as a pressure group outside Iran, and in support of resistance inside the country, some segments acting as an auxiliary for the armed movement, others forming a base for political groupings which did not have visible activities in Iran.[158]

By 1971, the transition and revival of the communist movement was complete, and the generational polarisation between the two strands of Marxists had taken place. While the whole movement went on the offensive against the imperial regime just when it seemed most secure, the generation that started armed struggle truly shook the system and surprised the older generation. From this point until the success of the 1979 revolution, the only revolutionary gauge for organisations was how they reacted to the issue of armed struggle, and their alternative if they rejected it. Repression and the lack of free dissent meant that armed action became the only way an organisation could maintain momentum. Right or wrong, for better or worse, the communist movement went on the offensive.

2

Offensive and Stalemate (1971–9): Violence and Suppression

> The vanguard is not able to organise the masses for the revolutionary cause if it is not itself the flaring torch and symbol of devotion and resistance.
>
> Bizhan Jazani, founder of the Fadaiyan

The 1970s was a glorious decade for the imperial regime, that is until the February 1979 revolution put an end to 50 years of Pahlavi rule and over 2000 years of empire. The Shah's reforms of the 1960s and consolidation of power had left him no rivals on the political scene. The United States had bolstered his power, and guaranteed the regime military and political support unknown before in Iran. In the 1970s, parallel to efforts to implement its version of modernity, the regime began to modernise the Iranian military in accordance with the Nixon doctrine. Here, aided by unprecedented oil income, the regime began to arm itself with the most modern conventional weapons the West could offer. The occupation of three disputed islands in the Persian Gulf, and the celebration of 2500 years of empire in 1971 marked the new place the regime was trying to find for Iran in the world. Parallel with this, relations with the socialist bloc began to improve, and the Soviet Union and its allies began to actively participate in Iran's industrialisation.

The regime's achievements in the 1970s would not have been possible if the Shah had not managed to consolidate his rule in the latter part of the 1960s. Despite the assassination of Premier Mansur and an attempt on his own life, the Shah managed to decimate the groups involved by striking at the Islamic Fadaiyan and Marxists. By replacing Gen. Hasan Pakravan, the relatively moderate head of SAVAK, with Lt Gen. Ne'matollah Nasiri, he signaled even more repression. Between 1965 and 1970, SAVAK managed to break a number of underground cells, both Marxist and Islamic, preparing for armed action. By the beginning of the 1970s, political power was increasingly concentrated in the Shah's hands, the cabinet playing a secondary role and the Majles acting as a rubber stamp for the monarch's decisions. With Iran achieving complete control of its oil industry and revenue in 1973, the regime was provided with the income needed to build up Iran's industrial infrastructure and military. The 1972 Nixon-Kissinger trip to Tehran in effect put the Shah in charge of implementing the Nixon Doctrine in the Persian Gulf region. By 1975, the Shah felt confident enough to abolish the two government-run political parties and replace them with the *Rastakhiz* (Resurgence) Party. Apparently the decision to create *Rastakhiz* was taken arbitrarily by the Shah himself, without consultation with any of the political leaders.[1] The forming of a single-party-system in Iran ran against the Shah's own pronouncement that a single party system could only create dictatorship.[2] During the same year, he made peace with Saddam Hussein of Iraq, winning Iran the right to share equally the Shatt al-Arab waterway in return for an end to Iran's support for the Kurdish rebellion in Iraq headed by Molla Mostafa Barzani. To celebrate its achievements, in 1976 the regime started the celebration of 50 years of Pahlavi rule in Iran.

Iran's relations with the Soviet Union improved greatly between the latter part of the 1960s and 1978, thanks both to the imperial regime and the new Soviet leadership under Leonid Brezhenev. For the Soviets, the demise of its opposite number, the Tudeh, the lack of any alternative to the Shah, and pure economic considerations were major factors in the *rapprochement*. Also, while dissatisfied with political repression inside Iran and the pro-Western nature of the Shah's policies, the Soviets saw the reforms quite positively, in that they were moving Iran from a 'feudal' society to a capitalist one.[3] For the imperial regime, while the USSR was still a threat not to be underestimated, the need to normalise relations with Iran's powerful northern neighbour and the Soviet willingness to participate in industrial projects at bargain prices were important factors. Hence, in 1966 the two countries signed a pact under which Iran provided natural gas, the Soviets made limited military sales and participated in industrial projects. The most important of these projects was Iran's steel complex in Isfahan, the country's first. The deal was followed by a five-year trade agreement in 1967.

By the beginning of the 1970s, the composition of Iranian Marxists, and their activities, had already begun to change. The more traditional parties, the Tudeh and its Maoist splinter groups, which had their efforts to establish a base inside the country frustrated by SAVAK, moved into the background, and their involvement, for the most part, became limited to anti-regime activities outside Iran. Between 1970 and 1979 the guerrilla groups moved to the forefront, and led anti-regime activities inside the country. The regime itself was perhaps the main reason for the switch to systematic violence. The reform programme was accompanied by heavy repression, and to many political activists, both Marxist and Moslem, the only remaining option, short of silence and forbearance, was armed struggle. The success of the Cuban and Algerian experiences and the on-going Vietnam War gave them inspiration, but were not the main reason for their move from political to military-political opposition. In attempting to understand the general socio-political atmosphere that resulted in armed struggle taking precedence over other forms of opposition, it is significant that Marxist opponents of the doctrine – the Tudeh and others who criticised the failure of armed struggle after the revolution – did not attempt to produce an alternative. The activists of the armed struggle had clearly come to the conclusion that no other avenue remained open. The theoretical justification for armed struggle came after this initial practical step. Right or wrong, the advocates of violence believed that inaction – with the hope that unforeseeable future developments might progress the cause – was unacceptable. For the other political parties or groupings that, for whatever reason, did not resort to violence the result was disengagement from independent political activity inside the country. This was the time of guerrilla groups, of bold offensives against the regime, of romantic heroism, and of a rationalisation of violence. The impact of the guerrilla movement was sufficiently widespread that it even appeared in the Shah's private conversations with his court minister. On one occasion, on 13 January 1976, he is reported to have said, 'The determination with which they fight is quite unbelievable. Even the women keep battling on to their very last gasp. The men carry cyanide tablets in their mouths and commit suicide rather than face capture.'[4] The Shah, while wanting to depict himself as an open-minded and modern leader, was known to view women as inferior to men. His amazement at the conduct of female guerrillas was a further example of the impact the movement had on the highest echelons of the imperial regime.

For Iranian Marxist groups struggling in this period, new problems, both theoretical and practical, joined the old ones, demanding solutions before progress could be made. Of these, one of the most imposing was an analysis of Iranian society: the Shah's reform programme, the nature of his rule, the role of foreign powers in Iran, and the past performance of the Iranian communist movement. A second was the methods of struggle necessary, while another was differences between the two communist giants and their role in Iranian affairs. Finally, there was a need to define what is known in Marxist terminology as the revolutionary stage. Here, three different analyses existed, dividing the movement in three. The first school of thought believed Iran was at a national democratic stage. This meant that a coalition against the imperial regime did not have to be led by communists, that development did not have to be a social revolution and that reform could be of a type commonly referred to as bourgeois-democratic. The second placed Iran in the people's democratic stage. This meant that any coalition against the imperial regime had to be led by the communist element, that the reforms that followed would necessarily be both bourgeois and socialist in nature, and that such development would be a social revolution. The third contended that the only social revolution was a socialist one, de-emphasised coalition with non-communist groups and pointed to the working class as the only class capable of bringing about real change. Below, the activities and history of the movement in the 1970s will be examined, and their response to these problems analysed.

THE FADAIYAN GUERRILLAS

The Organisation of Iranian People's Fada'i Guerrillas (OIPFG, *saz-man-e cherikha-ye fada'i-ye khalq-e Iran*) was officially established in late April 1971 by the union of the Ahmadzadeh-Puyan group and the remnant of the Jazani-Zarifi group, and renamed the Jangal group following the Siyahkal operation.[5] The gendarmerie post in Siyahkal, a village in the northern province of Gilan, was attacked by the Jangal group in February 1971, marking the start of the armed struggle against the imperial system. The operation was initiated by a team of 16 guerrillas headed by Ali Akbar Safa'i-farahani, but by the time of the attack four members had been already arrested.[6] The attack sparked eight years of intense armed struggle, led to the final establishment of the Fadaiyan,[7] signaled the beginning of what came to be known as the New Communist Movement of Iran (*jonbesh-e novin-e komonisti-e Iran*), and inspired many other politico-military groups, Marxist and Islamic, to take up arms against the dictatorship. Siyahkal was a failure in the sense that all the guerrillas were caught and the majority killed, but was a success in that it signaled a new beginning for the militant anti-Shah opposition.

Not all the original founders of the Fadaiyan had the necessary theoretical grounding needed to confront the problems facing them, although it is known that the published works of Fadaiyan theoreticians, written in jail or underground, were reviewed in group discussions. The original authors were Jazani, Ahmadzadeh, Puyan, Farahani, Zarifi and Hamid Mo'meni, the last of these having joined the organisation after its establishment but nevertheless contributing greatly to it. Ashraf, the main leader of the organisation between 1972 and 1976, also wrote a number of pamphlets, but was more an organiser and practitioner than a theoretician.

Among the members mentioned, Jazani, Ahmadzadeh and Puyan occupy a special place in Fadaiyan history. This is mainly due to the effect of their theoretical and practical work, not only on Fadaiyan programmes and policies, but also on the Iranian communist movement and on other guerrilla groups in general. The one theoretical essay written by Amir Parviz Puyan (1947–71), *The Necessity of Armed Struggle and a Refutation of the Theory of Survival*, was widely distributed among students and intellectuals, and had a profound impact upon them. In this essay, the first theoretical work on the armed struggle by an Iranian Marxist, Puyan attacked the passivity of those groups which believed in purely political opposition. He called this passivity the 'theory of survival', and put the case for armed struggle. To explain why the working class was not rising against the regime, Puyan developed the thesis of 'two absolutes' (*du motlaq*), which contended that the overwhelming power of the state, on one hand, and the total lack of working-class political organisation, on the other, had created a situation in which absolute strength met absolute weakness. Armed struggle, according to Puyan, would shatter this atmosphere and lead to the establishment of a vanguard and victory.[8]

Armed Struggle Both as a Tactic and Strategy, by Mas'ud Ahmadzadeh (1947–72), had by far the greatest effect in shaping the Fadaiyan's theoretical foundation for close to six years, and the theoretical foundation of the two Fadaiyan splinter groups after the 1979 revolution. Ahmadzadeh presented a socio-economic analysis of Iranian society and its class structure, addressing such issues as the working class and its allies, the organisation of the revolutionary movement, and the role played by the vanguard's armed struggle. The ideas of Latin-American guerrilla theorists, as well as those of Regis Debray, had clear influence on him, and Ahmadzadeh adopted from Debray the metaphor of the 'little motor' and the 'big motor' to describe the relation between the guerrilla force and the revolutionary classes. In explaining the necessity of armed struggle, Ahmadzadeh, like Puyan, wrote that armed struggle would pave the way for a people's awareness of their own historical strength, and for the vanguard organisation to become a mass army and lead the revolution to its final victory.[9]

Of the three theorists, Bizhan Jazani (1937–75) was the oldest, the ablest, and had the most effect on the communist movement in general, and the Fadaiyan in particular. Unlike most Marxist and Moslem activists, who were usually technical university students, Jazani was a bright philosophy graduate student when arrested in 1968, and is widely regarded as one of Iran's major Marxist theorists. A political activist since the age of ten, he was a member of the Tudeh's Youth Organisation and came from an activist family. He was sentenced to 15 years' imprisonment while trying to organise armed action, and in jail persistently organised resistance among other political inmates. His writings, mostly written in prison and smuggled out, covered a variety of issues, from analysis of Iranian society to the tasks of the vanguard party in organising armed struggle, to the effects of psychology and spontaneity in revolutionary movements.[10] Jazani had a deep understanding of recent Iranian history, rare among activists of his generation and the one which followed, his grasp of Iranian history giving him a political insight unmatched by others. For example, acknowledging Ayatollah Khomeini's popularity among certain segments of the population, he was perhaps the first person, in the early 1970s, to predict that Ayatollah Khomeini might lead the anti-Shah movement:

> With this background, Khomeini has unprecedented popularity among the masses, especially petty bourgeois businesses, and with his opportunities for relatively free political activity has an unprecedented chance of success.[11]

Also a painter, Jazani depicted the ideas of the movement and the conditions of prison in his work. His commitment to the revolutionary struggle was devotional, and his emotional and sometimes romantic words on the tasks facing the vanguard are perhaps the best expression of how the young revolutionaries felt when the movement took off in 1971.[12] Jazani's prime concern was creating and organising the vanguard, or revolutionary intelligentsia, but once this was done, he believed that the tactics should expand to include political propaganda as well as military action. He called political agitation the movement's second leg, and kept advising the Fadaiyan to pay more attention to this aspect. His assassination in prison in April 1975, along with six other original Fadaiyan founders, was a great blow to the movement and came at a time when it was preparing to adapt to his views.

Since he wrote from prison, he had no way of defending his views within the organisation. Indeed, it could be said that, unlike Ahmadzadeh and Puyan, he had already lost theoretical influence over his group by the time of the organisation's birth. With most of the experienced members arrested in 1968, the leadership of the group fell into the hands of Ashraf and Farahani, and with Farahani's death in the Siyahkal operation, Ashraf, youngest member of the Jazani-Zarifi group, accepted most of Ahmadzadeh's theses in the process of the Fadaiyan's formation. But it was only five years after the Siyahkal operation and one year after Jazani and his comrades were murdered in jail that Jazani's theses were accepted by the Fadaiyan.

The theorists of the two groups adopted significantly different analyses of Iranian society. Both groups acknowledged that the land reform programme had caused deep changes. Almost independently of each other, they concluded that what had replaced the pre-capitalist socio-economic formation was dependent capitalism. They both agreed that Iran's dependent capitalist system relied on state dictatorship and a capitalist class (comprador bourgeoisie) closely linked to that state, and that this arrangement was not in the people's interest. Hence, both groups agreed that the new social changes were fundamentally reactionary, their purpose to integrate Iran into the world capitalist system. Ahmadzadeh believed that the reform programme was imposed on society mainly because of the intervention and pressure of imperialism in the form of US interference. He saw the Iranian comprador bourgeoisie as a close ally of the international bourgeoisie, and therefore for the most part as equally imperialist. He also believed that the reforms, far from easing the class contradictions and conflicts in Iranian society, had intensified them and so brought about objective revolutionary conditions.[13] In contrast to Ahmadzadeh, Jazani believed that both an internal and external factor had led to the reforms, the internal one being that Iran's pre-capitalist socio-economic relations had reached a point of crisis in the late 1950s. This, he believed, was the main incentive for reform, imperialism playing a secondary role. Jazani suggested that reform had eased class contradictions and conflicts (in the 1960s), and that because of this an objective revolutionary condition did not exist,[14] but that in the nature of a dependent capitalist system such a condition would emerge in time, so that revolutionaries had to be ready for it.

Ahmadzadeh believed that the Shah's regime was merely a puppet of imperialism, created and maintained by it. Therefore, according to this analysis, the main enemy of the future revolutionary movement would be imperialism, the state being secondary. In contrast, Jazani believed that land reform had changed the nature of the regime, that although the Shah was installed by imperialism, his regime was a personal dictatorship. The Shah, although ultimately a puppet, had a certain amount of independence.[15] Therefore, the slogan 'Down with the Shah's dictatorship and his imperialist protectors' was suggested by Jazani as an alternative to the Fadaiyan slogan, adopted from both the Vietnamese experience and Ahmadzadeh's theses, 'Down with imperialism and its running dogs'. Farahani also believed in the relative independence of the Shah, but his early death ended his contribution to the conversion of the Fadaiyan to the Jazani thesis.[16] The two positions, then, differed greatly over the role of the external factor in Iran. While Ahmadzadeh saw it as the crucial element, Jazani consistently tried to put the foreign and domestic elements into a dialectical perspective.

The similarity between Jazani's proposed slogan for the Fadaiyan and that of the Tudeh, adopted after 1975 (see below), which read 'down with the Shah's dictatorship' caused controversy, the main issue being that Jazani's radical opponents, both inside the Fadaiyan and outside, accused him and his supporters of being doctrinally close to the Tudeh. It should be noted that the accusation of similarity to the Tudeh, whether correct or not, was one of the most damaging radical Marxists could throw at each other at this time. In Jazani's case, the accusation was false, but was repeated so frequently that it become popular belief, and has remained so to this day.[17] For Jazani, an organisation's slogans had to relate directly to its activities. Therefore he believed that since the Shah had become the absolute ruler of the state and the most evident symbol of state repression, the slogan 'Down with the Shah's dictatorship' would act as the best vehicle for the mobilisation of the opposition. Here, Jazani was analysing the situation from the perspective of those directly involved in the struggle, whose main preoccupation was the mobilisation of the masses and the overthrow of the state. Furthermore, Jazani was a firm believer in communist, that is proletarian, leadership in any coalition. He had come to the conclusion that the national and petit bourgeoisie were incapable of leading a social revolution. In Marxist terminology this meant that the Iranian revolution was at a people's democratic stage rather than a national democratic stage. Hence, according to Jazani, while the proletariat was not strong enough to stage a socialist revolution on its own, and had to unite with other classes, it must take charge for the revolution to be successful. The Tudeh's perception was very different, and will be analysed below, but suffice to say that the Tudeh slogans were designed to reach the ruling classes, since the party had neither the ability to, nor the intention of, overthrowing the regime as a whole. The Tudeh strategy in this period was to remove the Shah without necessarily removing the monarchy. Furthermore, the Tudeh believed Iran to be at the national democratic stage, which meant it could accept the leadership of non-communist forces.

On the history of the Iranian communist movement, especially recent experience, the Tudeh, Ahmadzadeh and Puyan did not offer an analytical view. Ahmadzadeh believed that the Tudeh was just a caricature of a Marxist-Leninist party, and they both believed that the past defeats and passivity of the movement in Iran were due, for the most part, to Tudeh opportunism. The devotions and sacrifices of armed struggle were supposed to help clear away the memories of past defeats, and to bring back the movement's lost prestige. The revolutionary heroism of the armed vanguard would clear away the memories of the Tudeh's cowardice. Ahmadzadeh's criticism of the performance of the Tudeh and its splinter group, ROTPI, in the 1960s was harsh. He saw the Tudeh's view – that the reform programme had some positive elements, and that growing relations between the imperial regime and the socialist camp would ultimately aid the growth of industry and the proletariat, and lead to less dependence – was simply a means of covering up an inability to act inside the country. Ahmadzadeh summed up the Tudeh's argument thus: 'What we can do is to adopt a number of reformist measures, gather strength, ask the regime to speed up its "positive" steps and try to force it into some tactical concessions. In current conditions, the main task is not the overthrow of the "Shah's dictatorship" and its replacement with the "people's dictatorship", but is to ask for the gradual change of the "Shah's dictatorship" into the "Shah's democracy"'.[18] As to ROTPI, Ahmadzadeh acknowledged its revolutionary tendencies but criticised it for not accepting that the reform programme had changed Iran from a feudal society into a dependent capitalist one, for the fear of being forced to accept the Tudeh's analysis and relinquishing armed struggle. By not seeing the reality, Ahmadzadeh suggested, ROTPI would be unable to fight for change.[19]

The Jazani-Zarifi group's arguments on the Tudeh – accepting that the Tudeh had been the communist party before 1953 – were more in-depth, though similar to those of the other group. Zarifi's view was: 'Our understanding of the Tudeh Party, on the eve of 19 August 1953, is that the Tudeh party was a communist party; this is why we consider the defeat of 19 August as being principally due to the inability of the party's leadership to carry out its revolutionary duties'.[20] In summing up the reasons behind the 1953 defeat, Jazani similarly believed that defeat was mainly due to the inability of the Tudeh leadership to react:

> The 19 August onslaught could have become a turning-point for intensifying the struggle and for the passing of the movement from a political phase to a military one. Had the Tudeh Party, with its inadequate forces, chosen to resist between 17 and 22 August, it might have been able to defeat the coup. This resistance could have become the beginning of a revolutionary movement for mobilising and arming the masses for a people's war against the enemy.[21]

Jazani, echoing the sentiments of his generation, praised the gallantry of the Tudeh rank-and-file, but attacked the Tudeh leadership:

> The Tudeh Party's principal weakness was not that it did not have devoted members. The resistance of many rank-and-file and some of the higher-ranking Tudeh Party members in the face of the enemy is still a source of pride for the working class and the people. There were a number of people who died under torture but did not reveal party secrets... At least 20 percent of the Tudeh Party and Youth Organisation members were willing to participate in an armed struggle and sacrifice their lives. This force was enough to start a revolutionary struggle. There is no doubt that in later stages thousands and tens of thousands, from among the toilers and the people who were mobilised, would have joined the armed movement against the regime. The principal weakness of the Tudeh Party was in that, from a year prior to the coup, it failed to use this ready force to prepare for violent resistance.[22]

Jazani acknowledged that the Tudeh's close relations with the Socialist camp, especially the Soviet Union, had provided it with some opportunities to act against the regime outside Iran, but he considered this close identification with the Soviet Union, at a time when relations between the Soviets and the imperial regime were improving, worked against the party. Jazani considered the Tudeh from the 1960s onwards as non-revolutionary and reformist, and ridiculed the party's efforts to depict itself as the working-class party. He rejected the Tudeh's policy of purely political means of confronting the imperial regime, and suggested that it was waiting for political openings while not doing anything to bring them about.[23] Jazani was much harsher than Ahmadzadeh on Maoist-Tudeh splinter groups such as the Tufan and ROTPI. He compared their situation to that of the Tudeh by criticising their reliance on China, the fact that some of their members had co-operated with the imperial regime after their arrest, their political infighting and their inability to organise and operate inside the country.[24] But he saved most of his criticism for the analysis of Maoist groups on the reform programme, vehemently attacking the theorists of these groups who, by relying on the Chinese model and Mao's writings, refused to acknowledge that the reform programme had changed Iran from a feudal society to a capitalist one:

> ... [we would like] to remind them that it is regrettable that some of the theorists of this analysis and a number of well-known supporters of these theses only put aside their dogmatism when it is too late and they are in front of the television cameras, and with 'guilty' consciences are admitting to their mistakes, and declare the end of feudalism... and accept the progressiveness of the regime and the victory of the 'white revolution.[25]

On the strategy and tactics of the revolutionary movement, and an analysis of the class structure of Iran, both positions agreed that the Iranian national bourgeoisie, of whom Mosaddeq was the political manifestation, was defeated and had entered a process of dissolution, and Jazani provided an in-depth analysis of how and why this was happening. None of the writers believed that the national bourgeoisie could play a leading role in the movement, and that the revolutionary classes consisted of the working class, the petit bourgeoisie and the remnants of the national bourgeoisie.

The deepest differences between the two appeared over the theory of armed struggle. Since Jazani and his group in jail had a different analysis of the results of land reform, their version of the theory differed in its view of the objective conditions of revolution. As noted before, both Ahmadzadeh and Puyan believed that the reform programme had intensified class contradictions in society, and so in analysing the causes of the lack of spontaneous movement, they both pointed to the role of the dictatorship as fundamental. Ahmadzadeh believed that the lack of spontaneous movement was due to violent and long-term repression and the weakness of revolutionary forces,[26] and that the objective revolutionary conditions did exist, so that the only other factor needed for revolution was a consistent attack on the dictatorship. Such an attack would gradually result in the creation of a people's army, and would bring the spontaneous revolt into the open. While Admadzadeh's theses were dominant, the Tudeh attacked the Fadaiyan on the very same point. Without any visible and significant activity inside the country, the Tudeh attacked the Fadaiyan as anti-Leninist, petit bourgeois revolutionaries launching an armed struggle in the absence of revolutionary conditions. The Fadaiyan insisted that such conditions were present in the Iran of the early 1970s.

Jazani saw the situation differently. He believed that land reform had indeed eased class conflict, and that objective revolutionary conditions did not exist. On the basis of this analysis, he suggested the 'armed propaganda theory', and divided the process of armed struggle into two phases. The first phase, he suggested, would be the establishment of the vanguard organisation. In this phase, that vanguard would attack the dictatorship, declare its existence to the people, and organise revolutionary elements ready to take up arms and join the struggle. Armed actions would be propagandist, and would prepare the vanguard militarily, organisationally and politically for the participation of the people. The second phase would be a mass-based revolutionary movement, in which a people's army would be formed.[27] Jazani saw armed struggle as both a military and political process. Although he saw armed action as the axis of all other tactics and strategies, he indirectly criticised Ahmadzadeh and the Fadaiyan for not paying enough attention to the political side of the movement, and warned them of the dangers of sectarianism and over-adventurousness.[28] It is obvious that he took an unorthodox view on this issue. Most Marxists, including Lenin, agree that the use of violent means as the main revolutionary tactic is legitimate only when objective revolutionary conditions exist. Jazani's heterodoxy was his theory of 'armed propaganda' whereby the vanguard uses armed struggle as a means, first, of establishing itself, and second, of preparing the movement for revolution, whether or not known objective revolutionary conditions may exist.

All national communist movements have a theoretical view of the international communist movement, and use it to determine their relations with other movements and countries. The Ahmadzadeh group did not write about this. What is known, however, is that, as noted before, the group had strong sympathies for the Chinese experience and Mao Zedong, but later rejected the Chinese model as not being applicable to Iran. The Fadaiyan, under Ashraf, showed strong Maoist sympathies, but the organisation managed to keep its independence from both China and the Soviet Union throughout the struggle against the imperial regime. The tendency to remain independent from international socialist camps was based on the Fadaiyan's belief that Tudeh dependence on the Soviets had adversely affected it. The fact that the Tudeh's Maoist splinter group had done no better than the main party only underlined the need for independence, and there was a historical tradition of Iranian hostility to the meddling of foreigners in national affairs. Although considering both the Soviet Union and China as progressive socialist countries, the Fadaiyan could not overlook the fact that they would always put their own national interest before international socialist solidarity. The Soviet Union's lukewarm co-operation with the imperial regime in the 1960s and 1970s, and China's normalisation of relations, which began in the 1970s, only emphasised this. Also, the new generation of Marxists found distasteful the demands put on the Tudeh by the Soviets in return for their support.

Jazani was very much aware of the split between the Chinese and Soviet communist parties in the 1960s, and suggested that the Iranian movement not take sides. He rejected the Khrushchev thesis that suggested peaceful coexistence as the main tactic for the international communist movement, favouring world revolution as the main vehicle of change.[29] Both Jazani and Farahani were critical of the Stalinist period, although their views never found a following among the Fadaiyan.[30] Jazani attacked the one-sided relationship between the CPSU and the Tudeh, both during and after Stalin, and considered it one of the reasons for the Tudeh's failures. On the role of the Soviet Union in Iran and its close relationship with the Shah, Jazani wrote:

> In this new situation, the Soviets gave their support to the land reform programme. Soon after, the economic relations between the two countries expanded greatly... meaning that right at a time when the

regime was repressing the people and strengthening the dictatorship, a honeymoon between Iran and the Soviets was starting. This development proved, once more, that the Iranian revolutionary movement must take an independent path vis-à-vis Soviet politics or any other foreign power, and rely on the power of the people. [This is so] since the Soviets and other powers and world movements have ignored the interests of our movement and have coordinated their relations with Iran according to their own needs.[31]

Throughout the anti-Shah struggle, the Fadaiyan may be considered Stalinist (despite the anti-Stalinist positions of Jazani and Farahani), although with no direct affiliation to any socialist state, being critical of what it saw as Soviet deviation from the revolutionary Marxist-Leninist path. On two occasions, Hamid Mo'meni and Ali Reza Nabdel even went as far as suggesting that capitalism was beginning to re-establish itself in the Soviet Union, but this analysis was theirs alone and was not the official Fadaiyan line.[32] The organisation's only affiliations were with other movements (eg the Palestinians), and it did receive financial support from countries such as Libya, but apparently without accompanying interference.

The Stalinist sympathies of the Fadaiyan had two implications. First, they showed that the Fadaiyan's Marxist education was highly influenced by the Russian revolutionary experience, as conveyed by Stalinist propaganda, as was also the case for most other Marxist organisations in Iran. Second, they showed that many of the Stalinist values of 'intra-party democracy' may also have been passed down to the Fadaiyan. Indeed, as we shall see below, the Fadaiyan did adopt many Stalinist norms on that point.

The Fadaiyan was the most active guerrilla organisation between 1971 and 1979. This is how the Organisation of Iranian People's Mojahedin (the main Moslem guerrilla group) described the impact of the Fadaiyan on society:

> ... in 1971, the Siyahkal guerrillas went into operation. This event forced the Mojahedin, in 1971, into action and to introduce themselves to society against their will and before they were ready. If they (the Mojahedin) had not come into action, the People's Fada'i would have been left as the sole vanguard organisation...[33]

Indeed the Mojahedin (established five years prior to the Fadaiyan) openly declared its existence, through armed action, in order not to fall behind the Fadaiyan in its quest for leadership of the revolution. The Mojahedin's assessment of the Fadaiyan's role in Iran is only one example of the impact of Siyahkal on the other guerrilla groups. Soon after the Siyahkal operation, other clandestine groups announced their existence as well. The Fadaiyan engaged the Shah's forces in intense, mostly urban, guerrilla activity which included assassination of those engaged in repression, bank robbery and the bombing of centres of the regime's power. It lost its entire original leadership (Jazani, Ahmadzadeh, Zarifi, Farahani, Puyan, Ashraf and others), but maintained a hegemonic role among guerrilla groups, in both the theoretical and practical spheres. Based on research done in the 1960s, the Fadaiyan also produced a number of studies on land and reform in Iran which were the only in-depth works of their kind by Iranian Marxists.[34]

The period 1971–9 may be divided into two stages. In the first, between 1971 and 1975, Ahmadzadeh's theses were the official line, and Ashraf was still alive. In the second, between 1976 and February 1979, the Jazani line was adopted. During this stage, the organisation had to recuperate from the loss of its leadership (Ashraf and others), adapt to the new line, and contain a challenge by a Tudeh-leaning splinter group.

The initial stage had two main characteristics. First, it was marked mostly by military operations devised by an organisation which had little experience of them. The Fadaiyan lost many able and dedicated members. Ahmadzadeh, Puyan, Meftahi, Farahani, and Ashtiani were all killed by 1972. Second was the expansion of the organisation, a process achieved both by recruiting new members and by uniting with smaller armed groups.

The Fadaiyan's military confrontation with the imperial regime in this period had a clear psychological, as well as political and military, aspect, in that the organisation chose its targets to deal psychological blows at the security forces as well as to make political points. With a self-confidence unique to that generation in Iran, the Fadaiyan under Ashraf would prepare and execute each attack with precision and care. It targeted the imperial regime's banks (for the movement's financial needs), and principal military or political leaders publicly known for their role in repression (an example was Gen. Zeinolabedin Farsiu, head of the military tribunal responsible for political trials, in 1971).[35] It bombed foreign interests in Iran (the Fadaiyan did not kill any foreigners and, unlike the Mojahedin, did not consider foreigners legitimate targets), and killed members of the bourgeoisie who had relied on the state to repress the workers, and SAVAK torturers. Examples of these activities were the bombing of the offices of American oil companies in the early 1970s, the assassination in 1974 of Muhammad Sadeq Fateh-yazdi, a factory owner who, by calling on the security forces to repress a strike, had caused death and injury to workers, and the assassination of SAVAK Maj. Alinaqi Nik-tab', a notorious torturer, in 1974.[36] Perhaps the biggest psychological blow to the imperial regime was the assassination, in March 1975, of the notorious Abbas Shahriari, who by this time had retired and was living in Tehran.[37] Each armed action was accompanied by the distribution of explanatory material, but since the Fadaiyan's perception of armed struggle was based on Ahmadzadeh's analysis, overall less attention was paid to political propaganda. The Fadaiyan paid dearly for its armed action, evident from the number of leaders and members killed, but it fought back, blow for blow. As long as Ashraf was alive, a kind of psychological contest existed between the Fadaiyan and SAVAK whereby every attack by one side was answered in kind by the other. The Shahriari assassination, which was preceded by others, was followed by the assassination of Jazani in prison. The Fadaiyan also became involved in other national liberation movements, and members of the organisation fought and died alongside Palestinians and the Dhofar revolutionaries.[38] With the imperial regime's involvement in the Omani civil war in the early 1970s, and the Fadaiyan's involvement on the side of the revolutionaries, Iranians were fighting and dying on both sides.

In the process of uniting with other groups, problems began to occur among the Fadaiyan, due mainly to the lack of clarity in its organisational structure. During its first three years, it was not clear whether the Fadaiyan worked within a set theoretical framework, and internal structure, or whether it was a front organisation for various Marxist groups which united to fight the imperial regime without a unified doctrine. The Fadaiyan did not call itself an organisation until 1972 – the group previously being known as the People's Fada'i Guerrillas – and its emblem emphasised this.[39] Jazani never referred to the Fadaiyan as an organisation, and he wrote two years after its establishment that it could be seen as a platform of unity for all Marxist-Leninists who believed in armed struggle.[40] The above hypothesis was confirmed by Mehdi Khanbaba-tehrani, a political activist of the period, who suggested that the term 'organisation' was added only during the Ashraf leadership after 1972.[41]

This lack of clarity in the status of the Fadaiyan later gave rise to the expulsion of Mostafa Shoa'ian (1936–75). An activist of the 1960s, by the early 1970s Shoa'ian had been a member of the

People's Democratic Front (*jebhe-ye demokratik-e khalq*), other well-known members of which were Nader Shaygan-shamasbi and Marzieh Ahmadi-osku'i.[42] While it is known that under Ashraf other smaller armed groups were invited to unite with the Fadaiyan, it is not known under what terms these unions were arranged. The People's Democratic Front, which also believed in armed struggle, joined the Fadaiyan in June 1973. Although by this time Shaygan had been killed, it was known that both he and Shoa'ian had strong reservations about Leninism, and considered it a deviation from Marxism, which meant that the group joined the Fadaiyan against a background of doctrinal disagreement. After Shoa'ian left, he claimed that he had been falsely assured by Fadaiyan leaders that he would be allowed to publish his views openly after unity. He also claimed that he was led to believe that the Fadaiyan was a front made up of all those groups which believed in armed struggle, and that a centralised Fadaiyan with a singular ideology was not what his group thought it was joining. A capable theorist, Shoa'ian wanted to put his views up for discussion and eventual adoption by the Fadaiyan, but the organisation was ill prepared for this sort of challenge. The leadership was made up mainly of practitioners, not theorists, and their preoccupation with day-to-day struggle and survival left them little time for this new dialogue. Yet, since the challenge could not remain unanswered, the task of responding to Shoa'ian fell to the only capable theorist, Hamid Mo'meni. A dogmatic and Stalinist thinker, and one of the few Russian-speaking members, Mo'meni engaged Shoa'ian throughout 1974 in a number of written discussions which were never published by the Fadaiyan, and came to an end with Shoa'ian's expulsion in 1974 and both authors' deaths in 1975.[43] After the expulsion, the rest of the People's Democratic Front adapted to the Fadaiyan ideology.[44] Shoa'ian was killed in an armed clash while trying to organise independent action. Shoa'ian's isolation, and his eventual ouster from the Fadaiyan, are an example of the organisation's Stalinist aspects, under which there was little or no room for internal democracy. This approach began to be consolidated into norms of the Ashraf leadership, and re-emerged again and again throughout the life of the Fadaiyan. Although the Fadaiyan started off as a front, it became an organisation during Ashraf's leadership, and the move was undertaken without much known discussion.

At the end of the first phase, the Fadaiyan had reached deadlock in its struggle with the regime. Although many sacrifices had been made, many military operations had been undertaken, and the organisation had established itself as a military-political force in Iranian society, it was unable to establish any kind of base among the working class, or the people in general. It remained basically a militant guerrilla group, whose members were mostly from the intelligentsia. Ahmadzadeh's idea that the 'little motor' was the way to start the 'big motor' had not materialised. Although the Fadaiyan had attacked the regime forcefully, the dictatorship had not cracked. As a result, as early as late 1974 or early 1975 a re-evaluaton of Fadaiyan strategy and tactics was initiated, the need for change being mooted while the organisation was strong, and Ashraf still alive. The result was the rejection of Ahmadzadeh's thesis and the adoption of Jazani's, a change which was officially published in the Fadaiyan publication, *Nabard-e Khalq*, in 1976.[45]

At the beginning of the second stage, at a critical juncture when Jazani's line was being adopted, two blows were dealt to the Fadaiyan. First, in March 1975, Jazani was murdered, along with six of the original members of the Jazani-Zarifi group and two members of the Moslem Mojahedin. Second, after a series of setbacks, in June 1976 came the deaths of Hamid Ashraf and nine other leaders and members in a long battle with the police in Tehran.[46]

Among political activists, Hamid Ashraf (1946–76) was famous for his organisational abilities, courage and expertise in dealing with the political police. Indeed, it is said that he had escaped police traps many times before his eventual death, and he was at the head of SAVAK's most-wanted list. The Fadaiyan had given him the title 'great comrade' while he was still alive, and there is no doubt that he was an idol to a generation of activists, but an evaluation of his role and leadership is complex, in that it had negative as well as positive aspects. His organisational abilities were instrumental in reshaping the Jazani-Zarifi group in 1968, after Jazani and his comrades were arrested, and he saved the Fadaiyan from probable annihilation after the death of Puyan and Ahmadzadeh in 1971 and 1972. Yet under his leadership the Fadaiyan came closer to Maoism and consolidated its Stalinist practices, both of which were against the views of older founding members, such as Jazani and Ahmadzadeh.[47] Ashraf's Stalinist practices – whether the lack of internal democracy or Machiavellian problem-solving – should not be confused with legitimate survival techniques arising from a violently hostile environment. It is true that a guerrilla organisation operating under constant threat of annihilation cannot be expected to respect all aspects of democracy and each member's rights to the letter. But in any collective effort, a balance should be struck between what the outside conditions dictate and attempts to preserve internal harmony. Once the Fadaiyan accepted the People's Democratic Front, despite its known hostility to Leninism, the fact that it did not keep to its agreement to tolerate that difference was simply established Stalinist practice. Consolidation of Stalinism in the Fadaiyan led to bloody internal purges of dissatisfied members in 1974. Although information about these and other purges is hard to obtain, due to the death of principal actors and the vow of secrecy taken by some former activists, enough information has become available for their existence to be established.[48] According to available information, the Fadaiyan under Ashraf and his second-in-command Ali Akbar Ja'fari executed some members for wanting to leave the underground life. This was revealed for the first time when in 1975 the home of Ashraf Dehqani was raided by the West German police for unrelated matters. Dehqani – sister of Behrooz Dehqani, one of the original organisers of Ahmadzadeh-Puyan Group in Tabriz – at this point shared the responsibility of running the Fadaiyan operation abroad. After Behrouz's arrest and death under torture, Ashraf was also arrested and tortured by SAVAK, but managed to escape and had to leave the country.[49] While the organisation was able to secure Dehqani's release, important microfilms were confiscated by the German police and passed on to SAVAK, which released contents of some of them, including evidence of these purges. In a letter, probably addressed to Muhammad Hormati-pur, co-director of the Fadaiyan operation abroad, Ja'fari confirmed the execution of three members for lack of loyalty and their demand to leave.[50] The content of the letter has been confirmed by Hasan Masali, a leading member of Communist Unity (*ettehad-e komonisti*), a well-connected group operating outside the country which was in the process of uniting with the Fadaiyan in the mid-1970s.[51] The idea of physically eliminating members seen as traitors was already a point of controversy between Ahmadzadeh and Ashraf in the early 1970s. It seems that as long as Ahmadzadeh was alive, he prevented any action against those who had a change of heart and wanted to leave,[52] but that after Ahmadzadeh's death in 1972, Ashraf followed his own inclinations.

Another piece of information provided by Masali has to do with the Fadaiyan's relations with the Soviet Union. As noted earlier, the Fadaiyan founders were from a new generation of Marxists which viewed past political and organisational dependencies on international communist affiliations as having been unhelpful to the movement. Against this background, between 1972 and 1976, Fadaiyan members outside Iran (Dehqani and Hormati-pur) were ordered by the leadership to approach the Soviet Government for military and financial aid. The contacts were made in secrecy, and even the ordinary members were not to know. According to Masali, while the Soviets dragged their feet and seemed unwilling to provide aid, they asked the Fadaiyan to provide intelligence on the Iranian military. This request was angrily refused by Ashraf. Masali does not know the outcome of the contact, since his group subsequently broke off close relations with the Fadaiyan,[53] but from the subsequent history of the Fadaiyan it is evident that the contacts with the Soviets did not go much further. The request for aid from the Soviet Union has two implications. First, while it was a direct contradiction of the Fadaiyan's declared policy of self-reliance and independence, Ashraf's response underlined the Organisation's sensitivity about any outside influence. Second, the Fadaiyan at this point had strong Maoist sympathies, so that asking for Soviet aid was incongruous, underlining the strong tendency for pragmatism under Ashraf's leadership.

Ashraf's death, in June 1976, left the Fadaiyan without authoritative leadership. The Tehran branch was badly damaged, which meant that the command centre was put out of action for a while. But other branches, especially those in the Khorasan, Gilan, Mazandaran and Isfahan, remained intact, although the Fadaiyan did not fully recover until after the 1979 revolution.

Under the Jazani influence, the Fadaiyan changed tactics and began to ascribe more importance to political propaganda and agitation, especially among the working class. Although it still believed in armed struggle as the axis of all tactics, it began to adopt what Jazani called the movement's 'second leg'. This meant giving more weight to the political side of the work, and to organising non-military agitation among the people.

With Ashraf's authority gone and Jazani's line not yet adopted, a split occurred in October 1976. Those who left were basically disappointed with the theory of armed struggle, and had come to accept the Tudeh approach. They called themselves OIPFG (the Splinter Group) (*goruh-e monsha'eb*) and were headed by Turaj Haydaribigvand, and as far as is known, numbered fewer than ten, Bigvand being killed a few months after the split.[54] Other members were Fariborz Salehi, Hosein Qalambar, Farzad Dadgar and Sima Behmanesh. The group abandoned armed struggle altogether, joined a Tudeh Party's branch established the year before, and helped to publish a paper called *Navid* (see below), becoming apparently the only active Tudeh branch inside Iran between 1976 and 1979.[55]

Once Ashraf's leadership was gone, the Khorasan branch claimed dominance inside the country and the Dehqani-Hormati team took control of operations abroad. The heads of the Khorasan branch, Ahmad Gholamian-langerudi (alias Hadi) and Qorban Ali Rahim-pur (alias Majid), came to believe that splinter group supporters had grown in numbers in the Isfahan Branch under Abdollah Panjeh-shahi. According to one source, in 1976 the trio asked Panjeh-shahi to go to Mashhad, and executed him in order to prevent the spread of the split.[56] It is not clear whether Panjeh-shahi was sympathetic to the splinter group, but apparently his removal brought the Isfahan branch under the newly emerging leadership from Khorasan. Under the new leadership, as the revolutionary tide was stirring, one last attempt was made to take on the splinter group and the Tudeh on the issue of armed struggle. But the new leadership simply repeated Jazani's views, revealing an apparent decline in the ideological health of the organisation at a time when analysis of a rapidly changing society was critical.[57]

The Fadaiyan's adoption of Jazani's theses coincided with the first signs of revolutionary momentum in Iran. Although the Fadaiyan's capabilities were limited, and it was still trying to recover from its reverses, it was the only armed group which participated in the revolutionary struggle in any effective and organised manner. Indeed, when the revolutionary struggle came to a head-on, violent clash on 9, 10 and 11 February 1979, the Fadaiyan, as well as other guerrilla groups, joined the people in storming military garrisons. When the rebellious air force base in Tehran was attacked by the 'immortals' of the Imperial Guard, it was the Fadaiyan which wholeheartedly and most effectively led the battle to overthrow the regime, losing in the process a leading member, Qasem Siyadati. The Fadaiyan was able to participate in the final days of the revolution more effectively than other guerrilla groups for two reasons. First, despite the setbacks of 1976, it was still the best prepared and armed group left inside the country. Second, the day before actual armed clashes started in the streets of Tehran the Fadaiyan were commemorating the anniversary of the Siyahkal operation in front of Tehran University. This coincidence meant that all its experienced members, including those recently released from prison, were gathered in one place and were able to arm supporters and send them into battle.[58]

What were the results of eight years of armed struggle (1971–9) as an urban guerrilla organisation? One notable failure was that the Fadaiyan was unable to take control of the revolution, and armed struggle did not become a mass movement. There were many reasons for this, the most important being that the founders of the Fadaiyan, although experienced politically and ideologically, started from scratch with very little practical experience. On this path of revolutionary agitation, they put their lives on the line in the hope that others would continue what they had started, and although they did, these newcomers were even less prepared, both practically and, especially, theoretically. In this environment, and alongside the adoption of Stalinist norms, dogmatism and inflexibility emerged from attempts to understand the realities of society and the struggle. For example, it took a long time for the Jazani theses to be adopted.

But guerrilla warfare had its positive aspects, despite the inability of the Fadaiyan to take charge of the 1979 revolution: as a direct result of the struggle, many radical intellectuals were attracted; the Fadaiyan fought the regime to a stalemate, and although it did not win overall, it was not destroyed by the state. The Fadaiyan emerged as a popular, prestigious social force after the revolution, transforming from a small group into the Marxist organisation with the largest number of supporters and a major opposition to the Islamic Republic of Iran for a time.

During this period, there were a number of groups and cells which were either in direct contact with the Fadaiyan or were members of it, but which departed after the revolution to establish themselves independently. Some of the original leaders of an organisation which came to be called the Worker's Path (*rah-e kargar*) after the revolution had been imprisoned Fadaiyan members who had rejected armed struggle. The members and leaders of a small intellectual cell which came to be called Fada'i's Path (*rah-e Fada'i*) after the revolution were former Fadaiyan supporters who adhered to Jazani's views from abroad. But perhaps the most famous cell, some of whose members had sympathy for the Fadaiyan but no apparent direct contact with it, was a group of intellectuals which came to be identified with two of its central figures, Khosrow Golesorkhi and Karamatollah Daneshian. The group was made up of 12 individuals arrested in 1972, allegedly for plotting to harm the royal family.[59] Not all the members were in contact with each other, or even knew each other prior to their trial. It seems that the trial of the group was an attempt by SAVAK to exaggerate the danger of the opposition and to achieve a perceived success against the guerrilla movement, with its accompanying propaganda value. The regime, evermore sure of its strength, sensationalised the event in its attempts to make an example of the case, putting the group on military trial in 1973 and 1974 and allowing national television to broadcast proceedings. A number of the group's members confessed to charges for which little evidence was produced, and asked for the Shah's pardon. But five, Golesorkhi, Daneshian, Teifur Batha'i, Abbas Ali Samakar and Muhammad Reza Allamehzadeh, refused to confess, even after extensive torture. Golesorkhi and Daneshian used the fact that the proceedings were televised to put the regime on trial, defend revolution and Marxism, and refute the charges. They refused to ask for the Shah's pardon, and were promptly executed. The other three were sentenced to life imprisonment, the rest to much lighter sentences.[60]

THE MOJAHEDIN (MARXIST-LENINIST): THE BIRTH OF THE PAYKAR

The Organisation of Iranian People's Mojahedin (Marxist-Leninist) was born in 1975 out of the Moslem organisation Mojahedin (holy warriors). Commonly called the Marxist Mojahedin, a majority of the organisation joined others to established the Paykar Organisation in 1979. The Moslem Mojahedin was established in 1965 by militant Moslem intellectuals with the intention of waging armed struggle against the regime.[61] However, it did not take any military action until after the Siyahkal operation by the Fadaiyan in 1971. The Moslem Mojahedin had its own version of what revolutionary Islam was, and how it related to armed struggle and revolution. Perhaps the best description of its founding fathers' perception of Islam is revisionist. Their idea was to adapt Islam to modern concepts and the revolutionary fever of the 1960s.[62] To do this, Marxism was studied and borrowed, and it was this borrowing from Marxism, and the revisionsism which followed, which prompted Ayatollah Khomeini, in exile in Najaf in Iraq, to deny the organisation his direct backing. In a number of meetings with Ayatollah Khomeini, between 1970 and 1973, the Moslem Mojahedin explained its views and asked for support, which Ayatollah Khomeini refused, being also unenthusiastic about the strategy of armed struggle. Years later, Ayatollah Khomeini suggested that he soon realised that although the Moslem Mojahedin relied on the Qur'an, they were in fact against Islam.[63] The two Moslem Mojahedin members sent to Ayatollah Khomeini in Najaf, Hosein Ruhani and Torrab Haqshenas, were later among those who changed ideology and created the Marxist Mojahedin.[64]

In September 1971, before the Moslem Mojahedin could stage any major armed actions, the security forces managed to deal it a massive blow. Sixty-nine members, including 11 leaders, were put on trial, creating a power vacuum in the organisation, and requiring a restructuring in order to lessen the possibility of future discoveries. The organisation was divided into three separate branches, the head of each making up the leadership council, which was initially Bahram Aram (1944–76), Reza Reza'i (1946–72) and Kazem Zolanvar (1947–75). Reza'i was one of those arrested, but had managed to escape. In 1972, he was killed in an armed clash, and Zolanvar was arrested (he was executed with the Jazani group in 1975). The two vacancies were filled with by Muhammad Taqi Shahram (1948–80), who was arrested in 1971 but escaped, and Majid Sharif-vaqefi (1949–75). Between 1972 and 1975, while the Mojahedin intensified its attacks on the regime, the branch under Shahram began to re-examine Islam, and soon came to subordinate it to Marxism-Leninism. Shahram converted Aram, and through him his branch, but met stiff resistance from Sharif-vaqefi and his second-in-command, Morteza Smadieh-labbaf. When persuasion failed, the Shahram-Aram union moved to eliminate Sharif-vaqefi and bring his branch into line with the rest of the organisation. Sharif-vaqefi moved to organise the remaining Moslem loyalists, but because his own wife, Leila Zomorrodi, had turned Marxist and was co-operating with the opposition, the plan was exposed. In May 1975, principally on Shahram's initiative, Sharif-vaqefi was murdered and Labbaf wounded in a shoot-out. Sharif-vaqefi's body was burnt and dumped outside Tehran, and Labbaf was arrested and executed by SAVAK.[65] The bloody purge created a feud between the Moslem and Marxist factions which was never resolved. Needless to say, the regime made full propaganda use of this bloody confrontation. Also, the contradictory term 'Islamic Marxists', frequently used by the regime, and the Shah's claim that the 'union of the black and red reaction' were his main enemies, were in fact confused references to the Moslem Mojahedin's receptiveness to Marxism, and the split that created the Marxist Mojahedin.

The Marxist Mojahedin declared its conversion to Marxism in September 1975, and continued to use its full, yet by this time contradictory, name until the fall of the imperial regime, keeping the Mojahedin emblem with minor changes.[66] As far as the scope of the split is concerned, it seems that the Marxist Mojahedin managed to gain control of the bulk of the organisation, although the Moslem Mojahedin maintained that only 20 percent sided with it.[67] At any rate, many prominent members turned Marxist. These included, beside Aram and Shahram, Haqshenas and Ruhani, who were in charge of the organisation's operations abroad, and would play a leading role in establishing the Paykar later on, and Ali Reza Sepasi-ashtiani, also a future Paykar leader.

In the first public communique on its conversion, the organisation wrote:

> In the beginning we thought it possible to combine Marxism and Islam and accept the philosophy of historical determinism without dialectical materialism. Now we realise that this thought is impossible... We chose Marxism because it is the correct and realistic path for the liberation of the exploited working class.[68]

By this time the organisation was under the firm control of Aram and Shahram, and kept silent about the purge. In recognising Marxism, the Marxist Mojahedin paid special attention to Mao's views, and the organisation was staunchly Stalinist-Maoist from its inception.[69]

The Marxist Mojahedin was a late-comers into the family of Iranian Marxists, but had strong views on how the struggle should be carried out. It appears that while the process of conversion to Marxism among key leaders was only two years old in 1975, the organisation's approach, and encounters with other Marxist groups, were self-assured. It must be noted that, unlike the Fadaiyan, the Mojahedin, whether Marxist or Moslem, never produced any systematic or in-depth analyses of the land reform programme, the changing socio-economic condition of Iran or, perhaps most importantly, armed struggle. What little analysis there was of Iranian society belonged to the pre-split Moslem period.[70] Moreover, although the conversion may not have been 'as sudden and unexpected as it at first appeared to the outside world',[71] this seems only to have been the case for key members, ordinary members being converted in a rather short period of time. In its *Manifesto*, the Marxist Mojahedin made it clear that the conversion was from top to bottom, and that those who refused to 'correct' themselves – up to 50 percent – were purged.[72] Also, according to Masali, when his group and the Mojahedin were co-operating outside Iran, he asked Hosein Ruhani, a leading member of the organisation, how it was that he had changed his ideology so suddenly, to which Ruhani answered, '... the leadership of the organisation has ordered us to criticise and reject our past metaphysical and idealistic thoughts and practices by analysing the mistakes which had been made, using Marxist methodology'.[73] It can be seen from this that the

Marxist Mojahedin was born when its understanding of Marxism was, at best, infantile, superficial and shallow when compared to that of the Fadaiyan or Tudeh, its understanding of Iranian society and history was very limited, and its theoretical output marginal. Religious dogma can be sensed in its approach. These characteristics were to remain with the organisation, and were passed on to the Paykar after the 1979 revolution.

The *Manifesto*, explaining the organisation's views, was published in September 1975, and is the first public declaration of its programme and goals. It kept silent on the bloody purge, instead suggesting that by 1974 a majority of the Moslem Mojahedin had concluded that the organisation's struggle against the regime had reached an *impasse*.[74] The Marxist Mojahedin also asked other groups, especially the Fadaiyan, to join it to form a united people's front.[75] The Fadaiyan generally remained silent on the internal purge, but began to engage the Marxist Mojahedin on their united front proposal, rejecting it as unsuitable.[76] The Marxist Mojahedin's response came in September 1976 in the form of an attack on the Fadaiyan on issues unrelated to their discussion, namely its close relations with the Communist Unity Group (see below) and alleged contacts with the Tudeh.[77] Communist Unity at this point was still co-operating with the Fadaiyan, and was the only group taking a hard line on the bloody purge in the Mojahedin. The Fadaiyan defended its relations with Communist Unity, and denied any relations with the Tudeh. But the encounter damaged relations between the two organisations. By this time Ashraf was dead, and the Fadaiyan had begun its process of reconstruction. The death of Aram, the Marxist Mojahedin's most experienced military mind, in October 1976, had the same effect on that organisation.

The most notable activities of the Marxist Mojahedin between its conversion and the revolutionary days of 1978 was the assassination of a SAVAK general and two American military advisors, and a failed attempt on an American diplomat's life, all in 1975.[78] But in 1976, after Aram's death and the capture and death of a number of activists, the organisation's activities declined sharply. As the revolutionary swell began in 1977–8, under the leadership of Haqshenas-Ruhani-Ashtiani, and perhaps because of pressure from other groups, the Marxist Mojahedin (which had begun to call itself the Mojahedin Splinter Group) ousted Shahram from its ranks.[79] It participated in the revolutionary events which led to the overthrow of the regime, but by its own admission its role was non-military and marginal compared to that of the Fadaiyan.[80]

THE TUDEH AND COMMUNIST SPLINTER GROUPS

The Tudeh's political struggle in the 1970s was more complicated than during the previous decade. With the coming of the 1970s, the party not only had to face the problem of reorganisation inside the country, but also the challenges posed by its own Maoist splinter groups, ROTPI, the Tufan and the guerrilla groups inside the country. The former challenged the party on issues related to the Sino-Soviet ideological split as well as those related to the actual Iranian situation, while the latter undermined the Tudeh's self-image as a revolutionary vanguard and the party of the working class. All these new and old problems had to be faced at a time when the party was more than ever engaged in factional fighting and its reliance on the Soviet camp was increasingly integral to its existence.

The December 1969 thirteenth party plenum was a show-down between the moderate and radical factions, with the ADP and the Soviets playing the determining role. Up to this point, Radmanesh was in charge of the party's Iran operations, and his position as first secretary of the party, alongside Eskandari and Kambakhsh on the secretariat, manifested a balance between the two factions, with the moderates enjoying a two-to-one control. The same balance existed in the executive committee, which was the highest body after the secretariat, and the one which made major decisions in the absence of a central committee. The only difference here was the presence of the ADP members. During the thirteenth plenum, Radmanesh's performance in the Shahriari affair was attacked by Kianuri, and a number of commissions were formed to assess the situation. In the end, the party admitted to SAVAK infiltration and its destructive consequences. Radmanesh was removed from his post after the plenum by the executive committee, and replaced by Eskandari.[81] Kianuri's move to remove Radmanesh and replace him with Eskandari was an attack by the radical faction on the moderate hold over the party, but the radicals were not yet strong enough to dominate. While Radmanesh's blunder in the Shahriari affair, and his refusal to listen to warnings from the Soviets, made his position vulnerable, it still does not explain why the moderates did not put up a fight. The explanation may be in the role the Soviets played in Radmanesh's removal. According to Eskandari, besides the consequences of his incompetence for inter-party politics, Radmanesh had angered the Soviets by refusing to take action when SAVAK infiltration had become evident, and by questioning the wisdom of certain Soviet policies.[82] Hence, when the radical move to get rid of Radmanesh came with Soviet support, the moderates backed off and settled for a compromise. According to Eskandari, the Soviets were instrumental in bringing peace between Kambakhsh and Kianuri, on one hand, and Daneshian, the ADP chief, on the other, so that the executive committee could remove Radmanesh with ease, and in ensuring that his punishment be limited to removal from office.[83]

The Tudeh's fourteenth plenum, in December 1970, confirmed the gains and loses of each faction. Eskandari was chosen as first secretary (which meant the moderates still held substantial power), but most of his responsibilities were given to radicals. Kambakhsh became second secretary, and was given charge of Iran operations, to be replaced after his death in 1971 by Kianuri. The make-up of the executive committee showed that the balance between the three factions had began to change, with the radicals only one step away from gaining total control.[84] The two Tudeh factions and the ADP had taken their starting positions for the confrontations of 1970s under Eskandari, Kianuri and Daneshian.

The Tudeh under Eskandari (1908–85) continued on a moderate path at a time when Iranian society and the opposition to the regime were becoming ever-more radicalised. A Qajar prince, Eskandari was an original member of the Group of Fifty-three and one of the founding fathers of the Tudeh. He was French educated, and a perfect example of an educated, cultured aristocratic Iranian intellectual turned communist. Eskandari was always associated with the moderate wing of the Tudeh, and like others had great admiration for the Soviet Union and the October Revolution. Perhaps his most important contribution to Iranian Marxism was his translation of Marx's *Capital*, the last volume of which he finished just before his death. Nevertheless, he maintained that his perception of the relationship between the Tudeh and the Soviets was different to that of individuals such as Kambakhsh and Kianuri, whom he alleged were outright KGB operatives. In identifying the two factions and their relations to the Soviets, Eskandari wrote:

> From the inception of the party two parallel lines existed, which can be called those of Kambakhsh and Radmanesh. This was the reality; I myself belonged to the Radmanesh line… We viewed the Soviet Union as a socialist country, the first socialist country, the Leninist country, a country which aided the world revolution, and finally the country with the biggest role in the great anti-imperialist struggle going on in the world. This is how we looked upon the Soviet Union, but I can say frankly that neither Radmanesh nor I simply accepted whatever the Soviets say as right.[85]

Eskandari may have sincerely believed this, and there may be some truth in it when his role and that of Radmanesh is compared to that of Kambakhsh and Kianuri. But the fact remains that at every decisive turn in Tudeh history when the Soviets interfered in the internal affairs of the party both Eskandari and Radmanesh deferred to Soviet wishes. When the Soviets forced the party to accept the ADP compromise, and when they asked for Radmanesh's removal, Eskandari agreed. Many more examples can be given, but perhaps the most ironic is when the Soviets backed Eskandari's own removal from office in 1979; he accepted his fate without resistance. Throughout Eskandari's memoirs, a self-appraisal of over 50 years of activism, he can be seen bowing to Soviet-supported stands which he had previously opposed.[86]

The Tudeh policy towards the regime during Eskandari's time was a continuation of the party's policy of the previous decade, which was based on demands for reform of the political regime, reinstatement of democratic rights and a return to constitutional rights and guarantees, as well as total support for closer economic ties between Iran and the Soviet Union, clearly moderate when compared to the militant groups. The Tudeh's policy toward the imperial regime can best be seen in its slogans, its evaluation of the revolutionary stage and its programme.

But before an analysis of the party's policy on the imperial regime in the 1970s, it is important to assess Tudeh organisational strength. This is important because only within the limits of its ability to challenge the regime could the Tudeh, or any other opposition political group, base its strategy and tactics. Outside Iran, the Tudeh was doing better than any other opposition political group. Based in the GDR, the party considered itself the new party of the working class, and the manifestation of its will. The Tudeh had the financial and logistical support of the Soviet Union and its allies. The ADP, the party's branch in Soviet Azarbaijan, enjoyed autonomy from the party central committee on many issues, and could rely on the support of the Azarbaijan Communist Party in Baku. This all translated into an anti-regime propaganda capability unmatched by Iranian student groups or parties active in Western Europe or the United States, or the supporters of armed struggle inside Iran. The Tudeh put its capabilities outside Iran to good use, broadcasting radio programmes (*Payk-e Iran* broadcast from Bulgaria until 1975) and issuing a number of publications. The party was also busy translating Soviet Marxist texts, as well as other material, into Persian.

The same assertion cannot be made about the party's strength and network inside Iran. As noted, that network had been effectively infiltrated by the SAVAK in the 1960s, and rendered worthless. In 1970, Kianuri was put in charge of party operations inside Iran, with the aim of revitalising the Tudeh. After the revolution, he claimed that the party had managed to organise 60 associated underground groups and cells in the 1970s.[87] The party leadership's assessment of the Tudeh's network inside Iran, based on confessions given to the security and intelligence forces after its arrest in 1982, suggests that the numbers and strength of these cells was exaggerated.[88] The overwhelming majority of less than 20 cells that the party leaders mentioned in their confessions did not take an active part in political activities. The only group which undertook publishing activities was Navid, which published an underground weekly of the same name after 1975. Headed by Muhammad Mehdi Partovi and Rahman Hatefi, Navid made its first contacts with the party in 1975, and by its own admission became the party's largest cell operating inside Iran.[89] In 1976 or early 1977, Navid was joined by the Fadaiyan Splinter Group, and managed to conduct limited publishing activity during the 1978–9 revolutionary period. Like the Tudeh, Navid, did not believe in armed struggle and, by its own account, played a limited and marginal role in the eventual armed clashes that brought the imperial regime down.[90]

The Tudeh's evaluation of its network in Iran in the 1970s should be viewed with suspicion. There simply is no evidence of the existence of the 60 cells the party claimed, or for that matter of the 20 mentioned after the leaders' arrest. Navid, with help from the Splinter Group, did publish and distribute party material, increasingly widely as the imperial regime began to crumble. But its participation in the final armed clashes can only be independently verified by the daily *Kayhan*, which was under Tudeh activists' influence (Hatefi was its assistant editor in the 1970s). The Tudeh's activities in Iran during most of the 1970s were at best marginal and insignificant. The myth about the party's active participation in the overthrow of the regime and the party's later claims of underground cells had more to do with improving its image among the people and countering the records of guerrilla groups.

Based on the above evaluation of Tudeh strength in Iran, the party's challenge to the imperial regime can perhaps be better understood. From 1953 to 1975, the Tudeh's main slogan was 'Down with the coup regime', which meant, in principal, a return to constitutional monarchy. In 1966, under Radmanesh's leadership, the party's answer to its Maoist splinter group, which accused it of not propounding the overthrow of the monarchy, was: 'In a national democratic government there is no room for a despotic monarchy'.[91] Although the party's purpose in this answer was to refute Maoist critics, it in fact confirmed its acceptance of the idea of a non-despotic monarchy. In the same year, the party's analysis placed Iranian society in the national democratic stage, of the three possible stages. It identified the proletariat, petit bourgeoisie, revolutionary intellectuals and national bourgeoisie as possible allies at this stage, and contended that the Iranian revolution was not at a socialist stage, in which the proletariat would be the sole participant, initiating socialist reforms, because the working class was weak both numerically and organisationally. The Iranian revolution was also not at a people-democratic stage, where the proletariat would play a controlling role in alliance with other classes, and would initiate semi-socialist semi-capitalist reforms, again because of the weakness of the working class, although the party stated that it would do its best to bring the revolution to this stage.[92] In layman's terms, since the Tudeh, as the sole working-class party, was weak, it could not impose its will in any anti-regime coalition. Hence, under the control of the moderates in the 1960s and the first half of the 1970s, the party was only asking for a lifting of despotism and a return to the constitutional rule of law.

Between 1970 and 1975, factional conflict within the Tudeh subsided, as a result of the party's lack of a social base in Iran, attacks from both its splinter groups and the guerrilla movement, and the regime's apparent stability and strength. These five years (between the Tudeh's fourteenth [1970] and fifteenth [1975] plenums) coincided with the intensification of the guerrilla movement's struggle. The moderate, radical and ADP factions within the Tudeh were in balance, and the moderate faction could still manage to pursue its strategy. As far as the imperial regime was concerned, the Tudeh was working towards the removal of the Shah's dictatorship without asking either for the overthrow of the monarchy or for any Tudeh-led government. The party saw itself as the sole vanguard of the working class, and put its energy into criticising the regime, defending Soviet policy in Iran and intense ideological struggle against the party's Maoist splinter groups and the guerrilla movement.

On Iran-Soviet relations in this period, the Tudeh shared a dilemma similar to that of other Iranian Marxists. At a time when the anti-Shah struggle was intensifying, the Soviet Union's relations with the regime, particularly in economic, technical and military fields, were improving. As noted, the Fadaiyan's policy was to maintain independence from the Soviet Union and pursue its own interests, since the Soviets were pursuing theirs. The Tudeh's policy was the exact opposite, defending Soviet-Iranian relations by pointing to its advantages for the Iranian people in the long run. The Tudeh maintained that Soviet aid to the imperial regime was financially profitable, technologically advantageous and economically progressive, and that through its relations with the Soviet Union the imperial regime was industrialising Iran and acquiring factories and technology denied to Iran by Western imperialists, while at the same time developing Iran's industrial and technological independence. The Tudeh's stand was that since Soviet policy on Iran was not based on exploitation, Iran could and should take full advantage of this opportunity and further expand its relations with the Soviet Union and its allies.[93] While questioning the overall industrial policies of the imperial regime, the party stated, 'The technical and economic aid of the Soviet Union and family of socialist countries to Iran's industrialisation in the past decade, despite the regime's and the Shah's subjective intentions, have been a strong base for strengthening the people of Iran's position in their struggle against imperialist domination and its neo-colonial policies'.[94] It remained silent on the political and social ramifications of this relationship, especially the effect it had on stabilising the very regime the party wanted to overthrow.

The factional harmony began to break down as the party started preparations for its fifteenth plenum, set to convene in June 1975. The two main factions had begun to develop different interpretations of current affairs in Iran, and how to confront the Government. Kianuri – who had become the undisputed leader of the radical faction and the Tudeh's second secretary, in charge of the party's network in Iran – and his associates began to see the situation in Iran changing from a non-revolutionary to a revolutionary one. Kianuri explained his change of attitude this way:

> A number of leading members of the party and myself began to feel that Iranian society was getting into turmoil and was heading for an explosion. In our opposition, a number of leading members (especially people like Eskandari, the first secretary) viewed developments in Iran as going in the opposite direction. In their view, the Shah's regime was consolidating and accumulating power, and the increase in oil income had given the Shah the opportunity to establish a stable capitalist system.[95]

The leading party members who Kianuri claimed supported the other line were from both the moderate and ADP factions, showing that they were in agreement on this. He named the following as supporters of the moderate policy: Eskandari, Davoud Noruzi and Hosein Joudat, all moderate supporters, and Daneshian and Hamid Saffari from the ADP. He also suggested that this policy advocated compromise with the Shah, working toward the betterment of Iran-Soviet relations and the legalising of the Tudeh. Tabari, a member of the radical faction, claimed that prior to the fifteenth plenum Kianuri suggested that the party adopt a new policy calling for the overthrow of the regime, and that the Soviets supported it. Opposing it, Eskandari called for the continuation of the previous policy of demanding the lifting of dictatorship and a return to constitutional guarantees.[96]

Eskandari's recollections only partially confirm this version of events. According to him, prior to and during the plenum two issues dominated factional differences. The first was whether or not to ask for the overthrow of the regime, the second how much to emphasise demands for democratic rights.[97] On the first issue, Eskandari suggested that his support for the removal of the dictatorship was in effect support for the overthrow of the imperial regime, the monarchy and its constitution.[98] This was clearly not so, as we shall see later. Eskandari saw the real difference between himself and Kianuri, or the radical and the moderate factions, in the extent to which they stressed democratic rights. He went on to suggest that in time this difference led one faction to support the Islamic movement led by Ayatollah Khomeini, the other to oppose it. It is important to note that the factions' different slogans implied different tactics and strategy. For Eskandari to suggest in the mid-1980s that the real conflict between the two factions was about democracy was simply an attempt on his part to settle old scores with such old adversaries as Kianuri and Tabari.[99] There is no reason to believe that the Tudeh, a Soviet-style communist party, would have been any more respectful of democratic rights than communist parties which had come to power elsewhere.

The fifteenth plenum was a compromise between the two factions. The party's slogan was changed to 'Down with the Shah's despotic rule', but the party programme demanded moderate reforms and respect for democratic rights, a standard procedure.[100] The compromise could not possibly have satisfied either faction. For example, while the party believed that the national democratic stage was the revolutionary one, it suggested that the only way such a

OFFENSIVE AND STALEMATE (1971–9): VIOLENCE AND SUPPRESSION

revolution could be really successful was for the proletariat to lead it. This was at a time when the party admitted to its own weakness, and was willing to accept the leadership of non-proletariat forces in a united front to bring about democratic revolution.[101] Another example is that while the party's programme called for the overthrow of the imperial regime it supported two trends in Iran's industrial development. One trend proposed more government control over industries, the other more private-sector control. The party viewed the former as the more progressive, and suggested its 'democratisation'.[102] While the overthrow of the imperial regime was the radical faction's policy, this policy was clearly in line with policies put forward by Eskandari and his comrades.

Clear contradictions in the party's policy were evident between 1975 and 1979, especially as the revolutionary tide began to shake the regime. In 1975, after the fifteenth plenum, the Tudeh's theoretical journal, *Donya*, published an article quite conciliatory towards some segments of the ruling classes. The article suggested that it was quite legitimate to make a distinction between the Shah's despotic rule on one hand and some segments of the ruling elite and the Iranian bourgeoisie on the other, and went on to state that the Tudeh preferred that the more progressive and realistic segments have power.[103] Looking to bring out the more realistic segments of the imperial regime at a time the party proposed the overthrow of the whole system was a clear policy contradiction and a manifestation of internal conflict. Also in 1975, after the plenum, the party, while generally favouring the overthrow of the whole system, asked and answered this revealing question: 'Does the overthrow of the Shah's despotic monarchical rule have to be accompanied with the overthrow of the monarchy as a whole? In our opinion no.'[104]

Perhaps the most revealing, and controversial, example of policy conflict was the Tudeh's direct overtures to the regime. According to Jahangir Behrouz, an Iranian journalist at this time, he was approached by the Tudeh on a trip to East Berlin in 1975. He had been invited by the GDR to attend an international youth conference as an independent journalist. As a young activist, he had been a member of the Tudeh and editor of a number of party newspapers before 1953. Behrouz's writings at that time suggest that he belonged to the radical faction, but he had been away from party politics since then. In Iran, he had been in trouble with the authorities, and was forbidden to practice his profession at the time of the trip. Nevertheless, because of his friendship with Premier Amir Abbas Hoveida from their journalism days, and because he was

81

allowed by SAVAK to attend the conference, the Tudeh wrongly assumed that he must have been sent by the regime. Behrouz was asked by Davoud Noruzi, in Berlin some time after the fifteenth plenum, to meet Eskandari, an invitation he accepted. Eskandari told Behrouz that the party believed that the Shah was reforming, was going to allow more democratic freedoms, and that under certain conditions, the Tudeh was willing to return to Iran and function within constitutional boundaries. He asked Behrouz to convey this message, and gave him a letter to deliver. Behrouz agreed, and passed on the message to the Iranian Government.[105]

In his memoirs, Eskandari mentioned a number of overtures he received from the imperial regime personally, but none to the party as a whole. He was invited to return to Iran, and receive a pension as an ex-minster, but remain out of politics; Eskandari rejected this.[106] While Eskandari made no mention of the Behrouz meeting, Kianuri presented it differently. He suggested that the imperial regime had sent Behrouz to the GDR to ask the Tudeh to return to Iran and function as a legal political party.[107] He added that Behrouz also had a meeting with him, that Eskandari reported the meeting to the party, and that the offer was rejected. Here, Kianuri was either presenting the event from a strictly factional view (he was against any overtures to the Shah), or bluntly misrepresenting the facts, or presenting them as reported to him and the rest of the executive committee by Eskandari. The policy of approaching the regime was clearly in line with the strategy of the Tudeh's moderate faction but in sharp contradiction with that of the Shah, who was very much in control, and seemingly invincible. He had turned Iran into a one-party system in March 1975, and was preparing to commemorate 50 years of Pahlavi rule. Also, his imperial court minister, Amir Asadollah Alam, does not mention anything about this policy, while clearly showing that every important decision was made by the Shah himself.[108] There was no real precedent on the Shah's part for any gesture towards the Tudeh.

The intensification of the revolutionary movement, and the gradual disintegration of the imperial regime during 1977 and 1978, turned the tide against the moderate faction. A Soviet change of policy resulted in the toppling of Eskandari and his replacement by Kianuri in February 1979. The Soviets, like the Americans, were slow to realise the magnitude of the Iranian revolution, and the speed with which the regime was disintegrating. Yet by December 1978 the Soviets had accepted the inevitability of the Shah's overthrow.[109] Here, the moderate approach of Eskandari and his colleagues did not fit with either the Soviet policy in Iran or the demands of revolutionary upheaval.

The policy of demanding the overthrow of the regime, while at the same time asking for the party to be allowed to function within Iran's constitutional boundaries, could only have created confusion, and hampered a party which did not have a solid base in the country to begin with. The contradiction hampered the Tudeh even more in 1977 and 1978. According to Eskandari, the main difference between the two factions as the revolutionary movement grew was not on the overthrow of the imperial regime – by this time the moderates had accepted the inevitable – but on what should replace it. The moderate faction kept emphasising democratic rights, and was suspicious of the Islamic movement under Ayatollah Khomeini, which it suspected would not respect those rights.[110] In practice, this policy meant siding with the more liberal segments of the anti-Shah opposition (the National Front and Grand Ayatollah Kazem Shari'atmadari) which did not necessarily demand the creation of an Islamic republic. The Tudeh's anti-regime communiques in the autumn of 1978 demanded the establishment of a secular republic at a time when the movement was clearly under Ayatollah Khomeini's leadership, and was demanding an Islamic one.[111] Kianuri confirmed the existence of two different views over the subject, and described his own view as being that moderate forces had no chance, and that the people's discontent could most effectively be channelled against the regime and America by Ayatollah Khomeini and his supporters.[112]

Two platforms were presented, by Eskandari and Kianuri, the list of supporters of each platform suggesting that the two forces were about equal in strength, with the ADP still siding with the moderates. But the change in Soviet policy shifted the balance.[113] According to Eskandari, his perception of Soviet policy toward the revolution was that the Soviets, while accepting the possibility of the overthrow of the regime, thought it more likely to come in the aftermath of a civil war which would involve both the United States and themselves. But as the situation became clear, the Soviets needed an ally to further their policies in post-revolutionary Iran.[114] Kianuri suggested that the Soviets changed their policy to support him because they realised that his position on the Iranian revolution was correct.[115] Both he and Eskandari agreed at the executive committee meeting on 14 January 1979 that he should replace Eskandari, because the ADP under Daneshian now supported him. Eskandari and Kianuri disagreed on what pushed the ADP to its new position.

According to Eskandari, the Soviet Azarbaijan Communist Party, under Haydar Aliev, pressured the ADP to accept Kianuri,[116] while Kianuri believed that a change of policy on an important country like Iran had to come from the top of the decision-making apparatus, the Politburo. He suggested that Aliev, as both the Azarbaijan Communist Party chief and a CPSU central committee member, was merely a messenger.[117] Whichever version is correct, here again the Soviet Union played a decisive role in the Tudeh's internal politics, gaving it a new direction.

Throughout the 1970s, the Tudeh's relations with its splinter groups, the Tufan and ROTPI, mirrored the Sino-Soviet split, and went from bad to worse. The similarities between the two groups made their attacks on each other rather abstract, and based on international issues rather than concrete Iranian ones. Both the Tudeh and its splinter groups were marginal to the intense armed struggle going on in Iran. While the Tudeh had relied on the Soviet Union for financial and logistical support, and as a source of ideological inspiration, the Tufan and ROTPI had similar relations with China and Albania.

China's foreign policy in the 1970s under Mao gave the Tudeh ample ammunition against its splinter groups. In theory, Chinese policy was based on confronting both imperialism (the United States and its allies) and social imperialism (the USSR and its allies). In practice, because of a long border with the Soviet Union and actual military clashes between the two communist poles, China often found itself emphasising the anti-Soviet side of its foreign policy, and Nixon's China policy and the gradual restoration of US-Chinese relations fostered this. The Tudeh attacked the policy, calling it anti-socialist and helpful only to imperialism.[118] The Tudeh attacked Iranian co-operation with China while defending links with the USSR.[119] The Tudeh became increasingly blunt in the 1970s, changing from general opposition to Maoism to outright attacks on Iranian Maoists, calling them anti-revolutionaries and SAVAK agents.[120]

The Tudeh's relations with the guerrilla groups was more careful and complex. A proposal to organise armed action and partisan resistance was discussed among the Tudeh leadership early in the 1960s, prior to the reform programmes that changed socio-economic conditions. Perhaps influenced by the experiences of Cuba and Vietnam, 25 members of the former Military Organisation in 1961 prepared for the leadership an essay outlining the possibilities, goals and logistical feasibility of partisan warfare in Iran.[121] The party appointed Hasan Nazari, a former military officer, to evaluate the proposal and report to the executive committee. It is important to note that the Tudeh at this point had no real network inside the country, and that any new strategy would have to start from scratch. Nazari supported the proposal, and suggested appointing operatives. The party leadership reviewing the proposal were against it for a variety of reasons. Perhaps Kianuri's November 1961 response to Nazari's suggestion that party members be appointed to the task shows most clearly the real reasons for the leadership's rejection of the proposal:

> The problem of a reliable volunteer who can take partisan action is important to me. As far as I know, there is no-one for this task in the GDR. Neither are there any volunteers among us, the leadership, or members who are working in party publications or the secretariat (except some of the officer comrades)... For example I myself, with my lung problem, cannot participate in this or lead it. This is true for all the leaders.[122]

When Nazari told the meeting that his intention was not to ask key leaders to directly participate, and that he was thinking of asking for volunteers, Kianuri replied that in 1957 such a call for volunteers resulted in only five or six responses. The issue of a lack of volunteers and leadership unfitness aside, the discussion about organising armed action in Iran soon turned to the role of the Soviet Union. Kianuri believed that only through all-out Soviet aid (eg modern weapons) could the party start anything, because 'only with the Soviet Union's aid can the revolution really be victorious in Iran, and all the movements which do not rely on the Soviet Union are anti-revolutionary'. Nazari offered the opinion that the leadership looked as if it was enjoying its stay in the socialist countries so much that it did not want to return to Iran. During the next meeting, Kianuri said that the Soviets were against guerrilla action in Iran, due to a lack of objective revolutionary circumstances, and that if the Tudeh wanted to pursue the idea, it would have to be with backing other than theirs.[123] The Tudeh rejected any possibility of starting a guerrilla movement in Iran. Nazari, the strongest supporter of armed action, summed up his view of seven meetings in 1963 by suggesting that the leadership's reaction to the proposal had convinced him that:

> ... the leadership intends to find the weak points of [arguments for an] armed movement and blow them out of proportion for the central committee members, so that the most important positive action in Iran's

current situation may be disregarded, and satisfy them [the central committee] with the current insufficient action. Heroic actions for the people, accompanied with suffering, devotion and acceptance of hardship, does not seem to conform with the taste of comrades who do not seem willing to make such sacrifices, which are the most important characteristic of any leader of a working-class party.[124]

It was against this background that the Tudeh was stunned by the Siyahkal operation in 1971. Of those engaged in armed struggle, the Tudeh was most focused on the Fadaiyan, the only violent Marxist-Leninist group until 1975, and between 1971 and 1975, the party's polemics against the Fadaiyan centred on the writings of Puyan, Ahmadzadeh and Farahani. The Tudeh kept silent about the psychological impact its own shortcomings and defeats had had on the new generation of Marxists, and instead dealt with the obvious shortcomings of the Fadaiyan's writings at a time when all its authors had already been killed in action. The guerrilla movement seems to have had a unifying effect on the Tudeh. The party's fourteenth plenum, the Tudeh's last before the Siyahkal operation, was held in 1970. The next was in 1975. Since these plenums were the most obvious place for factions to settle their differences, their absence for five years, during the most intense period of guerrilla warfare, points to a lessening of factional conflict over this period.

Tudeh attacks on the Fadaiyan centred on issues such as Puyan's 'two absolutes', Ahmadzadeh's discussion of armed struggle, and the need to continue the struggle through political agitation among the working class. As if offended by a new generation of Marxists challenging the imperial regime and the Tudeh's claim to working-class and revolutionary leadership, the party ridiculed the movement's claim to be the real communist movement.[125] The Tudeh called the Fadaiyan's theories alien to Marxism-Leninism. Calling Puyan's 'two absolutes' the strategy of defeat, the Tudeh suggested that the presence of the political police and repression made activity among the masses difficult but not impossible.[126] Completely ignoring the Fadaiyan argument that its intention was to establish a working-class vanguard by declaring war on the regime and sweeping away negative memories of the Tudeh, with its record of defeat, the Tudeh accused the Fadaiyan of excluding the working-class – the revolutionary class – from the struggle.[127] It remained silent on its own failures in the 1960s to establish any underground cell inside the country, and claimed that the Fadaiyan was trying to replace the working class with revolutionary intellectuals. Its attacks on

Jazani's views centred not on his armed struggle analysis, nor his evaluation of Iranian society, nor his position on the recent history of Iran and the role played by the Tudeh, but on the need for a working-class party in future revolutionary upheavals. Jazani and the Fadaiyan believed that the discussion of whether there should be a communist party (of the working class) before the struggle started was irrelevant. To the Fadaiyan, a working-class party was to be built in the process of struggle, not before. The Tudeh correctly saw in the Fadaiyan's analysis, among other things, an attempt to bypass the Tudeh's self-proclaimed role as the working-class party. Relying on Lenin's writings, the Tudeh emphasised that a working-class party was an inseparable part of any modern social revolution, and that the Tudeh was that party.[128] At the root of disagreement between the two groups were their analyses of Iranian society. The Fadaiyan believed that a revolutionary period was at hand (Ahmadzadeh), or would be in the near future (Jazani), so that the task of Marxists was to create a revolutionary vanguard to lead it, and that armed struggle, in both the Jazani and Ahmadzadeh theses, was the vehicle to achieve that goal. The Tudeh, while proclaiming itself the sole working-class party, and thus the vanguard organisation, was well aware of its lack of a base in Iran, and viewed the situation in the country as one of consolidation for the imperial regime, the revolutionary period being beyond the foreseeable future. There was no common ground between the Tudeh strategy – of wait-and-see and overtures to the imperial regime – and the radical armed-struggle approach of the Fadaiyan, but much of the Tudeh reaction was to do with the presence of a competitor on the political scene. This competitor, unlike groups which had diverged from the Tudeh, was ignoring the party and backing up its rhetoric with action. By pointing to the doctrinal weaknesses of the guerrilla movement, the Tudeh hoped to be able to recruit from among its number – a hope partially justified by the minor split in the Fadaiyan in 1976 – and to hide its own inability to act and organise working-class support.

ROTPI and the Tufan fared no better; in fact their performance was worse. As already noted, ROTPI began in the 1960s as a popular force among Iranian students abroad, but its two major attempts to create a foothold inside Iran had failed, and it had to contend with a split in 1967. The 1970s brought ROTPI no more success, and its two most significant attempts to establish a presence in Iran ended in disaster. A group associated with ROTPI, the Organisation For the Liberation of the Iranian People (*sazman-e raha'i bakhsh-e khalqha-ye Iran*), and headed by Cyrus Nahavandi, was discovered by SAVAK in December 1971. The group had been established outside Iran in the mid-1960s, had close theoretical and organisational relations with ROTPI, and had returned to Iran in co-ordination with ROTPI, in order to wage armed struggle in rural areas. After failing to organise in the rural areas, and contrary to its beliefs – the group attempted a few urban actions, such as bank robbery, and had failed in an attempt to kidnap the US Ambassador to Tehran just before being uncovered by SAVAK. The group's arrest – 22 members altogether – was followed by its principal members' co-operation with SAVAK.[129] In 1972, SAVAK faked Nahavandi's escape from prison, and in return he began feeding ROTPI false information. Groups from inside Iran, principally the Fadaiyan, raised doubts about Nahavandi, but ROTPI continued to support him, and even published his description of his escape and analysis of Iranian society and the struggle.[130] A number of ROTPI members who were sent into the country were compromised because of him.[131] In the early 1970s, Kurosh Lasha'i, a principal member of ROTPI, returned to Iran in order to organise resistance, and was arrested. ROTPI's expectation of resistance from him was unfounded, and in December 1972 he was shown on national television condemning ROTPI and Marxism, and claiming that any resistance to the imperial regime would be futile. He had realised when he saw it at first hand that everything ROTPI had said about the reform programme was wrong, that he and his comrades had not fully comprehended Iranian society, that as intellectuals they had demanded too much, and that democracy was a relative reality. Lasha'i asked his ROTPI comrades to return to Iran and see the realities for themselves.[132] It was cases such as this that prompted other groups to allege that ROTPI had been infiltrated by SAVAK, and added to the speed of its decline in the 1970s. ROTPI had started off as a popular group among Iranian students abroad, especially in Western Europe, but mirroring ROTPI's decline and failure in Iran, the organisation began to lose its popularity abroad as it was challenged by student supporters of the guerrilla movement and other Maoist groups which did not have its Tudeh background. Nevertheless, although SAVAK put its membership at around 200 in 1975, it continued to publish *Tudeh* and *Setareh-ye Sorkh*, and played a role in the anti-regime movement abroad.[133]

ROTPI continued to follow its Maoist line in confrontations with the Tudeh and the guerrilla movement. It received $20,000 annually from China, and sent teams there for training, and to help the Chinese run their Persian-language radio broadcasts.[134] From 1975, as the Chinese Communist Party moved to depict the Soviet Union as the main threat to liberation movements and international socialism, ROTPI became the only organisation supporting the Chinese line. It remained a staunch defender of Mao's teachings, attacked the Tudeh for its relations with, and defence of, the Soviet Union,[135] which it called a social-imperialist power, and accused the Tudeh of being anti-revolutionary.[136] But perhaps the most intense point of contention between ROTPI and the Tudeh on Iranian affairs centred on the use of violence in the struggle, and the need for the dictatorship of the proletariat as the only replacement for the regime. ROTPI accused the Tudeh of not wanting to use violence against the state, and of not wanting to replace the regime with a dictatorship of the proletariat.[137] In the light of ROTPI's own inability to organise inside Iran, these polemics were in reality part of a campaign for the hearts and minds of Iranians abroad. Ironically, for all its anti-Tudeh rhetoric about proletarian dictatorship, once the revolutionary tide began in Iran, it became a staunch supporter of Ayatollah Khomeini's Islamic movement.[138]

Like the Tudeh, ROTPI's attacks on the guerrilla movement centred on the Fadaiyan. But contrary to the Tudeh, which criticised the Fadaiyan for its over-emphasis on armed struggle, ROTPI attacked it from a radical angle. The ROTPI contention was that the reform programme had not brought any significant change to Iranian society, and that any armed action should be based on the Chinese model. This meant concentrating the efforts of the vanguard organisation on Iranian peasantry, and trying to encircle the urban areas from rural ones.[139] In accordance with Mao's view, ROTPI believed in the creation of a communist party to lead the revolution, and saw itself as a candidate.[140] Its failure to organise inside Iran had very little effect on its perception of Iranian society and armed struggle. It began to change its view only towards the end of the imperial regime's life.

The Tufan in the 1970s functioned, more or less, outside Iran. The group's only major attempt to establish a base in Iran was frustrated when SAVAK discovered its principal members and arrested several people. In the late 1960s, the Tufan sent Hadi Ja'fari to Iran in order to attempt to organise support. He managed to gather a number of people around him in Tehran and Mashhad, but in 1970 the whole group was arrested and the ringleaders convicted.[141]

Throughout the 1970s, the Tufan remained a Maoist Organisation, and opposed both the Tudeh and the guerrilla movement from a pro-Chinese and Albanian background. Between 1970 and 1977, it published *Tufan* and functioned as an exile group from Western Europe and the United States, its main concentration being in the Confederation of Iranian Students, where it was a minor player. It saw the Soviet Union as a social-imperialist power with only exploitative designs on Iran,[142] so its attacks on the Tudeh were also abstract, and unrelated to the anti-regime struggle. The Tufan considered the Tudeh a revisionist Soviet tool,[143] and its reaction to the land reform programme was, at best, confused and contradictory. Without mentioning whether or not reform had established capitalist relations in rural areas, the organisation considered the programme's effects devastating for the peasantry.[144] It believed that the peasantry was a revolutionary force with which the working class had to unite in order to lead a successful revolution. Like the Tudeh, the Tufan opposed the guerrilla movement on the grounds that a party of the working class was necessary to lead the revolution, and that armed action, such as that undertaken by the Fadaiyan, paid inadequate attention to political agitation among the masses.[145]

Early in the 1970s, theoretical disputes between Gholam Hosein Forutan and Ahmad Qasemi, the two leading members of the Tufan, started off a process of internal struggle which resulted in a split in 1977. The dispute between the two centred on the problem of the working-class party. Qasemi, the dogmatic and tough Stalinist theorist, took the orthodox line that in any given nation only one working-class or communist party could exist. Forutan, on the other hand, came to the conclusion that there could be two or more.[146] As long as Qasemi was alive, his line was observed, but after his death in 1975 the balance began to change, and other issues entered the fray. In 1977, the organisation's only gathering was held in West Berlin, where the dispute centred on three points, namely the dispute over the communist party, China's foreign policy and the Albanian criticism of it, and the rising revolutionary tide in Iran. Two main contending groups emerged, and precipitated a split. One group, under Forutan, continued with the multi-communist-party stand, continued to use the organisation's name, criticised Chinese foreign policy in its depiction of the Soviet Union as the main enemy while refusing to criticise Mao, and endorsed the Albanian Communist Party as the true revolutionary communist party. This group continued to function in student movements abroad, and its policy was to work towards union with ROTPI. The second group, under Ali Sa'adati (alias Sanjar) had declared its existence even before the split, and called itself the Party of Workers and Peasants (*hezb-e kargaran va dehqanan).*[147] This group had managed to secure the support of the Albanian Communist Party, criticised both China and Mao, and acquired control of *Tufan*. In 1978, this group split again, and a group of dissidents, under Fereidun Montaqemi, left to create the Militant Workers (*kargaran-e mobarez*). The remainder, under Sa'adati, began to call themselves the Party of Labour (*hezb-e kar*) just before the revolution.

MARXIST CELLS ABROAD

Besides these groups, organisations and parties which were, at one point or another, active in Iran, the 1970s saw the emergence of a number of groups which were active abroad. Their importance lay in the fact that they were a part of the general anti-imperial regime movement abroad, primarily concentrated in the Confederation of Iranian Students, played a role in supporting the guerrilla movement, or that they became active after the revolution.

Prominent among Marxist groups outside Iran was the Communist Unity Group (*goruh-e etehad-e komonisti*). The group originated among younger members of the National Front abroad who, during the 1960s, had turned Marxist, and functioned as the front's left wing, under the title National Front (Middle East Branch). Well-known founder members of the group were Hasan Masali and Khosrow Kalantari. With the Siyahkal operation and the advent of the guerrilla movement, these young Marxists began to organise independently under the title of Communist Unity. The group continued its activities within the Confederation of Iranian Students, but also, perhaps more importantly, began to support actively the guerrilla movement. In the early 1970s, because of its weakness abroad, the guerrilla movement, whether Fadaiyan or Moslem Mojahedin, welcomed the new group and its support. Between 1970 and 1973, Communist Unity co-operated with both organisations, and from 1973 accepted the command structure of, and entered a process of union with, the Fadaiyan. The two organisations, while co-operating closely abroad, exchanged written polemics on their differences which produced lively discussions rare in the history of communism in Iran, and which prevented merger. Communist Unity distanced itself from the Fadaiyan by propounding Leninism and using Trotskyite arguments against Stalin and Stalinism. The Fadaiyan, under Ashraf, believed firmly in Stalinism, and had put Hamid Mo'meni, a dogmatic thinker, in charge of debating these points. The result of these debates was published by Communist Unity under the title *Estalinism*, while the Fadaiyan published only its own side of the argument. To make unity even less likely, the next round of the debate centred on Maoism, and again the two found themselves at opposite ends of the spectrum.[148] The Fadaiyan's internal purges also aggravated the already tense relationship, and ties were broken in early 1976. Communist Unity maintained some links with the Moslem Mojahedin until 1975, when internal purges in the latter group brought the relationship to an end. Communist Unity was the only Iranian Marxist group to take a firm line on the Mojahedin's bloody purge and condemn the organisation openly.[149] The Marxist Mojahedin not only retaliated over the purge, but also began to criticise the Fadaiyan for continuing to maintain relations with Communist Unity.

As the revolutionary tide began to shake the imperial regime, Communist Unity had no visible presence in the country, and was one of the few Marxist groups, with the exception of the Iranian Trotskyites, which maintained that social revolution in Iran had to be socialist in nature.[150] This was in opposition to the overwhelming majority of other groups, which maintained that a democratic revolution would be acceptable if led by the working class. Communist Unity changed its name to the Organisation of Communist Unity (*sazman-e vahdat-e komonisti*) after the 1979 revolution.

Another group which was founded in the 1970s and played an important role in the post-revolution period was the Organisation of Revolutionary Communists (*sazman-e enqelabiyun-e komonist*) founded in Berkeley, California, in 1970. The organisation had emerged from a study-group founded in 1966 in Berkeley by Iranian students with a background of political activity abroad. Its founding members had mixed backgrounds, and included supporters of the National Front, former Moslem activists and some supporters of the nationalist Iranian intellectual Ahmad Kasravi.[151] By 1970, however, they had turned Maoist, had begun publishing *Komonist* as an official journal, and were primarily active in the Confederation of Iranian Students. Notable among the original members were Hamid Kosari, Siyamak Za'im, Parviz and Hamid Shokat, Faramarz Semnani, Hashem Mazandarani, Abbas Bozorg, Muhammad Amini, Ahmad Taqva'i, Fereidun Ali-abadi and Zhaleh Behrouzi.

As Iran's oil revenues increased, more and more students from the lower classes were able to go abroad for higher education. From 1972, as a result of government-sponsored financial aid and a strong rial, European and American universities were flooded with Iranian students. The Confederation of Iranian Students attracted many of these newcomers, and the Revolutionary Communists managed to build a base there. This base undermined ROTPI's student support, and indeed the Revolutionary Communists became ROTPI's main competition for the hearts and minds of Iranian students, particularly in America. The Revolutionary Communists recruited from among students of a lower-middle-class background, and this became its most important asset after the revolution, when many of these recruits became full-time members.

Although Maoist, the group had major differences with other Iranian Maoist organisations. To begin with, it did not believe in receiving help from other socialist countries or other communist parties. Unlike ROTPI and the Tufan, which copied the Chinese and Albanian experiences and tried to apply them to Iran, the Revolutionary Communists saw the Iranian situation as being closer to the Russian. Drawing on the experiences of Iran's constitutional revolution of 1906–11, it had concluded that Iran's revolution would be based in urban areas, rather than the rural areas of ROTPI's analysis,[152] and criticised ROTPI for its lack of action, depicting itself as an alternative to that group, which had failed to organise inside Iran. Its analysis of the reform programme was confused, and it saw Iran after the reform programme as a bourgeois-feudal society, indicating its remoteness from the realities of Iranian society. It opposed the guerrilla movement's insistence on armed action, and emphasised agitation among the working class.

In 1973, the remnant of the Palestine Group, headed by Hosein Riahi, alias Puya, joined the organisation. In 1975, it officially changed its name to The League of Iranian Communists (*etehadiyeh-ye komonistha-ye Iran*), publishing *Haqiqat* as its main journal and *Komonist* as its theoretical one. It continued to be active outside Iran, but was not able to establish a base in the country, and thus did not play any direct role in the revolutionary events of 1979.

The 1970s witnessed the birth of an Iranian version of the Trotskyite movement. The radical student movement in Europe of the late 1960s, in particular the anti-Vietnam movement and the 1968 movement in France, had its effects on a group of Iranian students in Britain. These students came from different political backgrounds (Maoist, pro-Cuba and others), but had accepted the views of the Fourth International, which adhered to the views of Leon Trotsky. Among the founding members of Iranian Trotskyites in Britain were Hormoz Rahimi and Hozhabr Khosravi-azarbaijani.[153] The group began the publication of *Kand va Kav* in 1974, becoming known as the Kand va Kav Group,[154] and throughout the 1970s was active outside Iran in human rights activities and as the International's representative in the Confederation of Iranian Students. Here, in line with the international Trotskyite movement, the group worked for the right of tendencies within the confederation to form factions, and because of this often clashed with the Maoist leadership and the majority of the Confederation.[155] At the same time as the establishment of Kand va Kav in Britain, another Trotskyite group was created in the United States with the help of the US-based Socialist Workers Party. The most important members of this group were an able speaker, Babak Zahra'i, and Afsaneh Najmabadi (also known as Azar Tabari), who after 1974 moved to Europe. Initially the two groups in Europe and the United States were unaware of each other's existence, but were brought together through the Fourth International. Iranian Trotskyites were few in numbers and limited in activities, and did not have an active presence in Iran until after the collapse of the imperial regime.

By the time the revolutionary tide began to shake the foundations of the state, the communist movement in Iran had reached a stalemate with the regime. In Western countries, the movement had organised mostly around such sensitive themes as human rights and the lack of elementary democratic rights. These activities were a constant nuisance to the regime and the Shah, who sought to depict himself as a modern progressive statesman of world stature. In socialist countries, the Tudeh had managed to divert resources and funds to put a parallel pressure on the regime. Inside the country, the guerrilla movement had begun challenging the regime at the height of its power. This challenge did not result in a popular revolution led by the devoted Marxist vanguard, but the regime had not managed to uproot the guerrillas either. In this stalemate, the movement had managed to score two points. First, it had shown that the regime was far from invincible, and that it could be challenged despite its financial and military resources. Second, and closely related to the first point, following the defeats of the 1950s and 1960s, the guerrilla movement had created a culture of resistance to the dictatorship.[156] In varying degree this culture of resistance helped maintain a spirit of defiance which had a direct bearing on the coming revolution. The stalemate, however, was upset by the revolution, and the regime was swept aside by a mass movement led by the Islamists. This development had not been anticipated by Iranian Marxists, and was in effect the ultimate challenge to the movement.

3

Revolution: The Dance of Death (1979–83)

Because of killing six Americans and many Iranians in the past five or six years, the terrorist groups enjoy popular support. During the past four years Iran's terrorist movement has emerged as two important organisations, namely People's Mojahedin and the Organisation of People's Fada'i Guerrillas, which in all probability receive aid from Libya, but that as far as we know not from the Soviets.

American Embassy Report

[The Left] did not contribute anything. They did not help the revolution at all... They were not decisive in the victory, they were not responsible, they did not contribute anything... The people fought for Islam.

Ayatollah Khomeini

REVOLUTION

The February 1979 revolution in Iran was a surprise to all its participants, both domestic and foreign powers trying either to bring the situation under control or to take advantage of it. The rapidity with which the last Shah of Iran and his imperial regime were consigned to history stunned the superpowers, paralysed the Shah and his imperial armed forces, and was totally unexpected, given the *ad hoc* nature of the coalition ranged against the regime. By September 1978, this coalition had come under the Islamists' leadership, with Ayatollah Khomeini as its undisputed leader. What was unique about the coalition was that it included almost all social classes and political forces, whether tied to the Islamists or not. With the possible exception of the upper layer of the Iranian bourgeoisie, the Shah had managed to alienate all other social groups and classes, so that by the time the upheaval reached its peak, there was no one left to defend the regime. A popular anecdote of the time was indicative of the regime's predicament. The Empress Farah was reminded, at the height of the unrest, that when King Louis XVI was in trouble his supporters demonstrated on his behalf in the Champs-Elysees, and when asked why the Shah's supporters were not doing the same, she replied that they were – in the Champs-Elysees. The story pointed to the fact that those who benefited most under the Shah's rule were those who abandoned him when he most needed them.

It seems that an American Democratic president with strong convictions on world-wide human rights had a profound effect on Iranian politics. The Shah, always an active supporter of Republican candidates in American politics, perceived Nixon's resignation, following Watergate, and also Ford's defeat by Carter, as a weakening of American support for his rule. With issues of human rights becoming increasingly important in American politics after Carter's inauguration in January 1977, the Shah moved to adapt the imperial regime's conduct in line with new international realities, although this is not to suggest that evidence exists of direct US pressure. With political power and decision-making increasingly concentrated in the hands of the Shah, any change in his perception of events triggered change throughout the regime. According to one observer, '... the Shah had come, over his years of rule, to depend on the United States for general guidance and orientation, for specific advice and even instructions, and to a significant extent... as a source of psychological well-being'.[1] Hence, the inauguration of a Democrat president, making human rights a cornerstone of US foreign policy, was a significant factor in persuading the Shah that the time had come for change, and for the liberalisation of Iranian politics.

The regime's moderate and radical opposition soon felt the change of atmosphere. In October 1977, a group of secular intellectuals, lawyers and judges addressed an open letter to the Shah asking for the constitution to be observed, the freeing of political prisoners, and the respecting of political freedoms and human rights. In November 1977, Ayatollah Khomeini wrote a letter to the *ulama* in Iran telling them of the unique opportunity created by Carter's human rights policy and, citing the secular intellectuals' letter, asking them also to start writing letters. He suggested, 'write about the problems and deliver it to them [the Government] like those who wrote of many things, and signed the letter without anyone bothering them'.[2]

The same month, the Shah's first meeting with Carter in Washington was disrupted by angry Iranian students. The demonstrators, mainly Marxist activists and supporters of various branches of the Confederation of Iranian Students, had been active against the regime for years. The sight of the Shah, Carter, their aides and wives suffering from tear-gas inhalation was unforgettable for the demonstrators, and was broadcast all over the world. The visit and Carter's return visit to Tehran in late December 1977, during which he called the Shah's Iran '... an island of stability in one of the more troubled areas of the world', seems to have had two results in the run-up to the turbulent days of 1978. First, the two men developed a working relationship, and the Shah was assured of strong US backing. Second, the Shah reaffirmed his resolve to push through reforms in Iran.[3] Issues such as human rights and political freedoms were discussed, but no pressure was exerted.

1978 witnessed a gradual quickening of events which resulted in outright revolutionary struggle by the summer and the collapse of the regime in February 1979. Although clashes with security forces and the army had been occurring through the spring of 1978, the Shah did not seem alarmed until mid-summer. As late as June, the Shah was still more concerned with buying new military equipment for the Iranian airforce than with opposition demonstrations and subsequent clashes.[4] Yet by autumn 1978, it appeared he had lost control of events. According to the US Ambassador to Tehran, from September 1978 the Shah began to ask the United States and British ambassadors for frequent visits, and actively sought their advice on the situation.[5]

Like many Iranians of his generation, the Shah was a subscriber to conspiracy theories based on the idea that many or all of Iran's troubles and misfortunes have a foreign element or power behind them.[6] Throughout the 1970s, the Shah and the imperial regime's ruling elite believed that the armed opposition, whether Moslem or Marxist, was in fact an 'unholy alliance between black and red', with the Soviet Union and the Tudeh playing a leading role from behind the scenes. The Shah sometimes referred to the armed opposition as

'Islamic Marxists', and dispatched the entire weight of the imperial regime's security forces to crush it. By 1978, he resembled a boxer reeling from punches from his blind side. The revolution was neither led by the armed opposition of the 1970s, nor by any Soviet-backed political organisation, partly because all these forces were kept in check by SAVAK. The revolution was spontaneous in nature, and had come under the leadership of radical Islamists led by Ayatollah Khomeini. This the Shah could not comprehend and, like a disoriented boxer, he went from one conspiracy theory to another to explain the situation. It has been noted that as early as November 1978 the Shah wondered if American and British intelligence services were behind the turmoil.[7] In the end, he blamed everyone and everything, from his attempt to raise the price of oil – which supposedly angered the Western powers – to his old favourite theme, the 'black and red'.[8]

The regime's paralysis in confronting the revolution was directly linked to the Shah's confusion, loss of will and inability to comprehend the reality of the revolutionary movement before him. This state of paralysis was partially linked to the inability of his traditional foreign backers and friends to understand the situation and to give him the general advice he so desperately needed. Here, the Carter administration's confused and contradictory policy toward the Shah and revolution played a major role in the regime's demise. Had US foreign policy been able to play a more decisive role in supporting the Shah and providing him with solid advice during early 1978, there is a strong possibility that the outcome of the Iranian revolution would have been different. There seem to have been three basic reasons for the American failure in Iran. First, as some American policy-makers of the time have noted, there was a sharp decline in US intelligence-gathering on Iran in the late 1970s,[9] based on a misguided trust in the regime's stability and the Shah's authority. The lack of adequate intelligence meant that American officials failed to realise the seriousness of the situation in time and, even more importantly, had very little information on opposition leaders and the way they operated. Second, American foreign policy was faced with a number of important issues in 1978 (SALT II and the Camp David Accords among others) which stretched its resources to the limit. According to one American policy-maker, 'Our decision-making circuits were heavily overloaded'.[10] This meant that the Iranian situation did not receive due attention until the revolution was well underway. Third, at the top of the administration there were two approaches to events in Iran, which translated into two sets of advice to the Shah. This factor was perhaps the most confusing one for the Shah, and most afected his will and morale in confronting the revolution. According to Carter's National Security Advisor, Zbigniew Brzezinski, the two different approaches originated from the National Security Council and the State Department, the former emphasising US and Western interests in Iran, the latter more preoccupied with promoting democracy.[11] Once events became more critical, from September 1978, the two policies sent contradictory signals. The fact that the US Ambassador to Tehran began to lose his standing within the US administration only added to the confusion. Once it became clear that the Shah's rule could not be sustained, the two policies became even more divided. The policy proposed by the National Security Advisor held that any government in Iran should enter negotiations with the opposition from a position of strength. Accordingly, the Iranian Government was constantly urged to show force, and Gen. Robert Huyser was sent to Iran to assure the integrity of the Iranian armed forces. This policy expected the armed forces to stage a coup if the civilian Government of Shapour Bakhtiar failed. The State Department, it seems, had more faith in the Bakhtiar Government, and wanted the armed forces to continue backing it.[12] By this time, the US Ambassador, William Sullivan, had completely lost the trust of Washington policy-makers, and increasingly carried out the policy he saw fit, one based on the premise that compromise with the opposition was inevitable, and a position should be reached whereby the imperial armed forces would maintain their integrity so that in the future they could be used as a counter-balance to the new revolutionary Government. It seems that regardless of where American policy was made, the widespread view was that radicalisation of the movement would allow the communists, and therefore the Soviets, to take advantage of the situation.[13] When the administration ultimately accepted as inevitable the collapse of the regime, it believed that the succeeding Islamic Republic would be composed of moderates who would maintain ties with the United States in order to safeguard Iran from Soviet aggression. In light of the lack of intelligence on Iran and the confused US policy throughout 1978, it is unclear how and why the American policy-makers came to these conclusions.

The Soviet Union's reaction to the Iranian revolution was no less confusing, and was the result of an utter misunderstanding of the realities. The emergence of Islam and the Shi'i clergy at the head of a mass revolutionary movement in Iran took the Soviets by surprise, as can be seen from Soviet scholarly work on Islam in pre-revolutionary Iran. Up to the end of the 1960s, Soviet scholars saw little or no progressive role for Shi'i Islam in modern times. These scholars, and indeed the Soviet Government, viewed the 1963 uprising against the Shah's reform programme as regressive. Yet this type of analysis began to change in the 1970s as a new generation of Soviet scholars began to analyse the subject.[14] The new approach depicted Islam as a positive mobilising force in a society trying to move from a feudal stage to a capitalist one, but still saw Islam's role in a capitalist society as reactionary. Hence, while the 1970s witnessed heated discussions in Soviet scholarly circles over the progressive nature of Islam, the overall view remained unchanged. One scholar has noted that as late as October 1978 Soviet scholars viewed Islam as being in a state of crisis.[15]

As noted earlier, the 1970s saw a mutually beneficial economic, and a stable political, relationship between the Soviet Union and the imperial regime. The Shah always mistrusted the Soviet Union's hidden agenda for Iran, and the Soviet Union, while recognising the Shah as an ally of the West, viewed the imperial regime as stable enough to allow accommodation rather than confrontation. Based on its analysis of Islam and coexistence with the imperial regime, Soviet policy-makers were slow to acknowledge the existence of the revolutionary movement, and its ideological character. Another reason for this lack of comprehension was a sharp decline in the Soviet intelligence performance in Iran, echoing the American intelligence position. According to Vlademir Kuzichkin, a KGB operative in Iran, the decline was due to 'the replacement of many officers, including the heads in the residency'.[16] Despite several bloody clashes between the Iranian military and the growing revolutionary movement in the first half of 1978, the Soviet Union's first public acknowledgment of the existence of such clashes was published in *Pravda* following the Black Friday clashes on 8 September. *Pravda* reported the clash on 9 September, and went on to analyse the mass demonstration of *Eid al-fitr* a few days earlier. The significance of this demonstration was in that it was the largest peaceful demonstration against the imperial regime yet, with over 200,000 people clearly calling for Ayatollah Khomeini's return, and the establishment of an Islamic republic. Ironically, the *Pravda* commentary missed the significance and character of the demonstration by suggesting that it was in defence of Iran's 1906 constitution.[17] Nevertheless, as the revolutionary upheaval grew, the Soviet Union began to pay more attention to the realities in Iran. In November 1978, the Soviets assessed the situation as sufficiently critical to warn the US Government against direct intervention.[18] On 7 January, *Pravda* suggested that while events in Iran were purely internal, Islam and religious circles were playing a significant role.[19] The reality, however, was that by January 1979, the clergy, headed by Ayatollah Khomeini, did not just play a significant role, but was leading the revolution. Until as late as 2 January, while *Pravda* warned the revolutionaries of the dangers of a military coup, it named Ayatollah Khomeini as leader of the revolution without mentioning his religious credentials. The article anticipated a victorious revolution and a government based on people's will, but made no mention of the distinct possibility of theocracy.[20] It was only towards the end of January that the Soviet press began to recognise clerical leadership of the revolution. Yet even here, and as late as 7 February (the imperial regime collapsed on the twelfth), the Soviets failed to acknowledge that the clerical leadership sought an Islamic republic, the *Pravda* commentary of that date referring to Ayatollah Khomeini as 'the leader of the national democratic and religious opposition', and suggesting that he sought the creation of a republic.[21] This was despite a much earlier call for a specifically Islamic republic.

The last Shah of Iran left the country at the height of revolutionary fever on 16 January 1979. The successes and failures of the revolution were confirmed in a referendum in April 1979, when an Islamic republic was confirmed by the overwhelming majority of the population over sixteen years of age. The creation of the Islamic Republic of Iran (IRI) marked the initial unravelling of the undeclared coalition formed to overthrow the old regime, as the Islamists sought to consolidate their power within a theocracy, and the opposition attempted to prevent or postpone that consolidation, in the hope of creating the right conditions for an attempt of their own to secure power.

In consolidating power, the new Islamist elite had two different interpretations of the meaning of an Islamic state. In the period under study, 1979–83, these two interpretations resulted in the gradual formation of two distinct factions within old and new state organs. One faction, which could in general terms be called 'Liberals', had a more Western-oriented interpretation of the Islamic state. They believed that once the revolution was successful, the affairs of the state should be entrusted to the hands of moderate and Western-educated figures who would run the country within limited parliamentary procedures, with Islamic ethics and morality gently applied, and an economy reformed, but along existing lines, to tread a path between East and West, though favouring the latter as a check to the ambitions of Iran's powerful northern neighbour. Clearly, in this interpretation of an Islamic state very little room was left for the clergy, whom the Islamic Liberals expected to play a marginal role. Among the leading Islamic Liberals were premier Mehdi Bazargan and his Liberation Movement colleagues, who ran the affairs of the state between February and November 1979, and President Abol Hasan Bani-sadr and colleagues, who came to office in December and were ousted in June 1981. Once the old regime collapsed, the Islamic Liberals, mandated by Ayatollah Khomeini, moved to secure the old regime's state apparatus. These were the ministries, the police and the armed forces, which the Islamic Liberals saw as caretakers.

In opposition to the Islamic Liberals were those with a stricter interpretation of the Islamic state. Better known as *Maktabis* (committed and doctrinaire), this faction saw a more active and dominant role for the clergy, and viewed the role of non-clerics as marginal. During the period 1979–83, the *Maktabis* had a more strict interpretation of 'neither East nor West', and opted for more independence *vis-à-vis* superpowers and a more clearly anti-American line. Personalities such as Ayatollah Muhammad Hosein Beheshti, Ayatollah Hasan Ali Montazeri, Hoj Muhammad Javad Bahonar, Hoj Ali Akbar Hashemi-rafsanjani and Hoj Ali Khameneh'i belonged to this faction, and dominated the revolutionary council and the Islamic Republic Party (IRP). As the Islamic Liberals took control of the state apparatus of the old regime, the *Maktabis* moved to create their own state institutions and legal entities in society, and soon gained control of the revolutionary council, the revolutionary 'komiteh' (security committees) and the Islamic Revolutionary Guards Corps (*sepah-e pasdaran-e enqelab-e eslami*). These parallel institutions, with increasingly more power than the old institutions, helped the *Maktabis* to overcome the Islamic Liberals.[22]

The period under study may be divided into two separate phases with distinct characteristics. The first phase, 1979–81, was a period of transition, in which the IRI moved from overthrowing the old regime through a process of consolidation. The main characteristics of this phase were, on one hand, a struggle between the IRI and its opposition, and on the other, a factional competition within the IRI's ruling elite, which inevitably involved the opposition as well. This phase was one of relative freedom for the opposition, in which newspapers were published, political meetings were held in the open, and opposition to the IRI was, for the most part, political. The scale of these political freedoms, however, became more limited as events came to a head in June 1981. Among the important social and political issues in this phase were the rights of national minorities, the nature of an Islamic state, the rights of women, the American hostage crisis and the Iran-Iraq War. The second phase, 1981–3, started with the June 1981 crisis, and ended with the elimination of the last legal Marxist organisation in 1983. In June 1981, the *Maktabi* faction, led by the clergy, and the IRP, supported by Ayatollah Khomeini, pushed the Islamic Liberals out of power, declared all opposition political activities illegal, and entered a period of practical civil war with the Moslem Mojahedin, in which Marxist organisations played a marginal role. Important social and political issues of this phase were the consolidation of the IRI, the continuation of Iran-Iraq War, and the effective repression of the opposition and the disintegration of Marxist organisations.

The political freedom which followed the 1979 revolution offered political organisations and parties, from the left to the right (with the exception of the pro-monarchy forces), the chance to organise. After 26 years of relatively consistent dictatorship, this newly-achieved freedom gave an important breathing-space to all groups and parties, especially those of the left. Since the Iranian communist movement was the main target of the repression, the post-1979 freedom was a particularly historic moment for it. During the months immediately after the downfall of the old regime, Marxist organisations found a chance to organise on a mass scale. Here, a movement which had fought the regime and the 1953 coup organisers for decades, and waged armed struggle since 1971, disjointed as it had been, found the chance to address its constituency directly, and to organise openly. The honeymoon was to be shorter than many may have expected. Almost immediately after the collapse of the Shah's regime, signs of confrontation with the new IRI leadership began to show, and as time passed the movement realised that the new Islamist leadership's tolerance was limited, and coming to an end rapidly. This period was one of *danse macabre* for the communist movement in Iran, in which the movement's very survival depended on its ability to adapt to the post-revolutionary social environment of the country. In this venture, the Iranian communists ultimately failed.

The issues and problems facing the Iranian Marxists were enormous. The movement had to function in a post-revolutionary society in which the leadership emphasised the consolidation of a theocratic state and a cultural revolution rather than any change in the relations of production, the ownership of the means of production, or democratic institutions. The political independence of the new state was perhaps the most important issue facing the Iranian Marxists, and the key factor in keeping the movement off-balance for the duration of this period. Here, two elements contributed to Marxist confusion. The first was factional conflict within the new Islamic elite, often arising from contradictory socio-political tendencies, the second the IRI's foreign policy of 'neither East nor West', regardless of different interpretations, which meant the state's independence *vis-à-vis* foreign powers.[23] For Iran, this was an immensely important development which went unnoticed by many political groups, including the Marxists. Until the 1979 revolution, Iran had been under the indirect influence of foreign powers, a process which began with the defeats Qajar Iran suffered during the Russo-Iranian wars at the beginning of the nineteenth century. Since that period, foreign embassies in Tehran had played a decisive role in the internal politics of the country. The foreign influence could be seen during such important events as the constitutional revolution of 1906–9, the Reza Khan coup of 1921, and of course the notorious anti-Mosaddeq coup of 1953. The dependence of the imperial regime and Reza Shah on the Americans and the British was an important factor in the regime's inability to gain legitimacy among the population at large and the intelligentsia in particular. A great proportion of the Marxist literature of the pre-revolutionary period was based on this, as were the sharpest attacks of the Islamists on the old regime.

The emergence of Islam as a political force – what many would call fundamentalism – was a surprise to all who encountered it. For the Marxist supporters and theorists of the post-revolution period, the problem of the new Islamic state proved insoluble and ultimately devastating. While a number of Marxist organisations (the Tudeh amongst others) interpreted the political independence of the IRI and especially the anti-Americanism of the *Maktabis*, as a sign of a possible drift towards an understanding with the Soviet Union, the overwhelming majority denied the obvious and attempted to depict the new regime as a disguised puppet of imperialism. In doing so, most of them (for example Fadaiyan factions and the Paykar) concentrated their efforts on the Islamic Liberals, with radical slogans and policies. While struggling for public support, and increasingly for their very existence, each Marxist organisation tried its best to outdo the others and the IRI leadership in their calls for drastic change. In this fever of radicalism, the Marxists were outmanoeuvred by the Islamists because they refused to accept the independent nature of the new IRI leadership at face value, a factor which played an important role in the movement's inability to cope with the IRI, and ultimately led to its downfall.

After the revolution, the number of groups, organisations and parties claiming to adhere to Marxism grew rapidly. While prior to the revolution there had been perhaps a dozen such groups, after it their numbers grew to perhaps over 80, and this number increased as Marxist groups began to fragment into smaller units. Indeed, after the revolution it became common for any gathering of a few Marxist activists to call itself an organisation or party and claim to be the rightful vanguard of the working class. Hence, it is neither possible, nor perhaps necessary, to produce an account of all Marxist organisations, parties and groups in the post-revolutionary era. It is safe to suggest that whatever happened to the major organisations and parties also broadly happened to the smaller ones, and the focus here will be on the conduct and activities of these major groups. Organisations may be divided in to two major categories, namely those which supported the IRI and those which found themselves firmly opposed. Obviously, each of these categories may be further sub-divided, but such sub-division would only complicate an already difficult task. It will be left to each individual major organisation to explain itself.

THE FADAIYAN AND REVOLUTION

Among the various Marxist organisations, the Fadaiyan emerged as the largest, and soon found itself the major opposition organisation to the IRI in 1979 and 1980. According to one account, when the organisation experienced a major split in June 1980, it had fewer than 100 members, but over half a million reliable supporters (those it could rely on to execute key policies).[24]

The Fadaiyan's opposition to the IRI was the direct result, on one hand, of its attempt to get involved in social issues with radical slogans and policies, and on the other of the IRI's move to consolidate its power. After the collapse of the old regime, it took the new one almost three years to achieve this consolidation, which it began almost immediately after the revolution. The first confrontation with the Fadaiyan came on 31 March 1979, when the Islamic leadership organised a referendum and asked the population to chose between the imperial system and an Islamic Republic. The Fadaiyan were among the few which boycotted the referendum, claiming that the notion of an Islamic state was vague and the election procedures undemocratic.[25]

The post-revolution Fadaiyan leadership which took charge of the enormous task of adjusting to the new realities of mass organisation and a revolutionary environment was a collection of unelected pre-revolutionary members. This new leadership was selected from two categories of members just before the collapse of the imperial regime. First, there were those who, in one way or another, had managed to stay out of prison during the struggle, those who had salvaged the organisation after Ashraf's death in 1976, attempted to adjust to Jazani's theses, and conducted the internal purges that followed. They were generally poorly trained in the theoretical sphere, being mostly practitioners and organisers. Second, there were those who had been put in jail and were released in separate groups during 1978, and who had used their time in prison to strengthen their theoretical knowledge. This group had mostly converted to Jazani's theses, although some hardcore Ahmadzadeh supporters still remained among them. While the scope of pro-Tudeh beliefs was limited among Fadaiyan members in prison, and the Fadaiyan Splinter Group had not found many converts among them, it is suspected that some Fadaiyan members had already accepted, or were leaning towards, the Tudeh before their release in 1978.[26] Chief among these was Farrokh Negahdar, who was arrested with the Jazani-Zarifi Group in the 1960s and had spent much time in the Shiraz prison where most of the old Tudeh Military Organisation prisoners were kept.[27] Negahdar led the pro-Tudeh split in the Fadaiyan in 1980, and has been accused of long harbouring Tudeh sympathies, but keeping them hidden so as to take a large section of the Fadaiyan with him. At any rate, jailed Fadaiyan members quickly took their places in the organisation on release from prison, and began to fill its theoretical and leadership vacuum.[28] The post-revolutionary Fadaiyan, then, comprised two sets of members who had not been in contact with each other for years. In fact, many members of one group had joined the Fadaiyan long after members of the other were arrested. This was the leadership which was in charge of converting the Fadaiyan from an underground guerrilla organisation into a mass political force.

The Fadaiyan's confrontation with the IRI during 1979 and 1980 was immediate and intense. In February, the organisation was accused of attacking and occupying the US Embassy in Tehran, an event which ended quickly as the Provisional Government intervened to restore order. During the winter and spring of 1979, the Fadaiyan was faced with growing tension between women's groups and the IRI over women's rights, and outright military confrontation

106

between Turkman and Kurdish populations and the Government. Because of the Fadaiyan's prestige as a consistently anti-imperial guerrilla group, these events put increased pressure on it to take a position and become directly involved. The leadership chose the path of compromise on the first two problems, but the magnitude and intensity of the Kurdish conflict started a major rift in the organisation.

The women's issue was among the first conflicts between the IRI and its opposition. In essence the conflict involved mainly middle- and upper-class women, who had benefited most from some of the modernising reforms of the former regime. These reforms had opened up education and job opportunities for women, and included family laws which provided some protection for women in divorce cases and the right to wear Western clothing. Despite the gains they had made, many of these women had actively participated in the overthrow of the old regime, objecting to dictatorship and the lack of respect for human rights. Now, they were faced with a regime which intended to enforce Islamic moral codes with laws which many felt were discriminatory against women. Immediately after coming to power, the IRI began to remove women judges from the judiciary, and demands were made that women observe the Islamic dress code in the work-place. In response, women's groups began to organise. Two major women's groups emerged in the process, the first of which was the National League of Women (*ettehadieh-ye melli zanan*), composed of students, teachers and nurses, the great majority of whom were Marxists and supporters of the Fadaiyan. It published the bi-weekly *Equality* and monthly *Women and Struggle*. The other group was called Liberation of Women (*Raha'i-ye Zanan*), and was composed mostly of non-aligned Marxists, publishing *Women's Emancipation*.[29] Women's demonstrations started on international women's day, 8 March 1979, and was attacked by pro-IRI groups known as *hezbollah*. The Fadaiyan initially defended the demonstrators, supporting their democratic right to defend their interests, and warned the IRI of the consequences of any violent action on its part, but took no concrete steps.[30] There were two major reasons for Fadaiyan failure to respond to the issue decisively. First, the organisation was developing two different views on the revolution, represented in two factions which would ultimately cause paralysis and a split. The second, and more fundamental, reason was that the organisation's attitude to the issue was based on a class analysis of society – which almost all Marxist groups in Iran shared – according to which women's oppression would be overcome by the elimination of the class system.[31] In 1979, as clashes between women's groups and the IRI were going on, and the Fadaiyan was condemning the attacks on women, the organisation reiterated its class-based approach to women's liberation, and implied that those who favoured any other approach were causing 'false agitation' among women.[32] The approach exposed some of the differences among members which were to lead to factionalism and a rift. The policy of defending women's demonstrations, while at the same time condemning the independent women's movement as 'false agitation', was in fact the genesis of the Fadaiyan's break-up.

Another crisis the Fadaiyan found itself faced with was the Turkman Sahra war, which unravelled in two phases, the first in 1979, the second in 1980. Turkman Sahra, in north-eastern Iran, was by the time of the revolution a mechanised agricultural area which had developed a unique system of peasant councils after the collapse of the imperial regime. This led the Turkman agricultural workers and peasants, following the collapse of central authority, to seize the land. This was followed by the establishment in Gonbad-e Kavus of Turkman Peasants' Councils (*showraha-ye dehqani-ye torkman sahra*), which soon took charge of the new socio-economic order in the area.[33] When in March 1979 armed clashes between government troops and armed Turkmans started, the Fadaiyan, which had only one representative in the area, was drawn in. The representative, Abbas Hashemi – one of the surviving members of the Fadaiyan's Tehran branch of 1976 – tried and failed to bring about reconciliation. The Fadaiyan soon found itself in a situation whereby the Turkmans expected it to become directly involved, and provide guidance, while the Government accused it of masterminding the whole enterprise. The Fadaiyan leadership, while talking tough and declaring that it would defend the rights of the Turkman councils violently if necessary, opted for a compromise and played an active part in arranging a ceasefire in Gonbad-e Kavus.[34]

The Kurdish war began in March 1979 and continued, on and off, throughout the period under study and beyond. The fundamental reasons for the war were, on one hand, the Kurdish movement's desire for autonomy within a democratic Iran and, on the other, the IRI desire to assert central control over the provinces. The Fadaiyan's involvement in the Kurdish war accelerated its internal division.

In May 1979, despite these three crises for the Fadaiyan, its first split was based on old issues, and involved those who still followed Ahmadzadeh's theses. Among the famous members who joined the split were Ashraf Dehqani, a woman guerrilla who had, for a while, been in charge of the Fadaiyan's operations abroad; Abdol Rahim Sabburi, who was recently released from prison and was known to have engaged Jazani in ideological discussions and led pro-Ahmadzadeh Fadaiyan members against him there; and Muhammad Hormati-pur, another well-known and recently returned guerrilla and co-director of operations abroad. The spokesperson of this group, which called itself the People's Fadaiyan Guerrillas (without using the term 'organisation') was Dehqani.[35] She accused the Fadaiyan leadership of having rejected armed struggle without clarifying its position to supporters and members. She claimed that the split was imposed on the group, and that it was ejected undemocratically, without being given the opportunity to explain and defend its position. The faction, which subsequently became known as Fadaiyan (Ashraf Dehqani), soon adopted a radical anti-IRI position and advocated armed struggle against it.

The split was relatively small. The well-known members of the departing group had not joined the Fadaiyan as active members, and Ahmadzadeh's doctrines had been rejected years before, so Dehqani's views found little support. But her claim of undemocratic treatment was valid, when put in the context of past experiences (for example Shoa'ian), and showed the continuation of undemocratic internal relations even after the lifting of the imperial regime's dictatorship. This group actively participated in the Kurdish war from its outset.

Besides the Dehqani split, from the very early days after the revolution, and especially once *KAR*, the Fadaiyan's weekly publication, was produced openly, two contradictory policies began to emerge, one calling for resistance to the IRI, the other conciliatory. For example, while the organisation supported boycotting the March 1979 referendum legitimising the IRI, *KAR* published a conciliatory letter, written by Muhammad Ali Farkhondeh (alias Ali Keshtgar, the organisation's spokesperson, a central committee advisor, and one of Negahdar's closest allies) to the Provisional Government.[36] It must be noted that at this stage, between February and August 1979, the Fadaiyan still had not confronted the Government openly, largely because of Ayatollah Khomeini's extreme popularity. In the post-revolutionary months, many, including the Marxists, saw him as a progressive figure, although this widespread belief still left room for the existence of two factions in the Fadaiyan.

During the early summer of 1979, the organisation was heavily involved in an assessment of its past. The central issue was whether armed struggle should have been used against the imperial regime.

This central question would have put the contending parties on different sides of the debate waged between the Fadaiyan and the Tudeh in the 1970s, and supposedly separated the radicals from the conservatives in the Fadaiyan. Issues and events during spring and summer 1979 gradually shaped the two contending groups into two factions. The radical faction had its organisational base on the editorial board of *KAR* and in a minority of the central committee. This faction became known as the 'Minority' (*aqaliyyat*). The conservative faction, which advocated reconciliation with the *Maktabi* wing of the new regime, was basically organised around a majority of the central committee, and became known as the 'Majority' (*aksariyyat*). When the Kurdish war began in August 1979, the two factions clashed head-on. Initially, the internal clash was kept secret, and a plenum was arranged to study the differences. The agenda of the first post-revolution plenum, held in October 1979 in Tehran, was first a debate on the organisation's past and then on the Kurdish war and policy towards it. The plenum was obviously controlled by the Majority faction, which also controlled the central committee. The exact discussions of this plenum were never officially revealed, but an unofficial version was circulated by the Tudeh, which had strong supporters and allies among the Majority faction. During the plenum, the two factions took definite shape, the Minority's grievances basically centring around the incompetence of the central committee. It charged the Majority with lacking a coherent programme of action to confront social crises. It saw ideological crisis in the Fadaiyan as the main cause of the inability to draft concrete strategy. The Minority proposed open ideological discussions on the roots of the crisis, and the nature of the new state and its class base. The Majority, under whose authority the plenum was called, wanted to limit the meeting to discussing the problems raised by the struggle in Kurdestan, despite the fact that it had been forced to call the plenum to heal the growing rift. It did not allow all the members of the Fadaiyan to participate, and invited only one member of *KAR*'s editorial board to take part. Evidently, undemocratic means of dealing with ideological opponents, a tradition within the Fadaiyan, persisted. At any rate, the new crises which followed the Fadaiyan plenum put an end to any reconciliation within the organisation, if indeed there had been any possibility of it.[37]

The first post-plenum political crisis which confronted the Fadaiyan was the occupation of the US Embassy, in November 1979. While the anti-American stand of the IRI was interpreted as progressive and anti-imperialist by the Majority, it was looked upon with suspicion by its rival. What came to be known as the American hostage crisis only added fuel to the process of division in the largest Marxist organisation in Iran. The second crisis was the second Turkman Sahra war, in winter and spring 1980. At this point, the Fadaiyan had become a major force and organiser in the region. The Turkman peasant councils, however, were a unique experience in Iran, and their situation was that of a small island in a large and hostile sea. Therefore, much like the Kurds, the Turkman councils soon came into conflict with the IRI, a conflict which intensified when, in February 1980, four top council leaders and Fadaiyan members were arrested after leaving negotiations with state representatives, and their tortured bodies found later.[38] The Majority position was to back down in the face of IRI aggression, the Minority chose to defend the councils. After two battles and much bloodshed, the councils were crushed by spring 1980, causing a deepening of the Fadaiyan's crisis.

In June 1980, the Minority broke away. By publishing its own issue of *KAR*, it officially declared itself independent. Calling itself OIPFG, it accused the Majority of opportunism, and of using bureaucratic, rather than democratic, means to deal with internal differences, insisting that under the circumstances it had had no choice but to leave. The Minority believed that the differences over the nature and class base of the IRI were the main reason behind the split. It also accused the Majority of rejecting the fundamental doctrines of the Fadaiyan's anti-imperial struggle, and of moving steadily toward the Tudeh.[39] It acknowledged past mistakes, but regarded general developments as positive. The Majority accused the splinter group of left-wing sectarianism, and of leaving without good reason. It rejected the accusation of a drift towards the Tudeh, but did not disguise its sympathy and support for the *Maktabis*. It did state, however, its rejection of past Fadaiyan theories, such as the validity of armed struggle against the imperial regime, or any repressive state. Indeed, the Majority soon dropped the term 'guerrilla' from its name, stopped using the Fadaiyan emblem, and called itself the Organisation of Iranian People's Fadaiyan (Majority).[40]

It is hard to establish what proportion of the organisation sided with each faction, since no statistics are available. The Majority claimed 90 percent support, to the Minority's 10 percent.[41] This claim is impossible to verify. What is known, however, is that the names 'Majority' and 'Minority' were chosen on the basis of the division within the central committee, not on the basis of overall support within the organisation. As far as it is known, the Minority had two representatives in the central committee. One of these two, alias Haydar, split from the Majority, but the other, Mostafa Madani, along with a number of other members, agreed with the principle views of the Minority, but did not believe that the timing of the split was right, and so did not leave with the Minority. He was to leave the Majority to form OIPFG (Left-Wing Majority) in March 1981 (see below).

After the split, each faction moved towards reorganisation and the declaration of their views on social issues. The Minority analysis was as follows: the IRI state was an organ of compromise between the industrial bourgeoisie, represented by the Islamic Liberals (for example Bazargan and Bani-sadr), the commercial bourgeoisie, represented by the clergy-bazaar alliance and the Islamic Republic Party (IRP), and the upper layers of the traditional petit bourgeoisie, represented by Ayatollah Khomeini and those around him. They announced that the revolutionary process was incomplete, and that to ensure its completion the IRI must be replaced by an alliance of revolutionary workers and peasants. The anti-American moves of the state were not anti-imperialist in nature, and the IRI was a dependent capitalist state. The Minority attacked both Islamic Liberals and *Maktabis*, but as the social crisis deepened, it began to concentrate its slogans and attacks on the IRP, although not defending the Islamic Liberals in any way. By June 1981, the Minority's main slogan was 'Down with the IRP', an indication that it viewed the IRP as the immediate enemy. As of September 1980, it considered the Iran-Iraq War an anti-people's war which should be stopped at once, having initially advocated participation in the war as an independent entity, and later advocated turning it into a civil war. The right of self-determination for national minorities, especially the Kurds, had to be defended (the Minority continued to participate in the Kurdish war). The Tudeh was an opportunistic organisation which unjustifiably claimed to be the workers' party of Iran. As for the Soviet Union, it was a socialist state, but with revisionist deviations.[42] The Minority's view, as far as factional conflict within the IRI was concerned, was to ignore the real struggle and differences of political and social view that existed between *Maktabis* and Islamic Liberals. For it, the struggle was between two different segments of a reactionary bourgeoisie, and it gradually came to the position of declaring that the people's democratic stage, where the leadership of the working-class vanguard was essential, had been reached.

The Majority analysis was as follows: the IRI was a petit bourgeois and, therefore, a progressive and anti-imperialist state, emphatically so, and this meant that its anti-democratic policies were of secondary importance. The Tudeh was a workers' party (the plenum of the Majority in March 1981 officially approved a process of unification between the Tudeh and the Majority), and the Soviet Union was viewed as a revolutionary socialist state. As the right of self-determination for national minorities was seen as only secondary to the IRI's anti-imperialist policies, the Majority pulled out of Kurdestan, and by June 1981 had made reconciliation between the Kurdish insurgents and the IRI a cornerstone of its regional policy. The IRI was seen as passing along a non-capitalist path towards socialism under Ayatollah Khomeini's leadership. Regarding the Iran-Iraq War, the Majority defended the right of the IRI to fight Iraqi aggression, and participated in the first three years of the war. The Majority experience was a larger-scale repetition of that of the Splinter Group. It rejected its own organisation's view of the past and accepted the Tudeh analysis of the period. In the internal IRI conflict, the Majority gradually accepted Tudeh policy, and began to side with the *Maktabis* against the Islamic Liberals. In 1980, in trying to win over the Moslem Mojahedin, which was siding increasingly with the Islamic Liberals, the Majority outlined its definition of reaction: 'A reactionary is one who is dependent on imperialism, the big bourgeoisie, the liberals and the feudals, and defends their interests. A progressive is one who struggles against imperialism, big bourgeoisie, the liberals and the feudals.'[43] In arguing against the Minority, which considered the IRI a dependent capitalist state supported by imperialism, the Majority pointed to the state's obvious political independence, asked the Minority how it explained the IRI's struggle with the United States, and suggested that the IRI's political independence and anti-imperialist stand were signs of the regime's revolutionary character.[44]

The events of 1981–3 confirmed the Minority predictions about the Majority, which rapidly capitulated to the Tudeh line. Less than a year after the split, the Majority divided again in order to secure approval of a policy of unity with the Tudeh. Tudeh policy, which the Majority came to accept, was of unconditional support for the IRI. This meant not only attacking other anti-Government groups, but also any spontaneous anti-IRI movement. The foundation of such a policy will be analysed later, but suffice it to say that it was based on the Tudeh's class analysis of the IRI, especially Ayatollah Khomeini's leadership, which in turn was closely linked to the Tudeh policy towards the Soviet Union.

As noted, in March 1981 a second split occurred in the Majority, minor compared to the previous one. The splinter group, which called itself OIPFG (Left Wing-Majority) was made up of former Minority members who by this time had irreconcilable differences with the Majority, over such issues as support for the IRI, unity with the Tudeh, and adherence to the Soviet Union. As already mentioned, this group did not join the Minority initially because it believed the split ill-timed, although its only significant argument with the Minority was over analysis of the class base of the IRI. This group, while considering the IRI reactionary, believed it to be founded on the petit bourgeoisie, and rejected the Minority analysis of the 'organ of compromise' (see above).[45]

By the summer of 1981, four separate organisations claimed to be the rightful heir to the pre-revolutionary Fadaiyan. This fragmentation diminished the organisation's hegemony among Marxist organisations, and also greatly weakened the communist movement in general. With three of the splinter groups opposed to the IRI and one giving it support, the Fadaiyan's prestige declined among the population. While the Fadaiyan might have been able to organise a viable opposition to the IRI had it stayed united, its chances were diminished without that unity. After all the splits and disintegration, it is not possible to see the Fadaiyan as a social force, but rather as just a number of organisations among other Marxist organisations and groups, without any substantial mass support.

The June 1981 crisis and its outcome was a turning point in the contemporary history of Iran, what little political and social freedom remained in Iran being destroyed by the IRI, which openly outlawed almost all the opposition. It was basically the climax of a year-long confrontation between an alliance made up of the Islamic Liberals and Moslem Mojahedin, and the *Maktabi* faction of the IRI, with Ayatollah Khomeini throwing his full support behind the *Maktabis*.

Before then, Bani-sadr was dismissed as President and the Mojahedin initiated full-scale urban guerrilla warfare in an attempt to overthrow the IRI. The crisis reached civil-war proportions when the Mojahedin determined that functioning within the legal boundaries of the IRI was no longer possible, and opted to attempt an overthrow. In doing so, it brought its massive organisational and military capabilities to bear, surprising all other political groups. From this time on, the social discontent which had previously manifested itself either in support for various opposition groups or spontaneously was repressed by the IRI.

The Marxist organisations in Iran, ill prepared for the magnitude of the crisis and the extent of the repression, experienced internal upheaval, division and disintegration. Elements beyond their control pulled them into a violent struggle for which they were unprepared both organisationally and doctrinally. The Fadaiyan, the largest Marxist organisation to come out of the revolution, was divided and weakened by its four-way split.

The Majority's support for the IRI was not all-encompassing, but only for the *Maktabi*, which it considered progressive, revolutionary and radical, with its strong anti-American tendencies (for example the students who had occupied the US Embassy in Tehran). When this faction, allied with a more conservative clerical faction, came into collision with Bani-sadr, along with his liberal supporters and the Mojahedin, the Majority supported the former. In return, when Ayatollah Khomeini outlawed all opposition groups, the Majority and the Tudeh were initially exempted. Majority activities toward the militant opposition had been limited to advising them against any leftist or anti-IRI activities, but it now moved directly into collaboration with the state in repressing these groups.

The term 'collaboration' needs some explaining. The many individual Iranian Marxists, both in the 1950s and later, who had turned to co-operation with the authorities after their arrest had obviously done so under physical and mental pressure. It was a very different type of co-operation to that now entered into by the Majority-Tudeh alliance and the IRI. It was implemented long before the two groups were dismantled by the IRI, in an organised manner, and after a clear and conscious leadership-level decision, and was clearly designed to buy favour. The Majority-Tudeh alliance offered its knowledge of the opposition, thereby helping the state uproot it. In the case of the Majority, its leadership initially declared its loyalty to the IRI's constitution and declared the opposition movements (Mojahedin, Kurdish movement and other Fadaiyan factions) counter-revolutionary, offering this guidance to its supporters in August 1981: 'The Organisation's supporters must be aware of their duties in this critical situation. Uncovering the policies of the counter-revolution in the work-place, in the family, and in any place where the masses are present is one of your most important duties'.[46] In December 1981, Rahman Karimi, a Majority member, and Ghani Bulurian, a Tudeh member, received a letter of appreciation from Col. (later Brig.-Gen.) Ali Sayyad-shirazi, commander of the army's Kurdestan division. In this letter, Col. Shirazi expressed his gratitude to the two for helping the army suppress the Kurdish movement.[47] When, in late January 1981, the Iranian Communist League (see below) attacked and briefly occupied the city of Amol, the Majority had this to say:

> The Iranian People's Fadaiyan (Majority) and the forces of Tudeh Party of Iran, from the very early moments of the attack by counter-revolutionary intruders, participated, shoulder to shoulder with the people, the Basij, and the security forces, in their suppression and defeat. Two of our comrades and Tudeh members were wounded... and are in hospital at this moment.[48]

The collaboration did not last long. As soon as the IRI was stable enough, and had managed to repress the opposition, it turned its attention towards the Majority and the Tudeh.[49] By early 1983, both the Tudeh and the Majority were declared illegal, and went underground. The Majority moved its base to the Soviet Union and Afghanistan. In Afghanistan, its members put their experience at the disposal of the country's Government, and soon became an important element in the war against the Afghan Mojahedin. As far as activities inside the country were concerned, unlike the Tudeh, its leadership and network survived, but did not have a visible and effective presence, and the group became an opposition abroad after 1983.

In December 1981, a division opened up within the Majority. The dispute with the new faction, headed by Negahdar's old comrade Farkhondeh, alias Ali Keshtgar, centred on the issue of unity with the Tudeh, the 'Keshtgar' faction being opposed to it and calling for a congress to settle this and other issues. In the communique announcing its departure, the new faction did not indicate any disagreement on the issue of the IRI. In fact, both factions still saw the IRI as a progressive regime. At any rate, the Keshtgar faction initially called itself the Organisation of Iranian People's Fadaiyan (Majority), so there became two organisations with the same name, publishing two different publications with the same name (*KAR*). In 1984, the Keshtgar faction dropped the term 'Majority' and began to call its publication *Fada'i*.[50]

Among those Marxist organisations and parties which began to challenge the IRI violently during and after the June 1981 crisis, the Minority was better organised, and was the largest opposition group. It lost two important figures immediately following the crisis: Sa'id Sultan-pur, a prominent poet and Fadaiyan activist since the anti-imperial regime period, was arrested and executed in June; in September, Siyamak Asadian, alias Eskandar, head of military operations and an experienced guerrilla from the Ashraf period, was killed in action, along with two other members, near Amol. Asadian's death came in the aftermath of the Minority's call for the creation of fighting squads (*jukhehha-ye razmi*) as a way of confronting the IRI.[51] The main theorist behind the call for armed action was an emerging sectarian and dogmatic theorist named Akbar Kamiabi, alias Abbas Tavakkol. But the call for armed action had come at a time when the Minority was ill prepared and, according to one account, it was the fact that Asadian was reluctantly rushed into producing results that led to his death.[52] It in effect signalled the end of the Minority's attempts to organise any serious armed resistance to the IRI outside Iranian Kurdestan.

Despite these events, while other Marxist organisations were either in retreat and or were being totally destroyed, the Minority managed to function, avoiding the state's security nets and publishing *KAR*. In December 1981, as Iran was in the midst of a civil war, the Minority managed to organise in Tehran the first Fadaiyan congress in the history of the Fadaiyan factions. At this congress, the leadership criticised itself for its inability to provide a coherent policy and its inactivity in the face of the new situation (the June crisis). But while the congress was supposed to unify and to set new policies, it revealed a deep ideological and political division in its ranks.

Before the congress could even turn to its agenda, six important and experienced members, headed by the chief theorist of the struggle against the Majority, Haydar, left and became known as the Resigning Group. Haydar was one of the editors of *KAR* before the Minority-Majority split, and one of the two Minority members in the Fadaiyan central committee. He was a leading member of the Minority, a member of its central committee from the time of the split, and one of its leading theorists. But it seems that by the time of the congress he had developed deep differences with the rest of the organisation, centred around the policy on the new situation, especially the failed attempts to organise armed action, which this group considered too adventurous, and issues surrounding the international communist movement. The differences were so deep that this group did not even participate in the discussions of the congress. The group later went abroad, and formed the Organisation of Freedom of Labour (Fada'i) (*sazman-e azadi-ye kar-Fada'i*), and started publishing an official publication in 1985, called *KAR*.[53]

Once the Minority congress started on its agenda, more differences appeared. It became clear that three lines of thinking and two factions, a majority and a minority, existed. Every vote divided along these three lines. There were differences on how to confront the regime, how to organise the working class, with whom to unite, and over the international communist movement. In general terms, one line, under personalities such as Mehdi Same' and Mohsen Modir-shaneh-chi, advocated union with the Moslem Mojahedin, the main opposition force at this point. The second line, under the sectarian theorist Kamiabi, believed that any merger with another organisation should be undertaken only after the Minority's programme of action and leadership had been accepted by the Mojahedin. The third line, under Abbas Hashemi, Muhammad Reza Behkish and a young theorist named Ali Reza Mahfuzi, was an uneasy union advocating a general change in direction, towards the organisation of workers' councils, and favouring non-alignment until strength and respect could be achieved. The first and second line united against the third, which became a reluctant minority. The congress gave short-term answers to long-term problems, deciding against further division by arguing that whenever possible a compromise resolution would be drafted, and the issue left for future discussion. In the meantime, it was decided that the differences would be discussed openly in special ideological bulletins.[54]

OIPFG (Left-Wing Majority) was invited to join the Minority, and after the congress some – an unknown number, headed by Mostafa Madani – did. Those who did not opt for union moved abroad and began to publish *Aqazi-No*, precipitating the group's dissolution.

The congress tried to contain the crisis by electing a new central committee which would represent proportionally the two factions, two from the minority, four from the majority.[55] This enabled the congress to pass a number of resolutions to cope with its internal differences and the general social crisis. It agreed a programme of action on how to continue its struggle against the IRI.[56] But soon after the congress, the situation changed drastically, and the Minority proved unable to cope. First, the chair of the congress and a member of the central committee, Mohsen Modir-Shanehchi (from the larger faction), was killed in a shoot-out with security police in late December 1981. Then government forces attacked and closed underground publishing and distribution centres in March 1982. In this process, alongside many rank-and-file members, two more central committee members were killed. These were Muhammad Reza Behkish (from the smaller faction) and Ahmad Gholamian-langehrudi (from the larger). This attack, from which the Minority was never to recover, had two effects. First, it severely damaged the organisational network, and second, only three central committee members remained, and they were unable to handle the situation. From this point on, the Minority no longer offered effective opposition. Instead of the planned ideological debate, the two majority faction members of the central committee expelled the rival faction, undermining the spirit of co-operation introduced by the congress. In June 1982, the minority faction distributed a communique, identifying itself as the OIPFG (Socialist Revolutionary Tendency) (*gerayesh-e sosialism-e enqelabi*) and offered its views on the purge.

The Socialist Revolutionary faction was a lost cause from its very inception, its members being only united in their differences with their former rivals. Most of those killed in the publishing and distribution centres had been supporters of the smaller faction. Some Socialist Revolutionary sympathisers had developed close ties with a small Trotskyite group called the Socialist Worker's Party (*hezb-e kargaran-e sosialist*), and were already in the process of theoretical re-evaluation. This faction was able to distribute a few issues of a publication named *Nazme-e Kargar* inside Iran, but it later moved abroad, where its differences deepened. Soon, Abbas Hashemi, a Socialist Revolutionary central committee member, left, and the rest of the group simply dissolved after 1983.[57]

After the purge, the two remaining majority faction members of the central committee began the task of reorganising the Minority. They managed to start publication and limited distribution of *KAR*, appointed two new committee members, Mastureh Ahmadzadeh-heravi, alias A'zam, and Hosein Zohari, alias Bahram, and arranged a plenum for June 1982. The organisation even managed to establish a radio station in Kurdestan, but its position was weakened by external attack and internal division. In 1982 and 1983, it lost the remaining networks – underground workers and neighbourhood committees – it had managed to save from the March 1982 attack. In Kurdestan, where it had kept a visible military presence, it had to accept military defeat as IRI forces recaptured the area. Internally, there was division between the very two committee members responsible for the purge. Same' was a pro-Mojahedin figure who had in congress advocated unity between the Minority and the Mojahedin under the latter's leadership. Kamiabi, on the other hand, was a strong sectarian who could only envision alliance with another group under Minority leadership, which was organisationally feeble at this point. Hence Same' sought closer links with the Mojahedin, and Kamiabi sought confrontation. In this round of infighting, Same' lost by the same means he had used to purge the

Socialist Revolutionary faction. In June 1983, Kamiabi, allied with the two temporary members of the central committee (pending elections in congress), purged Same', his wife (an advisor to the central committee) and their supporters. A year later, the OIPFG (in search of identity programme) (*peyroy-e barnameh-ye hovyyat*), with Same' as its leader, declared its existence.

The scope of the Same' purge was probably very limited, probably consisting only of himself and his wife. His support for the Mojahedin was a lost cause, since that organisation had by this time lost much of its own prestige and power. His views might have found an audience among Minority members and supporters during the initial phase of the June 1981 crisis. At any rate, his faction soon joined the Mojahedin-dominated National Council of Resistance and began to publish *Nabard-e Khalq*. Considering this faction's dependence on the Mojahedin, any independent existence can be seen as symbolic.[58] Meanwhile, the rest of the Minority continued its downward spiral toward its final disintegration in 1986, following a shoot-out between members.

In August 1981, a split also developed in the IPFG (Ashraf Dehqani). Details of the dispute are not clear. What is known, however, is that a faction headed by Dehqani developed a more or less revisionist view on the original Ahmadzadeh theses. The other faction, headed by Muhammad Hormati-Pur and Abdol Rahim Sabburi, took a more orthodox stand. The latter called itself IPFG (Iranian People's Liberation Army) (*artesh-e rahai'i bakhsh-e khalqha-ye Iran*), while the former continued to call itself the IPFG. From 24 August 1981, the Liberation Army faction began seven months of guerrilla warfare in the forests of Mazandaran and Gilan provinces. But after Sabburi's death on 4 March 1982, Hormati-pur's on the twenty-fourth, and the overwhelming force brought to bear against it, the group was defeated.[59] In 1983, some of those who survived joined the newly-formed Communist Party of Iran (see below) and further weakened the Liberation Army.[60] The IPFG (Dehqani)'s network was uprooted by the IRI, especially in the port city of Bandar-e Abbas and the southern provinces, where it was strong, and it moved to Kurdestan. After 1983 both groups disappeared as effective armed groups.

THE PAYKAR AND REVOLUTION

The Marxist Mojahedin was in a rather odd position as revolution overturned the old regime. It had shifted from Islam to Marxism in 1975, had violently purged its Moslem members, and lost some of its most important members in setbacks in 1976. Furthermore, it had purged Taqi Shahram, the mastermind of the ideological shift, rejected armed struggle a year prior to the revolution, and shifted its attention to agitation among the working class. Therefore it was in a weak position, both theoretically and organisationally, as the revolution shook the old regime. Now, it was faced with a popular Islamic movement, an emerging Moslem Mojahedin and a Marxist movement whose major popular groups were at odds with it. In February 1979, it officially changed its name to the Organisation of Paykar (Combat) for the Liberation of the Working Class (*sazman-e paykar dar rah azadi-ye tabaqeh-ye kargar*). The Paykar was relatively small, and unprepared for the revolution, and its activities during the final days of the imperial regime were limited to some political agitation. However, after the revolution it began to reorganise.

The actual membership of the Paykar was small, and it did not attempt to bring in new members. Members who played a role in directing policies probably numbered between 30 and 50, although there were thousands of supporters who were mostly former Moslem Mojahedin members who had turned Marxist either in prison or outside. The Paykar had a five-man central committee dominated by Hosein Ruhani and Ali Reza Sepasi-ashtiani. The names of the other three central committee members never became public, but other well-known members were Torrab Haq-shenas, Puran Bazragan, Mohsen Fazel, Qasem Abedini, Ebrahim Nazari, Morteza Aladpush and Afkham Ahmadi.

From 1979 until its disintegration in early 1982, the Paykar was the main standard-bearer of Maoism and Stalinism in Iran. Having rejected post-Mao reforms in China, it was extremely hostile to both the Soviet Union and China. Although it considered the United States the main enemy of the revolutionary movement in Iran, it called the Soviet Union a socialist-imperialist power, the Tudeh a Soviet fifth column, and considered the Soviet threat imminent.[61] Having rejected both the Soviet and the Chinese models, the Paykar looked to Albania for inspiration and as a role model. Indeed its view of the Soviet Union as socialist-imperialist was based solely on translations from Albanian sources, indicating a lack of doctrinal weight.[62]

The Paykar showed some sympathy for the Islamic liberal faction of the IRI during the early days, but soon changed its policy to one of opposition to the state as a whole.[63] It boycotted the referendum legitimising the IRI, but did participate in elections for the council of experts which drafted the Islamic constitution. One of the main confrontations between it and the IRI during the first two years of the revolution was over the arrest, in July 1979, and execution, in July 1980, of Taqi Shahram. The Paykar had expelled Shahram a year before the revolution, but his arrest and trial for the murder of Sharif-vaqefi inevitably placed the organisation centre stage. The Paykar's position, which differed from that of other Marxist organisations, must be seen in the context of the period, and was that he must be tried by a court composed of his former comrades. This meant that the IRI had to relinquish judicial authority to Marxist organisations. In the end, the case was used by the IRI to put the Paykar and Marxism on trial, and the Paykar and other groups were unable to prevent his execution.[64]

As the standard-bearer of Maoism in Iran, the Paykar and a number of other Maoist organisations and cells arranged for a conference of unity in Tehran in May 1979. The goal was to unite Maoist groups in a united front against both the IRI and other Marxist groups. Among the participants were the Kurdish organisation, the Kumoleh, and the newly-reorganised Communist League (see below), which was made up mostly of activists from abroad. The Paykar's position on unity was based on a belief that the communist movement was weak, and did not have a firm base among the working class, its main natural base. Its policy was that unity between Maoist groups should take place under Paykar leadership.[65] Because of this, union was not achieved, although the Paykar managed to co-opt two small cells without offering its members full membership.[66]

The Paykar's relations with other non-Maoist organisations was tense for the most part. In Kurdestan, the organisation maintained a tactical alliance with the Kumoleh, the region's Maoist organisation and second-largest rebel group. The Paykar, itself ideologically weak, acted as the Kumoleh's ideological mentor until 1981. As the war intensified, the Paykar, like other non-Kurdish Marxist organisations opposed to the IRI, directly supported the Kurds. The Kurdish movement, however, although fighting the IRI, was divided between two main groups, the Kumoleh and the Kurdestan Democratic Party (KDP), fiercely, sometime violently, competitive. This meant that the Paykar clashed both with IRI armed forces and the KDP. Like the Kumoleh, the Paykar considered the KDP a bourgeois party, and accused it of wanting to compromise with the central Government, rather than defending the rights of the Kurdish people.[67]

The Paykar's relations with the Fadaiyan were mixed, and talks between the two before the revolution had yielded little. After it, the Paykar acknowledged the mass base of the Fadaiyan and considered it the largest Marxist organisation in Iran,[68] although this mass base was perceived as including mainly the petit bourgeois rather than the proletariat. Early on, the Paykar noticed Fadaiyan factionalism, and put its support behind the Minority,[69] and after the split began treating the Majority with the same hostility as the Tudeh. It proposed unity of action with the Minority, but tense relations meant that no real alliance was possible.

As the June 1981 crisis approached, the Paykar developed even more radical slogans. At a time when it admitted that in general the communist movement did not enjoy mass support, it called for the overthrow of the IRI, and its replacement with a people's democratic republic, and was totally unprepared for the IRI repression which followed. Once the Islamic Liberals were removed from power, the Ruhani-Sepasi leadership took the organisation in a new direction, without consultation and despite opposition from the rest of the central committee. The new line shifted policy from hostility to the IRI to support for the Islamic Liberals.[70] As the new policy came at a time when political events were rapidly changing the balance of power, the result was internal division. Three factions began to develop: the first defended the new line; the second, calling itself the Revolutionary Line, and with no previous representation in the central committee, accused the leadership of right-wing deviation, and made a bid for leadership;[71] the third faction supported a continuation of previous policy, and with only one representative in the central committee called for a commission to oust the current leadership and reorganise.

The speed of events allowed no time for reorganisation. In June 1981, one of Paykar's experienced military members, Mohsen Fazel, was executed. Between August 1981 and February 1982, the Paykar was hit hard by security forces, and this, added to the internal division, sealed the organisation's fate. The most severe setback was the arrest of Ruhani and Sepasi in Tehran in February 1982. While Sepasi died under arrest, Ruhani co-operated with the IRI until his execution in the mid-1980s, helping it to uproot the Paykar.[72] The remnants of the new policy faction eventually joined the newly-formed Communist Party of Iran in 1983, but the other two, after losing more members to the security forces, moved abroad and gradually dissolved in the mid-1980s.

THE TUDEH AND REVOLUTION

Like other Marxist organisations and groups, the February 1979 revolution brought benefits for the Tudeh. Although the party was perceived as the symbol of communist threat by both the regime and its Western supporters, in reality it had been effectively uprooted and contained since the 1950s. Except for its self-indulgent claim to be the sole working-class party of Iran, it had never recovered from the 1953 coup, and was marginal in the revolutionary events of 1978 and 1979. The revolution gave the Tudeh, for the first time since 1953, the chance to openly organise and participate in the daily life of the people.

The leadership was firmly in the hands of the radical faction by the time the party began open activity in February 1979. The master-mind of the strategy for an era of revolutionary change and party revival was Nur al-Din Kianuri (born 1915), who inherited a party in 1979 with no social base inside Iran, which had had little, if any, meaningful impact on the revolution, had a negative image among the population at large, and the revolutionary intelligentsia in particular, and a reputation as the lever of Soviet policy in Iran. The new radical leadership of the party resorted to a number of reforms. The party's sixteenth plenum, the last gathering of the party leadership outside Iran, was held in February 1979, just after the victory of the revolution, and confirmed the radical victory, leaving the way clear for its new strategy. According to the plenum documents, the party announced its support for the leadership of Ayatollah Khomeini, confirmed the close association between the Tudeh and the Soviet Union, proclaimed support for the Afghan coup which had brought the communists to power in that country, and proposed a people's democratic front to counter imperialist threats to the revolution.[73]

The Tudeh reorganised its leadership and organisation inside Iran. The executive committee was replaced by a political committee which acted as a politburo. The 18 men and women of this politburo were led by a three-man secretariat, in which Kianuri was first secretary. Although some moderate faction supporters remained members of the new body, they were in a minority, and the most notable among them, Eskandari and Radmanesh, were demoted to the central committee.[74] The ADP faction was also neutralised, and Daneshian, its head, was given a ceremonial role, and replaced by Amir Ali Lahrudi, a younger member.[75] After the return to Iran, the ADP became marginal, as its leadership did not return to the country, and Tudeh branches in Iranian Azarbaijan had a new constituency. Organisationally, the Tudeh divided its network into two parts, one legal and openly active, the other underground. According to Kianuri, the party restarted activities in Iran by opening headquarters and actively asking old members to rejoin. But the Navid network, under Hatefi and Partovi, remained underground, kept most of the party arsenal, and established a clandestine printing facility.[76] The Tudeh also began to recruit supporters and members from among the armed forces, but did not create a separate military organisation, instead putting military personnel in touch with a designated party member.

Perhaps the most difficult task for the party was its image and lack of social base, and here the strategy was two-fold. First, a concentrated effort was initiated to falsify the party's history. Books and articles were published which attempted to rehabilitate the party's reputation in such important historical events as the 1953 coup, the party's appeasement of the imperial regime, and its relations with the Soviet Union. This effort was aimed at the younger generation, which was hearing contradictory versions from both the Islamists and Marxist opponents. Second, to remedy the lack of a mass base, the party resorted to recruiting from other organisations by exposing or exploiting divisions and splits. Between 1979 and 1981, while other Marxist groups, for example the Fadaiyan, showed off their support by holding mass rallies, the Tudeh was strangely silent. The mass organisations had lost their able theorists in the struggle against the old regime, and this meant that despite their apparently wide support, they were ideologically unprepared. The Tudeh had clear advantages here because its experienced members, both theorists and organisers, were available to the party in this new period of activity. It was able to resort to Marxist texts and Soviet support in order to promote its arguments and views on Iranian society among other Marxist groups, and here it was partially successful. The party promoted actively the Fadaiyan split, both openly and through contacts with the Majority leadership.[77] The Fadaiyan split in 1980, and Majority links with the Tudeh, provided the party with a much-needed support, which also partially compensated for its lack of a mass following. Nevertheless, the party's attempts to unite with and subsume the Majority failed, and even caused two splits within Majority ranks in early and late 1981. The Tudeh tried the same strategy with the KDP, but was less successful, only winning seven new members.[78] After June 1981 there were a few defectors from other organisations, but their numbers were insignificant.

The Tudeh's post-revolutionary activity in Iran was based on a strategy of 'loyal opposition' to the IRI, while also promoting closer relations between the IRI and the Soviet Union. Between 1979 and 1981, the party generally sided with the *Maktabis* against the Islamic Liberals, and asked for the strengthening of institutions under the former's control: for example, it demanded that the IRI arm the Revolutionary Guards with heavier weapons with which to defend the revolution.[79] Through its members in the military, the party helped the IRI prevent a monarchist coup in June 1980, commonly called the Nozheh coup.[80] Furthermore, the party supported the war efforts of the IRI against the Iraqi invaders, and acted as mediator, pushing for compromise in internal ethnic conflicts. Over the same period, the party openly and aggressively perused an ideological war against Maoist groups, and tried to isolate them by calling them agents of imperialism and the CIA.[81] After June 1981, it took a line similar to that of the Fadaiyan Majority, and was in fact that organisation's mentor and ideological guide. In the clash between the IRI and its opposition, the Tudeh sided with the regime. The party began to refer to the opposition as 'the united anti-revolutionary front', and took the unprecedented step of engineering close collaboration with the authorities in suppression of the opposition. The extent of Tudeh and Majority collaboration with the IRI was well known, and was even reflected in the Soviet Embassy's KGB reports on Iran.[82] Never before in the history of communism in Iran, and very rarely in other parts of the world, has a Marxist organisation collaborated so closely with the state in the suppression of other Marxist groups.

The Tudeh's strategy of siding with the *Maktabis*, to the point of collaboration, was based on theoretical borrowing from the Soviet Union as part of an ever-closer link between the party and the CPSU. Although the moderate and radical factions within the Tudeh differed on some aspects of the party's relationship with the Soviets, they were united on general strategy, and under radical control the Tudeh came to be identified more than ever with the Soviet Union. The cornerstone of Tudeh strategy was the theory of a non-capitalist path of development. CPSU theorists had created this theory, which they claimed was rooted in Lenin's thought. According to it, developing countries under the revolutionary leadership of non-communist elements – but with close Soviet collaboration – could either bypass capitalism or to put strict limitations on it, and eventually cross over to socialism.[83] According to Shahrough Akhavi, when it came to political Islam, Soviet theorists distinguished between 'progressive' and 'reactionary' tendencies in the movement, and suggested 'the clergy can play an objectively useful role to the extent that they are anti-comprador and anti-big bourgeoisie'.[84] Akhavi's study of Soviet perceptions of the Iranian revolution suggests a self-centred approach in which the IRI was viewed as abandoning revolutionary ideals when it moved against the Tudeh.

A few months before his arrest, Kianuri tried to over-simplify the non-capitalist path theory for the Majority: 'The non-capitalist path means any path that at any rate is not capitalist. This non-capitalist path has one characteristic, and that is it separates from normal capitalist development and takes a different path which means not allowing the unchecked development of capitalism'.[85] In earlier years, Kianuri had made it clear that in his opinion no revolutionary movement would be successful without close links to the socialist camp.[86]

The theory of the non-capitalist path was actively promoted by the Soviets, and the Tudeh had already become a firm believer before the revolution. But after the revolution, the party found the chance to put it into practice in Iran. Tudeh-Soviet relations during this period were overseen by a special department of the CPSU called the International Department. Rostislav Ulyanovsky, one of its chiefs, had a personal interest in Iran, and was a mentor to the Tudeh, which translated and published many of his writings on Iran, and borrowed heavily from them. According to a KGB defector, Kianuri sent the department news and analyses on a regular basis, and the answers came back with Ulyanovsky's signature.[87] Before the Tudeh came under attack by the IRI, Ulyanovsky wrote:

> A part of the clergy is aware of the need for carrying on a consistent struggle against the united front of international imperialism headed by the US and for implementing profound social and economic reforms in the interest of the working people... The further trend of the development of Iranian revolution will largely depend on whether the progressive and, first and foremost, leftist forces in Iran will succeed in establishing a united popular front to defend the gains of the revolution on the platform of a firm anti-imperialist course and of radical social and economic changes.[88]

Here, Ulyanovsky was suggesting that the Tudeh and Majority must forge a coalition with the radical wing of the IRI, and with Soviet help push the revolution towards a non-capitalist path. This guideline was given in 1982 when the other Marxist organisations were engaged in a life-and-death battle with the IRI, and only a few months before the IRI turned against the Tudeh. The party had been trying to create a coalition with the radical wing of the IRI from the very beginning, without success. A few years after the IRI attack on the Tudeh, Ulyanovsky wrote another article blaming the failure of the Tudeh on its inability to understand the situation:

> The Tudeh party and a large part of the Fadaiyan which was close to it... continued their policy of 'loyal opposition' toward the ruling clergy. These forces hoped that by supporting the regime, the objective situation would sooner or later bring about conditions whereby the achievements of anti-Shah, anti-imperialist revolution could be saved. On the other hand, the policies of the Mojahedin and the Fadaiyan 'Minority' had come closer to each other. These two had concluded that the clergy had lost its progressive character, and even more, had become an anti-revolutionary force... As time went by both policies proved to be wrong... supporting the regime, in the new situation, not only could have deviated the revolutionary masses, but also could have caused them to lose their own standing in the face of the government's repressive measures.[89]

In 1982, while the Soviet theorist encouraged the Tudeh to try to create closer links with the radical clergy, in 1985 he blamed the party for doing exactly that, without taking any responsibility himself.

The final episode in Tudeh-Soviet relations is closely linked to the party's demise. The relations between the two were not limited to the flow of theory from CPSU to Tudeh. According to Kuzichkin, Kianuri sent the CPSU, via the Soviet Embassy in Tehran, regular reports on the country's situation and political developments. The same source suggested that Kianuri often exaggerated the party's role, and that the Tudeh and its leadership received regular payments from the Soviet Union.[90] Kuzichkin, who defected to the West in early 1982, also said that he was put in charge of arranging for the escape of the Tudeh leadership – both the Soviets and party leaders had sensed the threat. Less than a year after Kuzichkin's defection, there were mass arrests of Tudeh leaders and members, and the party was banned.

The IRI attack on the Tudeh, which began in February 1983, surprised no-one. Already, in May 1981, the Fadaiyan Minority had published a secret document to the effect that the IRI had divided its opposition into three categories, to be dismantled consecutively.[91] The Tudeh and Majority fell into the third. But the timing of the attack coincided with the defection of Kuzichkin, the KGB operative in charge of the escape of Tudeh leaders. Without denying the Western press's allegation that his defection had a direct bearing on the Tudeh arrests, Kuzichkin later said, '... but I feel quite sure that whether I had been there or not, the fate of the Party would have been the same'.[92] This may be true, but the fact remains that the IRI moved swiftly to eliminate the Tudeh just when its leaders were about to leave the country, and so comprehensively that almost all were arrested, and both the legal organisation and underground network eliminated. While it seems the IRI attack on the Tudeh would have taken place eventually, the speed and effectiveness of the operation was directly the result of the defection. The Western press has suggested that the information provided by Kuzichkin was passed down to the IRI through Western intelligence.[93] The Tudeh arrests revealed that once again the party had managed to find supporters among the armed forces, as a number of officers – prominent among them Capt. Bahram Afzali, commander of the Iranian navy – were arrested.

As the Tudeh network was effectively dismantled, the party proved once more it was ill-prepared for activity under repressive conditions. Moreover, its leadership's performance proved even worse than the post-1953 period. During 1983, one by one the Tudeh leaders were paraded on national television to confess to their crimes, which included spying for the Soviet Union and planning the overthrow of the IRI. In some cases, party officials acted as star witnesses for the prosecutor, prompting other members when they refused to confess their guilt.[94] The most startling example was when Capt. Afzali tried to deny some of the charges, his party contact and head of the Tudeh underground network, Mehdi Partovi, acted on the prosecution's behalf and forced him to confess. The rapid disintegration of the Tudeh at the hands of the state, and its leaders' confessions, led opposition and remaining party members to ask why. Explanations ranged from ideological capitulation to the use of Stalinist methods of trial. The remnant of the party outside the country resorted to strange explanations that special drugs created by the CIA and MI-6 were used.[95] The simplest explanation came from a prison visit by a United Nation's human rights representative to Iran. Kianuri was reported to have told the representative that he had made the confessions under torture.[96] In the latter part of the 1980s, and after the IRI had made full use of the propaganda potential, some former Tudeh leaders, all still under state supervision, began to publish quite contradictory views. For example, Ehsanollah Tabari, the chief ideologue of the party until 1983, seemed to have become a devout Moslem, and published books on the superiority of Islam over Marxism.[97] This was at the same time as Kianuri, both in his memoirs and in a number of interviews, showed loyalty to his old views, denouncing the Soviet reforms under Gorbachev and defending most of the old policies.[98] Kianuri also suggested that on at least one occasion the Tudeh did pass on some military information to the Soviets.[99]

After 1983, the Tudeh ceased to exist as an active political entity inside Iran. With the majority of its leadership in prison, a few leading members in the Soviet Union and the GDR attempted to revive the party, but the result of their attempt was fragmentation and the creation of rival groups. The collapse of the Eastern European governments and eventually the Soviet Union cut off the remnant of the party from its financial and logistical support, not to mention its ideological inspiration.

KURDISH GROUPS AND REVOLUTION

Beside the major Marxist groups studied above, the revolution gave birth to a number of smaller or more regional groups and organisations, of which the more important should be mentioned.

Iranian Kurdestan produced two of the largest political organisations in the country following the revolution, although their popularity never went beyond Kurdish areas. The older activists and leadership of the larger of the two, the Kurdestan Democratic Party of Iran (*hezb-e demokrat-e Kurtestan-e Iran*), were members of the movement which created the Mahabad republic at the same time as the ADP's venture in Azarbaijan in the mid-1940s.[100] These, prominent among them Abdol Rahman Qasemlu and Ghani Bulurian, later joined the Tudeh and ended up either in jail or exile after the party's defeat in 1953. Between the 1950s and 1979 the KDP existed on paper more than in reality. Its leader, Qasemlu, was a Czech-educated economist who had been affected by Alexander Dubchek's reforms in Czechoslovakia, although he kept a cordial relationship with both the Soviets and the Tudeh.[101] The KDP never claimed to be a Marxist-Leninist organisation, but was a member of the Second Socialist International, and emerged after the revolution as a social democratic party with strong nationalist policies. Although its leadership was from the urban elite, the KDP became a popular party after the revolution, and spearheaded armed resistance to the Government in this region. It began publishing an official publication, *Kurdestan*, after the revolution.

KDP-IRI relations were tense from the very beginning: the KDP's main policy of democracy for Iran and autonomy for Kurdestan, and the IRI's desire to consolidate power centrally were mutually exclusive. The KDP went through a minor split in 1980, as seven members of the party, headed by Bulurian, left and adopted the Tudeh policy of compromise with the Government.

The second Kurdish group engaged in armed struggle in Iranian Kurdestan was the Revolutionary Toiler's Organisation of Iranian Kurdestan (*sazman-e enqelabi-ye zahmatkeshan-e Kurdestan-e Iran*). Commonly called the Kumoleh, the organisation traced its roots to the 1969 Kurdish revolt and claimed to have been active between 1969 and 1979, although there is no evidence of this.[102] It became active in February 1979, and there is no evidence that it played any role in the downfall of the imperial regime. After the revolution, like the KDP, it began to publish an official publication, *Pishrow*, and to engage IRI forces in the region. From the very beginning, the Kumoleh was a Maoist organisation with clear ideological weaknesses, reliant on non-Kurdish Iranian organisations, such as the Paykar, for theoretical guidance. It considered itself the vanguard of the Kurdish proletariat, despite the fact that Kurdestan was a rural peasant region, and depicted the KDP as representative of the bourgeoisie. In 1982, it joined a number of small non-Kurdish Iranian groups and cells to create the Communist Party of Iran (CPI) (*hezb-e komonist-e Iran*), which began publication of *Komonist*. Prominent among these small groups was the Communists for Unity and Struggle (*etehad-e mobarezan-e komonist*), which in practice replaced the Paykar as the Kumoleh's ideological guide. The arrangement which led to the creation of the CPI was similar to that between the ADP and the Tudeh in the 1950s. The Kumoleh provided the mass support and organisational muscle, while the smaller groups furnished the theoretical framework of the new party, and the Kumoleh became its Kurdestan branch at a time when the Kumoleh had little outside Kurdestan.[103] The Kumoleh kept its own separate leadership, chain of command and publication, and was given the right to make decisions independent of the new party leadership.

The confrontation between the IRI and Kurdish guerrillas, commonly called the *pishmargeh*, continued throughout 1979–81, with occasional brief pauses. After 1981, Kurdestan became a refuge for political groups forced underground. However, from 1982, as the IRI began to gain the upper hand in its war with Iraq, Kurdish teritory was retaken by the IRI's armed forces. The Kurdish groups were forced to retreat into Iraq, where they enjoyed the support of the Iraqi Government, and conducted occasional raids into Iran. Relations between the Kumoleh and KDP deteriorated in the 1980s, as each tried to dominate the movement, resulting in numerous clashes.

THE MARGINAL MARXISTS AND REVOLUTION

Besides the above Kurdish groups, the revolution gave birth to a number of small Marxist organisations. The significance of these groups was not in their organisational network or mass support. Rather, these smaller groups played a role by stimulating discussion through challenging the larger groups on social issues.

Chief among the smaller groups was the Organisation of the Worker's Path (*sazman-e rah-e kargar*), which was made up mainly of former Fadaiyan and Marxist Mojahedin members or supporters who had changed their views on armed struggle while in prison, and developed anti-Maoist positions.[104] After the revolution, these individuals came together and began publishing their views in *Rahe-e Kargar*, their official publication. They considered the IRI a religious-Bonapartist regime composed of traditional petit bourgeoisie, bazaar bourgeoisie, and semi-proletariat population, under the leadership of the clergy.[105] Between 1979 and 1981, the Worker's Path was a minor player in the opposition to both the Islamic Liberals and the *Maktabis*, before going into exile. It went through a split at this point as some members left to join the Tudeh. In the mid-1980s, it attempted to fill the gap left by the disintegration of some organisations (for example the Fadaiyan Minority) by merging with smaller groups and producing a coherent programme and policies, but as the whole movement had reached the point of breakdown, these attempts proved futile.[106]

Communist Unity started its activity inside the country with a new name. Calling itself the Organisation for Communist Unity (*sazman-e vahdat-e komonisty*), it continued its role as a small circle of intellectuals publishing its views and challenging and criticising those of other groups. Between 1979 and 1981, it published *Raha'i* as its official publication, opposed both IRI factions, and was not involved in mass activity. After 1981, it engaged in minor publishing activities.

132

The Organisation of Revolutionary Communists, which was active outside the country before the revolution, moved to organise inside after a minor split and under a new name. Calling itself the Communist League of Iran (*etehadieh komonistha-ye Iran*), it remained a Maoist group which generally saw the US threat to Iran's sovereignty as the most immediate danger to the revolution, and supported the *Maktabi* faction against the Islamic Liberals. Publishing *Haqiqat*, it failed to reach agreement with the Paykar over a possible merger, and become a minor player in the movement. After the events of June 1981, its leadership, under Siyamak Za'im, made an about-turn and suggested that a coup had occurred, and that the regime had lost all its progressive characteristics.[107] After this point, it began preparing for armed action against the IRI, its main action being an attack on the town of Amol in January 1982. The ill-prepared operation was intended to ignite mass uprisings throughout the country, but was instead disastrous.[108] Calling themselves the *Sarbedaran* (literally 'those who are ready to be hanged'), the attackers carried out the operation at a time when differences within the organisation had reached fever pitch, the vital disagreement being between those proposing retreat and those calling for an offensive against the IRI. The Amol operation showed the latter had the upper hand, but the fiasco engulfed both factions. After 48 hours the attackers retreated into the jungle, and by the summer of 1982 were uprooted by IRI forces, over 250 members being arrested and later executed.[109] Among those executed were such notables of anti-Shah activity abroad as Siyamak Za'im, Abdol Rahman Azmaiesh, Hosein Riahi (alias Puya), mastermind of the military operation, and Farid and Vahid Sari'olqalam.[110] After 1982, the league moved abroad, and its remnants joined the Maoist International, which also included the Shining Path of Peru and the US-based Revolutionary Communist Party.[111]

The revolution had a particularly negative effect on the popularity and effectiveness of the Tudeh splinter groups of 1960s. These groups, ROTPI and the Tufan, lost whatever popularity they initially enjoyed as a result of conflict with the Tudeh abroad. ROTPI changed its name to the Ranjbaran Party of Iran (*hezb-e ranjbaran-e Iran*) and began publishing *Ranjbar*. It was small, pro-Chinese, and an adamant supporter of the Islamic Liberals between 1979 and 1981, but after that, it lost some members, and by the mid-1980s had disintegrated. Only one Tufan faction became active inside the country after the revolution, and this changed its name to the Iranian Labour Party (*hezb-e kar-e Iran*), publishing *Tufan*.

Like the Ranjbaran, this party was a minor player, and vanished after 1981.

The Iranian Trotskyite movement established itself inside Iran for the first time after the revolution, under the name Socialist Worker's Party (*hezb-e kargaran-e sosialist*). It published *Cheh Bayad Kard*, and was the result of a merger between the two US and British Trotskyite groups. Differences developed, however, over how to confront the developments of 1981, as one faction, under Babak Zahra'i, came to support the IRI, the other, under Rahimi and Khosravi, to oppose it. The faction which came to oppose the IRI developed links with the Socialist Revolutionary faction of the Fadaiyan Minority in 1981 and 1982, but after Minority setbacks, no union ever took place, both groups ceasing to exist after 1983.

In 1983, with the Tudeh and the Fadaiyan Majority declared illegal, the last legal activity of Marxist organisations came to an end in Iran. During the rest of the 1980s some underground activity persisted, but as the decade came to a close these activities also evaporated, a direct result of disintegration and a loss of general support. The start of Gorbachev's reforms in the Soviet Union and the eventual collapse of socialism in Eastern Europe dealt the final blow to organised Marxism in Iran, but were not the root cause of its disappearance, since the process had begun long before *perestroika* and *glasnost* became household terms.

4

Why the Failure?

If you can only reflect like a clean mirror you'll be that magical spirit.

Mowlana Jalal al-Din Muhammad Balkhi (Rumi)

After 30 years of struggle and sacrifice following their re-emergence from the ashes of the 1953 coup, Iranian Marxists were once again soundly defeated in the 1980s. The communist threat, feared by the West and imperial regime alike, never fully materialised. Instead of constituting a real and durable threat to the IRI, Iranian Marxists proved too weak to survive the hardships of the 1980s. Unlike that in 1953, the defeat of the 1980s followed stiff resistance, but still resulted in disintegration and the dashing of an entire generation's dreams. As a result, an important element of analyses of post-1953 Iranian Marxist activity became irrelevant. The young Marxists of the late 1960s and the 1970s pointed to the Tudeh's inability to resist forcibly the 1953 coup, and the flight of its leaders as important reasons for the movement's defeat. They argued that defeated action was preferable to defeat through inaction, and that such resistance could have provided a foundation for future opposition. In the 1980s, despite resistance by Marxist organisations and many deaths, the movement was effectively and comprehensively defeated.

Furthermore, the demise of Marxism in Iran predated the age of Gorbachev, and therefore the eventual collapse of Soviet communism. This is important in that Marxism in Iran was not defeated by the collapse of its ideological well-spring. The causes of defeat must be sought in the inability of the Marxists to understand and adapt to Iranian society's internal dynamics.

The disintegration of the movement in the 1980s begs a number of questions. What were the reasons for such comprehensive failure? Why was the movement unable to seize political power prior to and during the revolution of 1979? Moreover, why was it unable to sustain itself after the June 1981 crisis? How much of this failure should be attributed to the movement's internal dynamics, and how much was simply due to the power of its adversaries (the imperial regime and the Islamic movement)?

In answering these questions, many factors must be examined, dividing into three categories. The first covers general factors affecting all Marxist groups in Iran. Among these are Iran's socio-economic peculiarities, class formation and geo-political position. The second covers particular factors concerning certain major groups. These groups could have played a decisive role in the communist movement, but were prevented because of these factors. The third, and perhaps most important, covers structural and ideological factors, such as education and the organisational structure of the groups themselves.

COMMUNISTS AND GENERAL FACTORS OF FAILURE

Among the general factors, the one which has contributed most to the repeated defeat of Marxists in Iran has been the relentless repression of the state. Between 1953 and 1979 the history of Marxism in Iran shows a direct relationship between state repression and political weakness. The movement grew rapidly, both numerically and structurally, between 1941 and 1953 under Tudeh leadership, and between 1979 and 1981, but was effectively contained during periods of repression. The imperial regime threw the bulk of its weight against the communists in the 1953–79 period, seeing Marxism as its biggest threat. In contrast, while no independent political activity was allowed during these 30 years, Islamic centres were not (and in large measure could not be) suppressed by the regime. According to Said Amir-Arjomand, in the late 1960s and 1970s, religious periodicals gained circulation, religious books became more popular, and a large number of religious associations mushroomed among laymen.[1] At the same time, an entire network of religious establishments, for example mosques and religious teaching centres, were allowed to function. Political religious leaders were jailed when they actively challenged the regime, but no limitation was put on religious activity. Consequently, at a time when a clear vacuum of legitimacy existed – the imperial regime certainly failed to establish its claim to it – Marxists were effectively prevented from reaching the people and addressing their constituency while radical Islamists had a ready-made network at their disposal. The regime's blindness to the potential of the Islamic movement significantly contributed to the movement's ability to gain control of the revolution in 1977 and 1978. Once revolution was underway, these established channels of communication were effectively used to convey messages and to organise a resistance movement. One the other hand, with some exceptions, Iranian Marxists were effectively prevented from disseminating their message and establishing a popular movement.

Most decisively in the confrontation between the Marxists and the Islamist leadership of the revolution, the Marxists were utterly out-manoeuvred by the Islamists on two issues, radicalism and anti-imperialism. This happened because all Marxist groups failed to reach a realistic understanding of the nature of the new Islamic state, on such issues as politics, ideology and foreign policy. The roots of this failure are in what some scholars have called the 'anti-imperialist paradigm' or the 'problematic of dependency'.[2] Because of the anti-imperialist paradigm, Iranian Marxists were ultimately unable to distinguish between the political independence of the IRI, *vis-à-vis* foreign powers, and the Islamists' intention of creating a theocracy. A majority of Marxists groups in Iran believed that the dependent nature of the imperial regime was a characteristic of Iran's capitalist system. In this equation no room was left for a situation whereby the same economic system could operate in a state free from direct foreign influence. When the revolution was successful, the Marxists were at first puzzled and then totally confused as to the nature of the IRI. To some, like the Tudeh and the Fadaiyan Majority, the fact that the IRI was politically independent and that it (particularly its clerical wing) was often hostile to Western governments, political systems and cultural values, meant that the new state was anti-imperialist and able to pursue a course which might ultimately bring it into the Soviet camp. To encourage the IRI on this course, the Tudeh and Majority were willing to ignore other essential elements of the theocracy, namely its lack of respect for democratic freedoms. To others, like the Minority or the Paykar, the absence of any meaningful change in Iran's economic system meant that the IRI was dependent on foreign powers, regardless of the evidence to the contrary. At any rate, because of the anti-imperialist paradigm, this approach also failed to defend democratic freedoms substantially. The Marxists' failure to defend democratic freedoms had other components which will be discussed below, but it is important to note here that the IRI's own grievances against the West, especially the United States, initially disarmed the Marxists. Episodes such as the capture of the US Embassy in Tehran in 1979, confronting US interests in the region, and numerous other examples of anti-imperialist sentiments proved the IRI to be, in its own peculiar way, as anti-imperialist as the Marxists, if not more so.

The pro-Soviet Marxists' subscription to the anti-imperialist paradigm may be partially explained in the context of Soviet interests. However, to understand the reasons behind other Marxists' inability to rid themselves of the anti-imperialist paradigm, theories of third-worldism, Iranian nationalism and the conspiracy theory must all be taken into account. Third-worldism has been suggested as one element in the Marxists' adoption of the anti-imperialist paradigm. According to Mashayekhi, the goal of this loosely-defined idea was for 'national independence' to be achieved 'through a policy of non-alignment, via a "third way", distinct from both Western capitalism and Eastern socialism'. One political variant of the theory, according to Mashayekhi, was Third-World Marxism, 'adopted by those liberation movements in the periphery, which were characterised by revolutionary socialist leadership'.[3] This Third-World Marxism envisioned the establishment of a culturally independent socialist state and the replacement, through violent means, of the imperialist-dominated state. The idea contained a strong element of nationalism where it was successful (for example Cuba, Vietnam and China). In Iran, with the exception of pro-Soviet and some pro-Chinese Marxists, Iranian nationalism and the perceived need to maintain the movement's independence were both in evidence. Jazani's plea for Fadaiyan independence from international communist camps in the fight against the imperial regime should be seen in this context. The idea was that the national liberation movement confront the imperialist-dominated state and bring about change by establishing an independent socialist nation-state.

The typical Iranian version of the conspiracy theory was also an important component in the intellectual make-up of Marxists. An understudied subject, the conspiracy theory has been a convenient way for many Iranians, regardless of context, to explain complex national and international issues. According to Abrahamian, the proponents of this theory share the belief that Iran has been the scene of a great game whose players are controlled almost entirely by foreign powers. These foreign powers, according to this theory, enjoy limitless power and substantial control over Iranian affairs.[4] Exponents of the theory blame Iran's misfortunes on foreign elements, and view their own leaders as essentially unable to challenge or overcome these elements. Iranian Marxists, of course, did not see themselves as unable to confront foreign influence, but nonetheless viewed foreign powers as a decisive factor in any political equation. By renaming the foreign-element imperialism, many Marxists gave it a life of its own independent from Iran's internal dynamics. A look at theorists such as Ahmadzadeh, writing before the revolution, as well as the theorists of post-revolution Marxist groups confirms the continued potency of the conspiracy theory in the Iranian psyche. The combination of third worldism, Iranian nationalism and the conspiracy theory played a major role in preventing the Marxists from fully realising the political independence of the IRI, and caused them to be disarmed by it.

Another factor which worked against Marxism in Iran was social class formation. In many Third World countries where a dictatorship leaves no non-violent avenue of political change open, it is often the case that the class structure provides the necessary conditions for protracted armed resistance in rural areas in support of or as a part of an urban resistance movement. Many victorious liberation movements (for example Vietnam, Cuba and China) were supported by a revolutionary peasantry willing and able to lend support, for a prolonged period of time, to an urban or semi-urban armed movement. They were usually active in societies where the majority of the population was rural and, more importantly (particularly in rural areas), highly susceptible to political and revolutionary agitation. Twentieth-century Iranian society has shown two general tendencies. First, urban areas have always been the determining factor in any major political change, violent or otherwise.[5] Second, the Iranian peasantry has lacked significant revolutionary potential, and has remained, for the most part, politically passive. According to Nikki Keddie, this inaction mainly results from an arid climate, which produces a poor and scattered peasant population very much under the control of landlords. To this must be added the weakness of crucial middle peasantry.[6] These two factors have naturally forced

Iranian Marxists to concentrate their struggle in urban centres, where the state was better able to exert political control.

As mentioned, Marxist activists were largely unsuccessful in their attempts to organise the rural population in the 1960s and 1970s: ROTPI's attempts to organise the peasantry on the Maoist model, and the Fadaiyan's attempts to organise both in urban and rural centres clearly failed. Furthermore, unlike some other Third-World countries, Iran has had very little experience in independent trade union activity. By the end of the 1960s, the imperial regime had managed effectively to control all trade unions, thereby closing them to opposition political activity. This lack of any meaningful avenue for the expression of political dissent, coupled with an absence of any means of organising the working class or the population as a whole, combined to convince younger Marxists to turn to violence and concentrate on theories of armed resistance. However, by deciding to wage urban guerrilla warfare, they were in fact taking on a task neither theoretically nor practically well-defined. For example, the Fadaiyan's only reliable source of experience was the study of movements based in societies where a revolutionary peasantry was a determining factor and, more importantly, where the armed movement was strengthened by urban political activities. The experiences of Cuba, China and Vietnam all suggested that Marxist guerrillas could rely on some support from semi-legal urban activists, and could retreat to rural areas and seek refuge among sympathetic peasantry. This was not the case in Iran. The only entirely urban guerrilla experience the Fadaiyan founders had knowledge of was that of some unsuccessful Latin American guerrillas like Carlos Marigla, whose manual on guerrilla warfare was translated into Persian.[7] Therefore, the guerrilla movement in Iran had no guidance on how to overthrow a powerful state under conditions where neither revolutionary peasantry nor semi-legal unions or political parties existed. Jazani was perhaps the only Iranian Marxist theorist with some vision of how to organise an armed revolutionary movement in urban areas. He believed it possible to organise both in rural and urban areas, and he saw armed action as a first step to the empowerment of the vanguard organisation, and emphasised the need to organise political activities independent of the guerrilla group. He called this second aspect the movement's 'second leg', and envisioned that a co-ordinated struggle would lead to the creation of a people's army which would bring the regime down. As noted, however, Jazani's views never received due attention until after the Fadaiyan was already considerably weakened.

The February 1979 revolution, and the decisive role the Iranian working class played in paralysing the imperial regime, changed most Marxists' perception of the revolutionary model. Until 1979, Third-World revolutionary models based on protracted armed struggle were current among Iranian Marxists, particularly in the guerrilla groups. After the revolution, these models lost their appeal in favour of the Bolshevik revolutionary model, based on general strikes and a sudden uprising in urban centres. The resemblance between Iran and the Russia of 1917, the role played by the revolutionary Russian workers in a society where urban centres proved decisive, and the Bolshevik Party's role in organising and maintaining state power, all contributed to converting many Iranian Marxists to the Bolshevik model. The use of the Bolshevik model and its implications will be analysed later. It is important to note, however, that the Bolsheviks had a solid grasp of Russian history and the mood of the proletariat which enabled them to communicate with and organise the working class, something the Iranian Marxists never managed to accomplish fully.

The language barrier was another general factor that worked against Iranian Marxists. Here, however, the problem was shared by the entire educated strata of Iranian society. In general, a language barrier seems to have existed between Iran's educated classes and the population, and was more acutely felt by Marxists. After all, the Marxists' survival in a hostile political environment largely depended on their ability to convey their message to the masses in general, and to the working class in particular. In this venture the Marxists failed, as they never really devised a method of communication simply with the masses. Their failure here stands in sharp contrast to other successful communist movements in which the leaders learned the language of the people. Many Iranian Marxists ridiculed Mao for the simplicity of his writings when compared to those of Marx. Mao's simplification of complex philosophical and political issues, and his constant reference to Chinese proverbs and traditional stories, was looked down upon by many non-Maoist Marxists, especially after China's revolutionary example lost popularity. Many Iranian Marxists showed a distaste for Mao's writings, as containing a peasant tone suggestive of the unsophisticated nature of the Chinese revolution. Needless to say, the usefulness of this simplicity, and its success in rallying the peasantry in support of the Chinese Communist Party, never received due attention, even by Iranian Maoists. In this sphere, Marxists lost badly to the Islamists. The *ulama*, who dominated the Islamist movement, had centuries of practice and experience in simplifying religious issues and making them accessible to the general population. When the revolutionary movement required the transmission of political messages, an already existing tradition was adapted to the task. Iranian Marxists, however, addressed their constituency through their newspapers and speeches in their own language, filled with foreign words and political jargon such as 'proletariat' and 'hegemony'. This approach in a society with low literacy proved fatal. One look at any piece of Marxist literature of this period shows how difficult it is, even for an educated reader, to follow the arguments.

Another general factor which seems all-encompassing, and applied to almost all political organisations and social classes, is the lack of tolerance in Iran's political culture. Similar behaviour can be detected among the nationalists, liberals, Islamists of different political inclination, and Marxists, both Stalinist and anti-Stalinist. The roots of this behaviour can perhaps be traced back to the prolonged and persistent presence of despotism in Iranian society since medieval times. Lack of tolerance is a phenomenon which seems to begin in the family and spread throughout the society. As we shall see, in this context the problems of Iranian Marxists were compounded when a dictatorial revolutionary model was superimposed on an already despotic national culture.

Finally, a mention should be made of personality differences and rivalry. A subject which has received too little attention, and is hard to document, this nevertheless played a role in Iranian politics, and Marxists were not exempt from it. In studying the process of policy-making, and in the memoirs of Marxist activists, the role played by personal distaste and rivalry among individuals is discernable, as is the extent to which this was allowed to interfere with objectives. It is also clear, however, that while personal differences continued to play a role among younger Marxists, the generation of the 1960s and 1970s was less susceptible to them than that of the 1950s.

A study of documents and memoirs of Tudeh leaders reveals that factional differences were clearly accompanied by personal dislike and rivalry among party leaders. For example, it was one of the differences among the five-man executive committee of the Tudeh in charge of the party during the 1953 coup. Letters sent to the leadership abroad by the executive committee suggest a set of personal differences between four of the committee members and Kianuri. These letters – four in all – depict the internal state of the party in 1953 and 1954 (after the coup) and the relationship between the executive committee members, and request mediation from the leadership abroad. They show the extent of factional in-fighting, and clearly manifest the party's state of paralysis.[8] The first letter, signed jointly by Bahrami, Yazdi and Joudat, blames the party's failures on Kianuri and his faction. It accuses Kianuri and Qasemi of wanting to turn the party organisation into their own 'tuyul' (Turkish term for medieval land grant, also known by the Arabic term 'iqta'). The use of this term is very interesting, as it suggests total control based on medieval concepts. It accuses Kianuri of sectarian, bureaucratic and opportunistic acts, and suggests that the nation-wide party organisation was in a sorry state. The letter then turns to personal aspects of the leadership's relationship. It suggests that the executive committee had observed morally corrupt (*fesad-e acklaq*) behaviour, on the part of Maryam Firouz, Qoreishi and Lankarani, and states that written evidence of this had been given to Kianuri, but to no avail. The term 'morally corrupt behaviour' in this context has strong sexual connotations, and suggests infidelity on the part of Firouz and two of Kianuri's lieutenants. Iranian political culture is not known for its openness in sexual and marital issues, and for such issues to have found their way into the underground correspondence of a communist party points to serious deterioration of personal relationships. The letter calls executive committee meetings intolerable due to Kianuri's behaviour. He is accused of openly calling his comrades such names as 'dishonorable thief and spy of imperialism' (*dozd-e bisharaf-e jasus-e amperialism*), and of saying to Yazdi, 'If you are not a spy then your brother is', to Joudat, 'Your wife is a spy', and to Sharmini, 'Your mother is a spy'. The party's fourth plenum criticised this, referring to it as a lack of 'revolutionary character' among executive committee members.[9] Needless to say, these differences played an important role in paralysing the party when faced with the coup.

Another example was when Radmanesh was removed as the Tudeh's first secretary in 1970. According to Mo'meni, after Radmanesh's removal, Kianuri approached the GDR authorities and asked that Radmanesh be evicted from his apartment since he was no longer Tudeh first secretary.[10] The authorities rejected the request, but the episode shows the extent to which Tudeh leaders were willing to go in order to humiliate opponents even after defeating them.

The continuation of personal differences and rivalry as a factor in Marxist politics, albeit with less intensity, may be traced among the younger generation. In the mid-1960s, after Qasemi, Forutan and Sagha'i were expelled from the Tudeh, and joined ROTPI in the

West, differences developed between them and younger ROTPI members. Tehrani records a tragic and yet comical scene in which Rezvani, a ROTPI member, used rent money (that the organisation had allocated to the trio) to humiliate them and make them do his bidding.[11] The trio and ROTPI had many things in common, and had personality not been allowed to interfere then a union was not entirely out of question. Differences in the Fadaiyan, between Shoa'ian, the theorist, and Ashraf, the practitioner, is another example. Shoa'ian had joined with the understanding that his differences with the organisation would be discussed. This never happened, and one can clearly detect a personal bitterness in Shoa'ian's account of the episode. Shoa'ian accused Ashraf of failing to keep his word on open discussions, and even of putting his life in jeopardy by failing to arrive on time for their planned clandestine appointments.[12] While it is hard to imagine how Shoa'ian could have remained with the Fadaiyan, considering his ideological differences, less personal tension between him and Ashraf might have aided a smooth departure and prevented his early death in isolation.

COMMUNISTS AND PARTICULAR FACTORS OF FAILURE

Among the particular factors, the Tudeh experience is unique in that its relationship with the Soviet Union was the element most detrimental to the party. Between 1941 and 1953, the party functioned in a more-or-less free political environment, and its subservience to the Soviet interest was not as evident as it became in later years. However, as the Tudeh lost its social base within the country, and became ever more reliant on Soviet protection and support, the relationship became the most important factor working against the party. In a society whose xenophobia had led to the development of simplistic conspiracy theories to explain complex national and international problems, the Tudeh's subservience to the Soviets was simply unacceptable. The Tudeh was viewed both by other Marxist groups and its mortal enemies as a tool of Soviet policy in Iran. As noted, to different degrees all Tudeh factions shared this subservience to the Soviet Union. Three factors contributed to this attitude. First, many Tudeh leaders looked upon Moscow as the Mecca of international communism, and saw the CPSU's analyses of international and Iranian affairs as unassailable, almost to the point of religious observance. Second, all party factions believed that any revolutionary movement would ultimately be unsuccessful unless

1. Bizhan Jazani (1937-1975): major Marxist theorist and Fadaiyan founder, assassinated in prison.

2. Hamid Ashraf (1946-1976): founder of Fadaiyan and a main organiser of guerrilla activity in the 1970s, killed in shootout with police.

3. Mas'ud Ahmadzadeh-Heravi (1947-1972): founder and theorist of Fadaiyan, executed.

4. Amir Parviz Puyan (1947-1971): founder and theorist of Fadaiyan, killed in shootout with police.

5. Khosrow Roozbeh (1915-1958): leading member of Tudeh Party's Military and Intelligence Organisation, executed

6. Mostafa Shoa'ian (1936-1975): independent Marxist theorist and guerrilla, killed in shootout with police.

7. Nur al-Din Kianuri (b.1915): a leading member of the Tudeh Party and its former first secretary (1979-1983).

8. Bizhan Jazani's painting 'Siyahkal' was produced while he was in prison, where his visionary zeal evidently remained undimmed.

supported and protected by the Soviet Union. Third, there were some genuine Russophiles among Tudeh leaders and members, and their love for Russia and its culture was beyond any known in other national communist parties. For example, Eskandari records a startling incident in Baku in the late 1950s. During a dinner party given by the Azarbaijan Communist Party for Tudeh and ADP leaders, a Tudeh activist invited everyone to a toast in honour of the Turkmanchai Treaty of 1828, which relinquished parts of the Caucasus to Russia. The treaty is considered one of the most humiliating events in modern Iranian history, and to toast to it would be unimaginable for many Iranians. Even Eskandari, with all his respect for the Soviet Union, refused the toast, and registered his objections with his hosts.[13] The Tudeh-Soviet relationship was very much in the minds of the new generation of Iranian Marxists who initiated guerrilla warfare in the 1970s. They viewed as entirely negative the Soviet role in the Marxist struggle for the liberation of the country. These groups tried to remedy the interference by either turning to Maoism and showing outright hostility towards the Soviet Union or by maintaining their independence by not asking for Soviet help. According to Iraj Nayyeri, a former guerrilla and the only survivor of the Siyahkal team, while the Ba'th regime of Iraq was more than willing to provide dissident groups with money and weapons, the original Fadaiyan leadership refused these offers, and purchased what little weaponry it could on the open market at a great cost.[14] In a period when even minimal Soviet funding would have made a great difference, and while the Tudeh enjoyed generous Soviet support, the price of guerrilla independence was indeed high.

The Tudeh's reliance on the Soviets continued after the revolution, and younger communists brought into its camp began to lay aside the hard-won political independence of the 1970s and embark on a similar relationship with the Soviet Union. The account of one of the Fadaiyan Majority members of his experience in the Soviet Union illustrates the depth of the disappointment these younger activists must have faced when introduced to the realities of life in the Soviet Union. According to Parviz Mansur, when the time came for him to flee Iran, in early 1984, he and a central committee member crossed the border to Soviet Azarbaijan.[15] To Mansur, the crossing represented arrival in the Socialist fatherland, the home of the first proletarian state, an indication of the extent of the illusion. Apparently they were kept in a camp similar to a prison, with great limits on movement and activity. A point in his story of greater comedy, but also of greatest personal disillusionment, was when he was treated poorly by local hospital workers, having enthusiastically introduced himself as an Iranian communist: 'The most interesting development was the negative reaction to those who called themselves communists. Those who frequented the hospital were in danger of not receiving care. They realised that bribery was a more effective way of receiving care than insistence on communist and militant credentials'.[16]

Another particular factor which applied to the Tudeh, and later the Fadaiyan Majority, was conduct after the revolution. As noted, the general Tudeh strategy was to defend and promote a faction within the IRI which it saw as revolutionary, anti-imperialist and the best equipped to spearhead a future transition to socialism, with Soviet aid. The Tudeh defended the *Maktabi* faction against the Islamic Liberals, promoting division among its opponents and working to ease dissent, trying in effect to buy its way into the role of loyal opposition and, as its conduct showed, willing to pay any price for it. For example, the party was active in promoting the destruction of the largest Marxist organisation after the revolution, the Fadaiyan, and causing the split in the KDP and a number of other organisations. After June 1981, the party and the Majority joined in the repression of those opposed to the IRI, a strategy which, without doubt, had many repercussions, the most important of which was to tarnish the hard-earned image of Marxism among the population.

One particular factor related to the guerrilla movement, and to the Fadaiyan in particular, was a clear lapse of theoretically grounding and capable leadership. The founders started the movement from nothing, and in the process created a movement with a theoretical framework that strove gradually to acquire experience. The theoretical output of the Fadaiyan founders, with all its shortcomings, was original, new and creative. For example, the organisation conducted research in rural Iran in order to understand the socio-political effects of the land-reform programme of the 1960s.The violent political climate, however, caused the death of many of the founders, and this led to a decline. Under the Ashraf leadership in the first half of 1970s, the Fadaiyan's emphasis was to recruit those willing to engage in armed struggle, and very limited attention was paid to theory. According to one Fadaiyan member, during the Ashraf leadership new recruits were taken underground and armed immediately, without appropriate doctrinal training.[17] This was why the organisation was unable to generate capable theorists who could answer the criticisms of other groups and adapt the Fadaiyan to the new socio-political situation. This was in a sharp contrast to the Tudeh, which did maintain continuity among its stalwarts between 1953 and 1979. Indeed, a majority of post-revolutionary Tudeh leaders were those who were in leadership during the 1953 coup. The Tudeh put this evident advantage to good use, especially in relation to the Fadaiyan. Experienced Tudeh theorists, backed by the vast ideological and material resources of the Soviet Union, disarmed many younger Fadaiyan leaders in theoretical discussions. The decline of Fadaiyan doctrinal output was also clear in its post-revolution activity, the creative thinking of Jazani giving way to mere repetition of classical Marxist texts with little direct relation to the Iranian situation.

COMMUNISTS AND STRUCTURAL FACTORS OF FAILURE

Among the structural factors, three stand out. The first was the movement's relation to its main constituency, the working class of Iran. Perhaps the factor most instrumental in the Marxist defeat was the failure of the movement to create a strong base among the working class of Iran, which communists saw as vital to their plans. All communist organisations and parties appealed to the working class, depicting it as the class which would largely carry the burden of social revolution. The question of what kind of theoretical and political relationship existed between the movement and the working class is therefore vital to an understanding of Marxist failure. The second factor was the political and theoretical education of Iranian Marxists. Here, the ramifications of a Stalinist approach to socio-political problems was paramount. Third, closely related to the second factor, was poverty of philosophy. Here, over-simplification of philosophical and political issues was the main characteristic.

The February 1979 revolution in Iran lifted 25 years of relentless political dictatorship, and allowed the organisation of different political groups and parties. For Iranian Marxists this meant a chance to address the working class, which they considered their natural ally. Here, the theoretical approach to the working class and the social base of three major Marxist organisations will be examined. The three have been chosen because of their significant social influence, and because they each represented a different trend in the movement, although all were ultimately unsuccessful in establishing strong support among the working class. With the new freedom of operation, Marxist groups moved to try to find new theoretical and practical ways to organise followers, with a natural emphasis on their natural constituency. Each organisation began by claiming to be the rightful vanguard of the working class, or at least to have the potential to become so, thereby coming into competition with the others (sometimes antagonistically) and the Islamic state for the attention, and ultimately leadership, of the working class.

The three organisations under study here – the Tudeh, Fadaiyan and Paykar – were either highly active before the revolution or had a long history of activity. This meant that they had either popularity or experience to bring to the task of building support.

The three differed in more than background, and these differences had a direct effect on their perception of how to approach and organise the working class. They were all introduced to Marxism through the experience of the Russian Revolution as seen in Soviet propaganda. Yet even here the three differed, in that the Tudeh came to accept the changes of the post-Stalin period, while the other two still clung to the image of Stalin as the iron will of the international proletariat.

The Tudeh's pro-Soviet role made it effectively an instrument of Soviet policy in the Islamic state. This meant particularly support for the Islamic state's anti-American emphasis, but it also meant support for a regime which was gradually removing political freedom. As the inevitable showdown with the opposition loomed, Tudeh support for the Islamic state brought the party into conflict with the rest of the opposition. The non-aligned Fadaiyan had relied on its own resources throughout its struggle with the imperial regime, while the Maoist Paykar saw the Soviet Union as an aggressive, expansionist and reactionary social-imperialist power. The Soviet role in Iranian history, and the harmonious relationship it enjoyed with the imperial regime only fuelled Paykar antagonism. It looked instead to China, but after relations between China and the imperial regime improved, it turned to Albania as a role model. International allegiances were instrumental in casting the Paykar and Tudeh as mortal enemies.

Under the Shah, the Iranian working class grew tremendously. Asef Bayat's study of the working class before and after the revolution suggests that the workers made up 'well over 50 percent of the economically active population'.[18] Industrial workers were among the last to join the revolutionary struggle (in the second half of 1978), but once they did, their mass nation-wide strikes crippled the Iranian economy.[19] Although these workers came late to the struggle, their contribution was arguably the killer blow. The main reason for their late involvement may be in that the imperial regime paid them special attention, ensuring that their economic needs were catered for, fearing successful Marxist agitation.

Because of the lack of independent trade unions in Iran since the 1953 coup, workers turned to the *showra* (council) as the main vehicle of industrial organisation.[20] According to Bayat, '... the shuras also differed from syndicalism, which fought a political battle to change the social structure through industrial activities. The shuras lacked a clear political objective... They restricted themselves to demanding workers' control and transformation of power relations in the industrial arena.'[21] Bayat suggests that *showras* were a spontaneous development, and that leadership came from within the working class during the early stages of the strikes. Only in late 1978 were outside political groups significantly represented on these councils.[22] His study clearly shows the absence of the Marxist vanguard among the working class until immediately before the collapse of the old regime.

The role of the working class in the 1979 revolution was noted by the Marxists early on, and they moved to harness this force for a second revolution, but no serious study of the situation – with an assessment of its strengths and weaknesses – was produced. While all three Marxist organisations acknowledged the decisive role of the working class in bringing down the old regime, they differed on the relationship between this class and others, and thus on what role they should play. These differences centred on divergent interpretations of the revolutionary stage.

The Tudeh, oldest of the three, had an extensive network and social base, especially among the working class, between 1941 and 1953, and saw itself as the sole working-class party of Iran. According to Ladjevardi, by 1945 Tudeh-affiliated workers' organisations had a membership of between 100,000 and 150,000.[23] This, in a country with a pre-industrial economy, undoubtedly included the bulk of the country's working class.

The effective uprooting of the Tudeh after the 1953 coup left the party as an opposition outside Iran, sustained by the Soviet Union and its allies. It did not play a role in the overthrow of the imperial regime, other than in the use of its propaganda machine outside Iran, and agitation to a small degree inside the country. But after the revolution, it moved to Iran and put the experience of its membership and its international backing into rebuilding its organisation.

After 1975, the Tudeh considered Iranian revolutionary conditions to be at a 'national democratic' stage.[24] This meant that the proletariat and other democratic classes (the petit bourgeoisie, progressive intellectuals and middle bourgeoisie) would have to unite against the regime. According to the Tudeh, the proletariat could not immediately lead this union because of its weakness of numbers and consciousness, but nonetheless the coalition direction should be socialist. How could this be possible? How could the coalition have taken a socialist direction without working-class leadership? The Tudeh filled this apparent gap with the Soviet-developed theory of the non-capitalist path of development. As far as the Tudeh was concerned, closeness to the Soviet Union was the key to passing from the national democratic to the socialist stage.

After the victory of the revolution, the Tudeh put this theory to work. Announcing itself as the New Party of the Working Class (*hezb-e taraz-e novin-e tabaqeh-ye kargar*), the Tudeh put its support behind the new Islamic leadership in the hope that a coalition could be implemented. When the Islamic leadership began to polarise, and the Islamic liberal faction came into conflict with the more doctrinaire faction headed by the IRP, the Tudeh sided with the latter, because of its more anti-American and radical views.

Between 1979 and 1981, the role of the Tudeh, despite its claim to be the party of the working class, was one of state appeasement and attempts to reconcile the differences between the regime and the working class.[25] The party saw itself as acting on the behalf of the working class. In March 1981, it supported the revolutionary prosecutor-general's rules setting out which parties could be active in the IRI and forbidding parties from inciting strikes. The Tudeh justified this stand on the grounds that strikes and other activities were anti-revolutionary and could only help American interests in Iran.[26] Clearly, this policy put the party in conflict with other Marxist groups. This policy neutralised efforts to gain working-class support, since the Tudeh was appeasing the state at a time when the working class was confronting it. Indeed the Tudeh's absence among the working class was readily apparent in 1983 when the IRI turned against the party, dismantling its organisational network, which was extensive only in the IRI military and administration. The Tudeh's own evaluation of its role among the working class speaks for itself. In a report commemorating the Tudeh's fortieth anniversary, the chapter on the party's role among the working class concedes that the party had nothing to show for its post-revolution activity.[27]

Tudeh policy toward the IRI delayed the party's suppression, but did not prevent it. While the rest of the opposition was declared illegal in 1981, the Tudeh and Fadaiyan Majority were tolerated until 1983, after which, from outside Iran, both tried to give new analyses of their role in society and the place of the working class. In 1986, the Tudeh's national congress, held in the Soviet Union, revised its perception of the revolutionary stage. While still maintaining the national democratic formula, it came to see the middle bourgeoisie as playing no progressive role while the petit bourgeoisie was to be encouraged to join the coalition, though not in a leadership role.[28]

With the Fadaiyan's emergence as the largest Marxist organisation in post-revolutionary Iran, the growth of support simply overwhelmed the organisation's pre-revolution structure. The prestige and popularity of the Fadaiyan, combined with the relative freedom of the period immediately after 1979, provided a unique opportunity for the further broadening of this support. Indeed in every social confrontation of 1979 and 1980, Fadaiyan presence was consistent. The Turkman case is perhaps a good example of the party's overall potential to find a constituency among rural labourers. Turkman land confiscation was followed by the establishment of peasant councils which soon took charge of the new socio-economic order in the area. The Fadaiyan was the main organiser of these councils for the duration of their brief existence, and differences within the Fadaiyan – which led to its break-up – helped weaken the Turkman councils when they came into conflict with the IRI.

In June 1980, at the height of social tensions, and at a time when unity was an essential part of any political organisation's success, the Fadaiyan began to break up, the split dividing working-class support. From June 1980, the Fadaiyan Majority steered a course parallel to that of the Tudeh on every social issue, including that of working-class organisation. It seems that between June 1980 and early 1981, the Majority faction still had its own interpretation of the situation, and hence of how to approach the working class. Initially, while admitting working-class weakness because of a lack of any nation-wide organisation (that is working-class party) to support its demands, the Majority pursued a policy of support for the establishment of trade unions at a time when the working class was engaged in the *showras*.[29] At this time, the Majority faction attacked the Islamic Liberals for seeking to contain the spread of unions, and the *Maktabis* for wanting to eliminate them and other left-wing organisations for mixing union duties with those of *showras*.[30] The

Fadaiyan Majority's insistence on unions was related to its gradual acceptance of the Tudeh's overall analysis of the situation. According to the Majority, if the *Maktabis* were in fact revolutionary, then the working class needed institutions to work within the system, and it thought *showras* unsuitable as instruments of revolutionary change. After the June 1981 crisis, the Majority made two basic changes in its approach. First, it dropped its insistence on unions and accepted *showras* as the the order of the day, but insisted that it be allowed to agitate freely within them.[31] Second, it came to accept the Tudeh analysis completely, and moved to co-ordinate its strategy with that of Tudeh. From this point until its suppression in 1983, the Majority's policy, as far as the working class was concerned, was to reconcile this class and the state. In sharp contrast to its earlier suggestion that the greatest weakness of the working class was its lack of nation-wide organisation, seldom did it mention working-class weakness. It even began calling itself by the odd name of the New Organisation of the Working Class at a time when it admitted that the Tudeh was the New Party of the Working Class.

The Minority split with the Majority faction primarily over the approach to the IRI. On the working class, the Minority believed that in the absence of a communist party – that is a working-class party – the workers continued to confront the IRI without a central command. The Minority viewed the revolutionary stage as being 'people's democratic', a stage at which proletarian leadership was essential.[32] The main question was how this leadership could be asserted at a time when the working class's biggest problem was the lack of a communist party. How could the job be done when the self-proclaimed vanguard organisation admitted to a weak working-class base? In a report on the struggle of the working class from February 1979 to May 1981, the Minority tried to show the direction the working-class struggle was taking.[33] The report clearly showed the spontaneous nature of strikes and the minimal role played by vanguard organisations. Indeed, before the major setbacks which resulted in disruption of the Minority's underground network in the winter of 1982, the organisation could produce many reports on the activities of the working class, but nothing on its own role as the active vanguard.

During the first post-revolutionary period, 1979–81, and after its split from the Majority, the Minority's activities were given over to trying to forge a coalition with other Marxist groups, and to participation in day-to-day events, while at the same time trying to overcome theoretical and organisational shortcomings which had resulted from the split. The result of these activities was that by the end of the period it emerged as the largest Marxist opposition to the IRI, but without a strong foothold among the working class. In the second period, 1981–3, it began to disintegrate. Attacks on it by IRI security forces disrupted its underground network and removed the majority of its central committee. The effects of such actions were evident in the disappearance of reports on the activities of the workers from the pages of *KAR*. Ironically, as the Minority lost its organisational abilities its assessment of its role in society grew more unrealistic. In view of other Marxist groups' disappearance from the scene, the Minority began to portray itself as the largest and most popular of all Marxist groups,[34] and therefore to demand that other groups accept its leadership, even though it had no power-base.

Like other Marxist organisations, the Paykar saw the lack of a revolutionary and popular communist party as the working class's biggest weakness, and admitted that Marxist organisations did not have much of a base among the workers.[35] It also saw revolutionary development as having reached 'people's democratic' stage, in which working-class leadership was essential. But a striking difference between the Paykar and the other two groups was its lack of a strong theoretical base for its claims and analyses. For example, while the Paykar's second congress, held in August 1980, made statements about general social conditions, it lacked even minimal evidence for its claims.[36] Despite their common position of opposition to the IRI, one of the problems that prevented the Paykar and Fadaiyan Minority allying meaningfully was their differences on how to approach the working class at factory level. The Minority accused the Paykar of anarchism, and suggested that Paykar behaviour had led workers to expel its members from factories on a number of occasions.[37] Paykar disintegration put a stop to its attempts at working-class organisation.

All the evidence of Marxist organisations and the working class suggests that, despite a relatively long history and the unique opportunity of relative political freedom following the collapse of the old regime, Iranian Marxists failed to obtain the necessary degree of support from the working class. There were many factors involved. Certainly repression was one important factor, but there were also internal reasons. None of these groups produced any serious and comprehensive study of the working class, which had changed profoundly since the 1940s when the Tudeh was able to agitate among it. By the time of the revolution, its numbers had increased, but it was still very much affected by its peasant past. The essential questions that Marxists failed to address were how this peasant background affected the political consciousness of the worker, and why the working class joined the revolution later than other groups. Did the Shah's reforms and accommodation of the working class have an effect, and if so what was this?

While some aspects of failure were shared by the three groups, others were particular to each. The Tudeh had the most experience in working among and organising the working class, but after the revolution started to reorganise to a different agenda. The strategy was no longer to organise the working class to seize political power from below. At best the party sought to use the workers as bargaining chips in a game with the state, in the hope of achieving change from above. It had penetrated the IRI administration and military, but had little support among the working class. Fadaiyan break-up, and the Majority's adoption of Tudeh strategy only weakened the Marxist base, as an already-limited working-class support was divided. Next, there were the self-indulgent titles, New Party of the Working Class and New Organisation of the Working Class, which served only to preach to the converted and indicate an inflated self-image.

An unrealistic self-image was also a feature of both the Minority and the Paykar; the Minority saw itself as the sole vanguard of the working class at a time when most of its underground network and a good number of its members had been eliminated. As for the Paykar, there is the example of the Militant Workers, a cell which joined in the summer of 1979. When writing about its own history and reasons for joining, the Militant Workers wrote that despite its name it originated among university students in the mid-1970s.[38] Nowhere in the history of the cell is there justification for the name 'Militant Workers'.

Finally, while Marxist groups admitted that the working class, for the most part, struggled to further its own economic interests, the presence of various Marxist groups in the work-place perhaps added to an already confusing situation. Imagine a situation in which workers are preparing for a strike: one group is arguing against the whole idea, another is proposing ideas so unrealistic that it has to be ejected from the meeting, a third is more concerned with isolating the first than with organising the strike, all of this at a time when workers and management loyal to factory owners are doing their best to stop the whole venture.

A study of Marxist groups and organisations in Iran must conclude that, from a theoretical point of view, none of them approached the working class realistically. Those who were in support of the IRI had no intention of mobilising workers for social change or confrontation, and insofar as they were effective, acted as a disrupting force within workers' organisations. Those Marxists who opposed the IRI ultimately proved unable to mobilise the working class in that confrontation because of their inability to address the workers' demands, an inability caused by theoretical and organisational fragmentation.

If Marxist organisations lacked a strong working-class base, then what was their social base? Studies such as Asef Bayat's on the social background of Marxists may shed some light. From a limited study, conducted before the revolution, and a list of members of various groups opposed to the IRI, some understanding of the social background of some groups is possible. Research done on Marxist organisations before the revolution suggests that the majority of members were not working class. Abrahamian's study of the Tudeh before the 1953 coup suggests that based on partial information on 2419 former rank-and-file members, 1276 were from the new middle class, 169 from the traditional middle class, 860 from the urban working class, and 69 from the peasantry. The author concludes:

> Thus the intelligentsia, who formed less than 8 percent of the country's labour force, constituted more than 53 percent of the party's rank and file; and urban wage earners and town peddlers, who together totalled as little as 15 percent of the labour force, made up as much as 36 percent of the rank and file. Conversely, the rural masses, who totalled over 54 percent of the labour force, contributed only 3 percent of the rank and file.[39]

Abrahamian's study suggests that before the 1953 coup, when the Tudeh was able to function openly, the party appealed to the middle class, and was able to create a base among the working class. Azadeh Kian's study of the same period confirms this observation.[40] Abrahamian's study of the guerrilla groups in the 1970s was based on information available on 172 Fadaiyan (Table 1) and 30 Marxist Mojahedin (Table 2) members killed during the anti-imperial period.[41] Of 172 Fadaiyan members, only 12 (8 percent) were working class, while 73 (42.5 percent) were university students. Out of 30 Marxist Mojahedin members, only 1 (3.5 percent) was working class while 15 (50 percent) were university students. Abrahamian's study, limited as it is, leaves no doubt that the guerrilla movement appealed to the more educated sectors of society.

Based on available information, the social base of the Marxist groups after 1953 gets farther away from the working class, despite the early popularity of some organisations. According to information available on 30 Tudeh members (Table 3), while 6 (20 percent) were workers, 19 (66 percent) were university students, and 4 (13 percent) were high-school students.[42] Information on the Fadaiyan includes 160 members belonging to various factions (not including the Majority).[43] Of these, 21 (13.1 percent) were workers, while 38 (23.7 percent) were university students, and 57 (35.6 percent) were high-school students. In table 5, of 60 Paykar members 12 (1.6 percent) were workers, 15 (25 percent) high-school students.

A comparison of the information available on the social background of the three Marxists groups yields the following conclusions: the data on the Tudeh supports the notion that these groups were most successful when they were able to organise in a less repressive political environment. The Tudeh before the 1953 coup proved the most successful at establishing and growing a base among the working class. The information also suggests that Iranian Marxists never managed to establish a firm base among the working class after 1953, and at all among the peasantry. The appeal of Marxism seems to have been limited to more educated, new middle class strata, especially students. If this is correct, then clearly Iranian Marxists failed to link up with the main class able to understand their ideology and bring about social change.

Table 1
Gender and occupational background of
pre-revolution Fadaiyan based on information
available on 172 members

	%
22 women	12.8
12 workers	8
5 army personnel	8
4 intellectuals	2.3
3 doctors	1.7
7 office workers	4
19 engineers	11
17 teachers	9.9
1 high-school student	0
73 university students	42.5

Table 2
Gender and occupational background of pre-revolution Marxist Mojahedin (Paykar) based on information available on 30 members

	%
8 women	26
1 worker	3.5
2 engineers	6.6
3 teachers	10
15 university students	50

Table 3
Occupational background of post-revolution Tudeh based on information available on 30 members

	%
0 women	
6 workers	20
8 military personnel	26
2 office workers	6.6
1 engineer	3.3
4 teachers	13
4 high-school students	13
19 university students	66

Table 4
Gender and occupational background of post-revolution Fadaiyan based on information available on 433 members by gender and 160 by occupation.

	%
39 women	9
21 workers	13.1
6 military personnel	1.8
2 intellectuals	1.2
3 doctors	1.8
7 office workers	4.3
9 engineers	5.6
21 teachers	13.6
57 high-school students	35.6
38 university students	23.7
2 university professors	1.2
6 lawyers	3.7
9 others	5.6

Table 5
Gender and occupational background of the Paykar based on available background on 231 members by gender and 60 by occupation

	%
36 women	18.7
12 workers	20
1 doctor	1.6
2 office workers	3.3
11 engineers	18.3
10 teachers	16.6
15 high-school students	25
4 others	4.8

A recent study by Asef Bayat on the urban poor during the 1979 revolution also suggests an absence of Marxists among this important segment of Iranian society.[44] The author defines the urban poor as migrants from rural areas who began to settle in large numbers around major Iranian cities in 1960s and 1970s. These became the disfranchised of the Shah's modernisation programme, inhabiting slums and squatter settlements. Marxists would refer to them as the urban poor or 'lumpen proletariat'. Bayat's study suggests that, in contrast to common belief, the urban poor did not necessarily represent a source of support for the Islamists, and that as time went by they came into direct conflict with the new order.[45] At the core of the dispute was the urban poor's attempt to hold on to property confiscations (land, houses, etc) and the IRI's attempt to reverse this. This situation should have made the urban poor susceptible to Marxist agitation and social mobilisation, and indeed communist publications did take frequent note of this social strata's activities, but the study shows that there was a clear lack of any effective Marxist presence among this class. Bayat does document, however, a Moslem Mojahedin presence.[46]

An important factor behind Iranian Marxists' failure was the education they received in what Leon Trotsky called Stalin's School of Falsification. Of course communism in Iran was not the only movement highly affected by Stalinism. Other Marxists, especially in the Third World, had adhered to many Stalinist norms, and yet were successful in securing state power or sustaining long-term agitation. Communists in Vietnam and China are good examples. Stalinism was not the only reason for the failure of Iranian Marxists, and perhaps not even the most important one, but it was nonetheless a factor.

In general, all Iranian Marxist groups believed in the validity of the October Revolution in Russia and its lessons. An overwhelming majority of Marxist groups in Iran adhered to Stalinism, and referred to him in such hallowed terms as, 'great proletarian teacher' and 'the steel will of the world proletariat'. The remainder were a small number of intellectuals considered socialist but not Marxist-Leninist or revolutionary Marxists.

Accepting the validity of the Russian Revolution model meant that none of the Marxist organisations believed in any type of political democracy, which Marxist literature often referred to as bourgeois democracy, and regarded it as a given that a vanguard party with a firm hold among the working class could bypass or shortcut the capitalist phase and build socialism. As noted, the only exception here was the Tudeh, and later the Fadaiyan Majority, which believed the cross-over to socialism achievable by a non-proletarian force with close Soviet collaboration. The Russian Revolution became even more of a model after 1979, when many Marxist groups concluded that Iran's socio-economic condition resembled that of 1917 Russia, and began to emphasise the need for a vanguard communist party which could unify the working class and seize political power.

Most Iranian Marxist groups and organisations adhered to Stalinism, and this had a negative effect on their approach to social issues, especially democracy. Only marginal groups, such as Iranian Trotskyites and Communist Unity, were not Stalinist, and they followed the pre-Stalin Bolshevik Party model. Stephen Cohen has defined Stalinism as 'not simply nationalism, bureaucratic rationalisation, absence of democracy, censorship, police repression and the rest in any precedent sense... Instead, Stalinism was excess, extraordinary extremism, in each'.[47] In this sense, Iranian Marxists were not Stalinist. Marxists in Iran never held power, the ultimate test of a theory, and so were not in a position to show excess even had they been inclined to. The Stalinism Cohen describes was perhaps unique to the Soviet Union between the 1930s and the early 1950s. But if Stalinism means a small bit of each of the above, without the outright excesses, then Iranian Marxists were indeed Stalinists, or had strongly Stalinist characteristics.

Stalinism is most obvious when compared to democracy. Stalinist norms not only preclude free political activity in society at large, but demand ideological and political uniformity within the party itself. Stalin's final encounter with the Bolshevik left-wing opposition during the CPSU's fifteenth congress in 1927 is a good example. In the course of discussion, the Stalinist faction demanded that the left-wing opposition give up opinions which ran counter to those of the majority. When Lev Kamenev, an opposition leader, rejected the demand, Stalin stated, 'Kamenev asserts that there is nothing in the traditions of our Party, in the traditions of Bolshevism, that justifies the demand that a member of the Party should give up certain views that are incompatible with our Party's ideology, with our Programme. Is this correct? Of course not. More than that, it is a lie, comrades!'[48] In internal CPSU politics, Stalin's demand was, of course, a clear break from Bolshevik tradition, and set the stage for his faction's consolidation of power and the bloody purges of the 1930s. At this point, the Bolsheviks were indeed changing character, and were in the process of becoming the stagnant and terror-stricken party of Stalin. What is important here is that this behaviour became the norm for intra-party relations in the international communist movement.

From 1941 on, Iranian activists were introduced only to Stalinist Marxism, and therefore saw it as the norm. Three generations of Iranian Marxists learned about the Russian experience through the lens of Stalin's School of Falsification. For example, throughout the period under study, the main reference text on the history of Russian Revolution was a Persian translation of *History of the Communist Party of the Soviet Union (Bolsheviks)*, written in the 1930s.[49] This text offered Iranian Marxists a highly distorted version of Russian history which endorsed the actions of the Bolsheviks, led by Lenin and Stalin, while condemning their opponents. Even the Tudeh, which had accepted the post-Stalin reforms in the Soviet Union, used as a reference its own translation of a Brezhenev-era version of the Russian Revolution which is only slightly more objective. Even when more objective studies of Stalinism did find their way into Iran the Marxists rejected them. A rare lively ideological discussion on Stalinism occurred between the Fadaiyan and Communist Unity in the mid-1970s. At one point in the discussion, the latter referred to Issac Deutscher's biography of Stalin to counter Hamid Mo'meni, the Fadaiyan theorist, but he dismissed Deutscher as a bourgeois propagandist.[50] Except for the Tudeh, which adapted its policies to those of Stalin, Khrushchev and Brezhnev, most Marxist groups dismissed the post-Stalin reforms as revisionist. As a result of their Stalinist training, not one Marxist group or organisation in Iran in practice respected the right of individual members in internal disputes. The history of the Tudeh shows that serious party differences were resolved in a manner similar to those used by the CPSU, either by silencing ideological opponents or purging them. The record for other Marxist groups is similar if not worse. The Fadaiyan resorted to purging ideological opponents (for example the Shoa'ian affair) either by forcing them to leave or by physical elimination, and in the most notorious case, Marxist Mojahedin leaders conducted a bloody purge of their Moslem opponents when persuasion failed.

Tragically, these undemocratic practices persisted after the 1979 revolution when, more than ever, respect for democratic rights had become a social issue. The Marxists' failure to prove themselves in this respect played an important role in their inability to gain public support. As mentioned, the bulk of Iranian Marxists soon found themselves facing the IRI as defenders of the people's democratic rights. But could this defence be sustained by organisations which were themselves undemocratic? Tudeh and the Fadaiyan Majority support for the IRI in the midst of the struggle for democratic rights, and the vacillation of other groups, were partially rooted in their own lack of respect for democratic rights. After all, would the Marxists have treated the Islamists any differently had their postions been reversed?

Iranian Marxists' Stalinist training and the despotic nature of Iranian society was a potent combination. In a society where various types of dictatorship have long been prevalent, a despotic or repressive culture will take root. This repressive or despotic culture has a direct bearing on all social groups and classes, even intellectuals who espouse democracy, and liberation for all, and goes beyond the intra-party relations of any given organisation. In the case of Iranian Marxists, had they been successful, democratic rights would not have been generally respected, if the history of world or Iranian Marxism is taken as the model.

Iranian Marxists' training in Stalin's School of Falsification was not limited to the history of Russia or democracy, and included a variety of other issues such as an oversimplified perception of philosophical and political issues, itself a product of the Stalin era, which resulted in a kind of poverty of philosophy among Marxists in Iran. For the most part their knowledge of Marxism was limited to some of the writings of Lenin and Stalin, especially the latter. Very few of Marx's original writings were available and studied. The Marxists' knowledge of world or contemporary Iranian history and social structure was even more limited. No serious study of Iranian history was produced by any of them, with the exception of Ehsanollah Tabari, the Tudeh ideologue, and Bizhan Jazani, the

Fadaiyan founder. Tabari wrote a number of pamphlets on Iranian history, but these were often ignored due to the antipathy many had for the Tudeh. Furthermore, his writings were usually moulded to conform with the general Soviet historical and philosophical world view. Jazani's writings were mostly written while the author was in prison, a position which carried certain limitations. The Tudeh translated and distributed the writings of the Soviet historian Ivanov, although Eskandari dismissed him as a KGB agent. Ivanov was known for his distorted historiography of Iran, and Kianuri conceded that Ivanov twisted Iranian history to fit Soviet interests.[51]

The Marxists' poverty of philosophy had disastrous results after the revolution, and at a time when the movement was in desperate need of creative thinking and analysis of politicised Islam. All Marxist organisations showed an apparent inability to comprehend the new situation. The creative thinking of Fadaiyan founders was replaced by simple copying of some classical Marxist texts or, in the case of Tudeh, Soviet-produced literature. Each organisation simply borrowed the literature of whichever revolution or situation it saw as having a bearing on the present. Thus, the post-revolutionary polemics of various Marxist organisations became a mere repetition of, say, comparisons between the 1848 Revolutions in Europe and the 1905 or 1917 Revolutions in Russia. Heavy borrowing from classical Marxist texts suggest that the movement was unable to address key social questions. The issue of how to link up with the working class, how to address it, and other questions always remained unanswered.

Another symptom of the Marxists' poverty of philosophy was dogmatism and self-righteousness. After the revolution, the lack of creative thinking led many Marxists into dogmatic behaviour which in turn resulted in an inability to forge simple coalitions, even when faced with great danger. A good example in this is the armed clashes in the jungles of northern Iran. Between summer 1981 and spring 1982, about four guerrilla teams, belonging to various communist organisations, plus the Mojahedin, were facing security forces. All the guerrillas, perhaps as many as 300, were uprooted by the IRI without ever having established simple co-ordination among themselves.

The lack of respect for democratic rights and this poverty of philosophy showed its effects when the rights of women became a point of contention between secularist and leftist parties and the IRI. As noted, the attitude of most Marxist organisations on the women's issues was confined to a class analysis. This analysis held that women's oppression would be overcome by the elimination of the class system,[52] a Marxist generality which got around the need for creative thinking. The Marxists' lack of respect for democratic rights showed one of its side-effects when various organisations failed to provide solid support for popular grass-roots democratic organisations. According to one observer, 'The left's incorrect approach to women's struggle and demands was not just because it did not correctly understand the women's issue. Not paying attention to demands of the democratic struggle was a general weakness and a characteristic of most left and progressive forces'.[53] Accordingly, when faced with popular grass-roots organisations, most Marxist groups put pressure on them to declare solidarity with their own position.[54] This contrasted with the experiences of other revolutions, in which popular organisations were supported and strengthened by the communist party in order to foment unrest helpful to change.

Symptoms of Stalinism were not unique to Iranian Marxists. Other liberation movements, notably China and Vietnam, also accepted Stalinism, yet succeeded. This was because the communists of China and Vietnam were able to recognise the realities of their society and adapt accordingly. Iranian Marxists never managed to do this, although serious attempts were made.

The demise of Marxism in Iran followed the disintegration of various groups and organisations in the aftermath of the June 1981 crisis. As had happened after the 1953 coup, the Marxists were overwhelmed by a greatly superior foe without, once again, having chosen the moment of attack. The history of the last 40 years suggests that Iranian Marxists were never really poised to take power, although the architects of the 1953 coup feared it. The Tudeh never had any serious plan of action to secure power. Indeed, according to one study, the Tudeh opted for legal opposition between 1941 and 1953.[55] The guerrilla movement considered itself a serious contender for revolutionary leadership, but its mass armed revolution never really materialised. In 1981, however, the Iranian Marxists were drawn into a battle they did not want but could not stop.

The June 1981 crisis was essentially one which other non-Marxist elements had brought about, these being on one hand the Islamic Liberals, with the Moslem Mojahedin, and on the other the *Maktabis*, the IRP and state apparatus, backed by Ayatollah Khomeini. In this battle Marxist groups which supported the *Maktabis*, such as the Tudeh, joined the battle consciously. Those who opposed the *Maktabis*, the majority of whom also opposed the Islamic Liberals, were simply drawn into battle without preparation. The two-and-a-half years since the revolution had failed to bring about even minimal unity, and now each group had to face repression on its own.

By the mid-1980s, the organised activity of most Marxists was reduced to Kurdish areas, and by late the 1980s, as the Iran-Iraq War came to a close, even these pockets of activity were over-run by government troops. Unlike the 1970s, however, this time Marxists failed to revive any kind of anti-IRI activity, either inside the country or abroad. There are two fundamental reasons for this. First, the magnitude of the defeat was so great that many survivors left active political life, and the remaining ones, having lost many supporters, were reduced to gathering into small groups in exile. Kurdish groups were an exception. Second, the reforms unleashed by Gorbachev in the Soviet Union resulted in the collapse of the October Revolution model, which undermined the theoretical foundation of Iranian Marxistm.

In what is now a post-Soviet era, it is becoming clear that the concept of leftist political activity, for so long identified with revolutionary Marxism, is going through a metamorphosis. The collapse of the Eastern-Bloc socialist model has resulted in doctrinal revisions in many ex-Communist parties and liberation movements. What the end-result of this process will be in the new century is not clear. What is clear is that unlike before, much of the ex-radical left seems content with a modified notion of social democracy, so long attacked by it as having betrayed the cause of the international working class. Rahnama's collection of interviews with major Marxist activists and thinkers in exile opens a window to the ongoing discussions. While all of the personalities interviewed offer a degree of criticism of the past, three general categories are distinguishable. First, there were those critical of the past performance of Marxism in Iran, but who still viewed the world within the Soviet model, that is Marxism-Leninism. This category may want to modify the Soviet model but not break its boundaries.[56] Second, there are those critical of the past but more concerned with the future and the notion of social democracy. To this group, social democracy is a taboo, a code-name for the acceptance of bourgeois order and the loss of revolutionary credentials.[57] Finally, there are those who have broken with the past but are naturally uncertain about the uncharted future.[58] To this group the shortcomings of the past and international realities are insurmountable, and this appears to be the increasingly dominant trend in Iranian Marxism. While some hardcore activists refuse to accept the realities of the international and Iranian situation, most former and current activists have already begun a process of metamorphosis. While it is doubtful that the generation of the 1979 revolution will play a decisive role in the future development of Iran, it will no doubt play a role in passing on the experiences of that time and defining some for the problems of the coming century.

APPENDIX
CHRONOLOGY OF EVENTS (1941–83)

This chronology runs between 1941 and 1983, the period covered in this study. 1983 was the year in which the last communist organisations were either up-rooted or went underground. This chronology is based on the author's research and on the following sources: Baquer Aqeli, *Ruzshomar-e tarikh-e Iran: az mashruteh ta enqelab-e Islami* (*A Chronology of Iran: From Constitutional Revolution to the Islamic Revolution*), 2 vols (Tehran: Goftar Publishers, 1993); Gholam Reza Nejati, *Tarikh-e bist va panj saleh-ye Iran* (*The Twenty Five Year History of Iran*), vol. II (Tehran: Rasa Cultural Institute, 1992) 497–560; Nicholas M. Nikazmerad, 'A Chronological Survey of the Iranian Revolution', *Iranian Studies*, vol. XIII no. II, 1980, 327–68.

1941
26 August: Iran invaded and occupied by the Allies.
3 October: The Tudeh Party of Iran established.

1942
The establishment of the Central Union of Worker's Councils, dominated by the Tudeh.

1943
Iranian Government, under Sa'ed, opened talks with British and American oil companies regarding new concessions; Tehran Conference brings Stalin, Churchill and Roosevelt to Iran in order to decide the post-war fate of the world; Iran promised evacuation after the end of the war by all three powers.

1944

The Military Organisation of the Tudeh established.

March: Election of Tudeh members to the fourteenth Majles.

September: Kavtaradze mission arrived in Tehran to negotiate the northern oil field concessions.

August: The first congress of the Tudeh. Reza Shah died in exile.

1945

August: The rebellion of Tudeh officers in army's Khorasan division.

September: The establishment of the Azarbaijan Democratic Party (ADP) by Ja'far Pishehvari and his comrades. Tudeh branches and organisation in Azarbaijan were dissolved and joined the Democratic Party with Soviet approval, but without the knowledge of the Tudeh leadership.

December: The ADP declared an autonomous government in Azarbaijan and elected Pishehvari as its leader.

1946

Navvab Safavi established the Islamic Fadaiyan.

May: Three Tudeh leaders, Eskandari, Yazdi and Keshavarz, joined Ahmad Qavam's cabinet.

June: The Soviet army withdrew from Iran.

14 July: A Tudeh-led mass strike by oil industry workers.

December: The ADP defeated as the imperial army occupied Tabriz.

1947

February: Muhammad Mas'ud, a popular anti-imperial court journalist and publisher of *Mard-e Emrooz* was assassinated.

July: The mysterious death of Pishehvari, the exiled ADP's founder, in Baku.

December: Qavam's cabinet resigned.

1948

January: The first large-scale split in the Tudeh. Personalities such as Khalil Maleki, Anvar Khameh'i, Jalal Al-e Ahmad, Nader Naderpur and Ebrahim Golestan were among the departing party.

25 April: The second congress of the Tudeh party.

1949

February: Attempt on the Shah's life. The Tudeh was declared illegal.

October: Muhammad Mosaddeq and colleagues established the National Front.

1950

May: Ahmad Dehqan, Majles member, anti-Tudeh journalist and publisher of *Tehran Mosavvar*, was assassinated.

June: Haj Ali Razmara became Prime Minister.

APPENDIX: CHRONOLOGY OF EVENTS (1941–83)

15 December: Ten top Tudeh leaders escaped jail. Nur al-Din Kianuri and Khosrow Roozbeh were among the escaping group.

1951

7 March: Razmara assassinated by the Islamic Fadaiyan.

20 March: Oil nationalisation day.

30 April: Muhammad Mosaddeq became Prime Minister.

1 May: Mosaddeq enacted the Oil Bill.

May: Creation of the Toilers' Party of the People of Iran.

14 July: Averell Harriman, Truman's representative, arrived in Tehran to help mediate the Anglo-Iranian oil dispute. His arrival coincided with Tudeh-led demonstrations in Tehran which led to confrontation with security forces. From this point on, the Tudeh sharpened its propaganda against Mosaddeq and accused him of reaching a secret agreement with the United States over the oil dispute, despite his rejection of Harriman's offer.

October: Mosaddeq traveled to the United States.

1952

16 July: Mosaddeq resigned in dispute with the Shah.

21 July: A bloody uprising in support of Mosaddeq. The Shah reinstated him as Prime Minister. The Tudeh changed strategy and started to support Mosaddeq.

August: Maleki and company left the Toilers Party to establish the Third Force.

October: Mosaddeq broke diplomatic relations with Britain.

1953

March: Stalin's death.

April: Assassination of Gen. Afshar-tus, the pro-Mosaddeq chief of national police.

16 August: Mosaddeq dismissed the seventeenth Majles. The first coup attempt against him failed. Mosaddeq asked for a referendum on the future of Iran.

19 August: The second coup attempt – with the backing of the CIA, MI-6 and imperial court – was successful, and Mosaddeq's Government was overthrown.

12 November: The first post-coup mass demonstration organised by the Nationalists. The Tudeh participated.

7 December: University students demonstrated against Nixon's trip to Iran. Three students, Qandchi, Bozorg-nia and Shari'at-razavi, were shot dead. This day has been known as University Student's Day (rouz-e daneshju) by the opposition ever since.

1954

The arrest and death, under torture, of two rank-and-file Tudeh activists, Vartan Salakhanian and Mahmmud Kuchak-shushtari.

August–September: The Military Organisation of the Tudeh was discovered.

August: Iran resolved its oil dispute, reaching an agreement with the international oil consortium.

26 September: Tudeh's main printing hideout, publishing *Mardom*, was confiscated.

October: The first group of Tudeh military officers were executed.

1955

The arrest of Muhammad Bahrami, The Tudeh's first secretary, Ali Olovvi and Amanollah Qoreishi, Tudeh central committee members. Qoreishi was in charge of the Tudeh's Tehran organisation, and his arrest signaled the decimation of an important section of the Tudeh network. The remains of the Tudeh Military Organisation, under Khosrow Roozbeh, was discovered and decimated.

February: Explosion of the Davoudiah depot by the opposition.

March: The arrest of Morteza Yazdi, executive committee member, and Nader Sharmini, head of Tudeh's Youth Organisation.

August: The last group of Tudeh military officers were executed. The Shah's trip to the Soviet Union resulted in minor trade agreements between the two countries.

November: Iran joined the Baghdad Pact.

1956

February: A Tudeh delegation, under Radmanesh, participated in the CPSU's twentieth congress. The party accepted the introduction of de-Stalinisation initiated by Khrushchev.

1957

SAVAK, the Shah's notorious secret police, was founded with the aid of CIA and the Israeli MOSAD.

July: Khosrow Roozbeh arrested after a shootout. the Tudeh central committee's fourth plenum held outside Iran. The two factions in the party compromised by reinstating Radmanesh as first secretary, endorsed limited criticism of past party policy and attitude to Mosaddeq's Government, and made Roozbeh, captive in Iran, a central committee member.

November: the Tudeh's clandestine radio station (*peyk-e Iran*) started to broadcast anti-regime programmes from the GDR and later (1959) Bulgaria.

APPENDIX: CHRONOLOGY OF EVENTS (1941-83)

1958

27 February: Attempted coup against the Shah discovered, and its principal advocates, including Gen. Valiollah Qarahni, arrested.

May: Khosrow Roozbeh was executed; organised Tudeh activities inside Iran ceased.

1959

5 March: Iran-US bilateral defence agreement. The United States committed itself to Iran's defence against aggression.

May: Ali Olovvi became the only executive committee member of the Tudeh to be executed.

1960

January: One thousand high school students staged a demonstration criticising minimum-passing-grade policy, and chanted anti-Shah slogans.

June: Beginning of period of relaxation of repression by the Shah, which lAsted until 1963.

June: Tudeh seventh plenum approved unity with the ADP. Tudeh officially embraced Marxism-Leninism as its party ideology. Elections to the twentieth Majles, a new four-year term.

July: The Second National Front was formed by some of Mosaddeq's colleagues.

August: Unity Conference between the Tudeh and the Azarbaijan Democratic Party.

1961

January: Inauguration of US President Kennedy.

March: Grand Ayatollah Muhammad Hosein Borujerdi, dominant Shi'i figure (*marja'-e taqlid*), died in Qom.

2 May: Teachers' strike for better wages turned political.

9 May: The Shah dismissed the Twentieth Majles and ordered a review of electoral laws and new elections.

11 May: The Iran Liberation Movement (*nehzat-e azadi-ye Iran*) was founded by Mehdi Bazargan, Ayatollah Mahmmud Taleqani and their associates.

February: Twentieth Majles convened, of Shah's supporters, with only Alahyar Saleh of the National Front elected from the opposition.

2 May: One person killed at a teachers' demonstration.

6 May: Ali Amini became Prime Minister.

1962

January: Amini's cabinet approved a land reform bill.

10–18 April: Shah visited Washington and met President Kennedy.

19 July: Amini resigned, to be replaced by Amir Asadollah Alam.

27 January: The Shah's 'White Revolution' declared.

171

1963

5 June: Mass uprising against the reform programme, and in support of Ayatollah Khomeini, violently put down by security forces.

1964

Bahman Qashqa'i initiates armed rebellion in central Iran, which continues into the following year.

February: Youth members of the Tudeh split from the party to form the Revolutionary Organisation of the Tudeh Party of Iran.

March: Hasan Ali Mansur appointed Prime Minister.

October: Majles approved what came to be known in the United States as the Status of Forces Agreement (SOFA) and in Iran as the Capitulations Agreement.

November: After vehemently attacking the granting of capitulation rights to US personnel in Iran, Ayatollah Khomeini sent into exile in Turkey, form where he went to Iraq.

1965

January: Tudeh's eleventh plenum. Following the worsening of the Sino-Soviet dispute, a group of Tudeh leaders and members were ousted from the party. They formed the Marxist-Leninist Organisation of Tufan.

January: Premier Mansur assassinated by Muhammad Bokhara'i and replaced by Amir Abbas Hoveyda, who would hold the post for the next 13 years.

April, An attempt on the Shah's life failed. The assassin had contacts with a group associated with the Revolutionary Organisation.

September: Organisation of Iranian People's Mojahedin founded.

October: Trial of the group, associated with the Revolutionary Organisation, in connection to an attempt on the Shah's life.

1966

January: As relations improved, Iran and the Soviet Union agreed on the sale of Iranian natural gas to the Soviets in return for military equipment and industrial projects.

1967

Armed rebellion began in Iranian Kurdestan. It would continue until 1969.

March: Five-year trade agreement between Iran and the Soviet Union signed.

5 March: Mosaddeq died in internal exile.

July: Trial and conviction of Tudeh members Khavari and Hekmat-ju, who had returned to Iran clandestinely, but were compromised due to SAVAK infiltration.

26 October: Shah's imperial coronation.

December: Following the mysterious death of Gholam Reza Takhti, a popular and internationally-known wrestler and medalist, a large

APPENDIX: CHRONOLOGY OF EVENTS (1941–83)

demonstration, organised by Marxist university students, became an occasion for anti-regime sentiments.

1968

February: The Jazani-Zarifi group, one of the two founding pillars of the Fadaiyan, discovered by the SAVAK and its leaders arrested.
September: Death of Samad Behrangi, a revolutionary writer and teacher.

1969

December: Tudeh thirteenth plenum. Radmanesh attacked for mishandling of SAVAK infiltration.

1970

Beginning of the Shah's massive military build-up in accordance with the Nixon Doctrine.
December: Tudeh's fourteenth plenum. Radmanesh removed as first secretary, to be replaced by Eskandari.

1971

Beginning of period of intense armed struggle between opposition groups and imperial regime. Continued until 1976.
8 February: Jangal group initiated guerrilla activity against imperial regime by attacking the gendarmerie post in the village of Siyahkal.
April: Establishment of the Organisation of Iranian People's Fada'i Guerrillas. Gen. Zeinolabeddin Farsiu, military prosecutor general, assassinated by the Fadaiyan.
May: Amir Parviz Puyan, founding member of the Fadaiyan, and another member killed in clash with security forces.
17 August: Iran recognised the People's Republic of China.
September: 69 members of the Moslem Mojahedin, including 11 leaders, arrested.
October: Shah's extravagant celebration of 2500 years of Iranian empire.
November: Following British evacuation of the Persian Gulf region, Iran occupied three disputed islands, Abu Musa, Lesser and Greater Tumbs. This signaled Iran's dominance in the region at the height of the Shah's power.

1972

March: Mas'ud Ahmadzadeh and Abbas Meftahi, both Fadaiyan founder-members, and eight other activists executed in Tehran.
May: Nixon and Kissinger arrived in Tehran and informed the Shah that the United States was prepared to sell Iran any conventional weapons systems it wanted. Moslem Mojahedin attempted and failed to assassinate an American general.

1973

March: Iran took complete control of its oil industry.

July: The Moslem Mojahedin assassinated Louis Hawkins, an American colonel, in Tehran.

1974

February: Fadaiyan bombed the command centre of Iranian gendarmerie.

August: The Fadaiyan assassinated industrialist Muhammad Sadeq Fateh-yazdi.

December: Fadaiyan assassinated Maj. Alinaqi Nik-tab', a notorious SAVAK torturer.

1975

February: Fadaiyan bombed a gendarmerie command centre and a police station in Tehran, the central police station in Mashhad, and two gendarmerie stations in Babol and Lahijan, in commemoration of the Siyahkal operation.

March: By the Shah's decree the *Rastakhiz* party became the sole legal political party in Iran.

3 March: Fadaiyan assassinated Capt. Yadollah Noruzi, head of a university security squad, and bombed a police station in Tehran. Shah and Saddam Hussein signed the Algiers peace accord ending hostilities between Iran and Iraq.

5 March: Fadaiyan assassinated Abbas Ali Shahriari.

20 March: The Mojahedin, now dominated by the Marxist faction, assassinated Gen. Reza Zandipur, head of SAVAK-police joint committee.

18 April: Bizhan Jazani and six other Fadaiyan founders assassinated by SAVAK along with two members of the Mojahedin. The nine had been serving prison terms since the mid-1960s and early 1970s. Ali Akbar Ja'fari, Fadaiyan second in command, died in an accident.

May–September: After a bloody internal purge, which resulted in the assassination of Majid Sharif-vaqefi, a Mojahedin group establish the Organisation of Iranian People's Mojahedin (Marxist-Leninist).

16 May: The Marxist faction of Mojahedin assassinated Majid Sharif-vaqefi, head of the Moslem faction.

21 May: The Marxist Mojahedin assassinated two American military advisors in Tehran.

June: Tudeh's fifteenth plenum. The party's new programme approved, and a new generation entered party leadership. The Marxist Mojahedin failed to assassinate an American diplomat in Tehran.

1976

The beginning of official celebrations commemorating 50 years of Pahlavi dynasty rule. The Shah ordered the change form the official solar calendar to an imperial one.

January: Navid, the Tudeh's only active branch in Iran prior to the revolution, created.

APPENDIX: CHRONOLOGY OF EVENTS (1941–83)

February: Mostafa Shoa'ian, an independent Marxist by this time, killed in a street battle with security forces; in Mashhad, Fadaiyan assassinated Hosein Nahidi, a SAVAK interrogator.

June: Hamid Ashraf and a number of Fadaiyan leaders and members killed after a long gun-battle with security forces in Tehran.

October: Bahram Aram and two other Marxist Mojahedin members killed after a street battle in Tehran. Splinter Group broke away from the Fadaiyan to join the Tudeh.

1977

20 January: Inauguration of US President Carter.

May: Death of Dr Ali Shari'ati.

August: Prime Minister Amir Abbas Hoveyda replaced by Jamshid Amuzegar, as the imperial regime tried to improve cabinet performance.

September: Amnesty International criticised the imperial regime for violating human rights.

October: Publication of an open letter by a group of Iranian intellectuals asking the Shah to observe the constitution, free all political prisoners, and respect political freedoms and human rights.

November: Arrival of the Shah and Empress in Washington DC met by a violent and organised demonstration by Iranian student opposition. In a letter to the *ulama*, Ayatollah Khomeini asked them to follow the example of the secular intellectuals and write open letters to the Government demanding change.

December: Fadaiyan bombed the city administration building in Zanjan and Shahr-e Rayy in Tehran.

1978

January: President and Mrs Carter spent new year's eve in Tehran. Carter called Iran under the Shah an island of stability. Fadaiyan bombed the US-Iran cultural centre to mark the occasion.

7 January 1978: An article insulting to Ayatollah Khomeini appeared in a Tehran daily. This triggered revolutionary events that led to imperial regime's overthrow.

9 January: Demonstration by Qom theological school against the insulting article on Ayatollah Khomeini. In clashes with security forces a number of people were killed or wounded.

9 February: Fadaiyan bombed a police centre and the building of *Rastakhiz* Party in Qom.

18 February: During the commemoration of the fortieth day since the killing in Qom, Tabriz, Shiraz, Mashhad, Kerman and Isfahan witnessed violent demonstrations. A number of people were killed or wounded in Tabriz.

17 March: Fadaiyan bombed a police centre in Shams-e Tabrizi Ave in Tabriz.

30 March: During the commemoration of the fortieth day since the killing in Tabriz, Qom, Jahrom, Yazd, Kerman, Shiraz, Isfahan, Tehran, Mashhad and Ahvaz witnessed anti-imperial demonstrations.

31 March: The 'unholy alliance' of the red leftists and the black religious reactionaries was attacked by the *Rastakhiz* party. Fadaiyan bombed a police patrol in Mashhad.

6 April: Government announced the uncovering and destruction of a Soviet espionage network. It claimed to have proof of Soviet involvement in extremist dissent.

9 April: Hunger strike by Qezel Hesar political prisoners.

11 April: Demonstrations by Tehran and Science and Industry university students. A number of people wounded.

30 April : Marxist coup in Afghanistan.

9 May: Renewed anti-Government rioting swept across some 34 cities.

11 May: Large crowd of demonstrators in Tehran called for the overthrow of the regime and clashed with the security forces.

5 June: Demonstrations in Qom, Tehran and other cities in commemoration of the June 1963 uprising. The Shah dismissed Gen. Nasiri, the notorious head of the SAVAK, and replaced him with Gen. Naser Moqaddam.

5 August: The Society of Iranian Writers demanded the release of a number of political prisoners. The Shah declared that the next elections would be totally free.

6 August: With the start of the holy month of Ramadan, pro-Khomeini demonstrations intensified.

11 August: Mass violent demonstrations in Isfahan resulted in a number of dead and wounded. Martial law was declared in a number of cities in Isfahan province.

20 August: Large fire in the oil city of Abadan destroyed the Rex movie house and killed 327 people.

23 August: Demonstrations in Tehran: banks, cinems and cabarets were prime targets.

26 August: Amuzegar resigned as Premier, to be replaced by Ja'far Sharif-emami.

28 August: Liberation Movement demanded Shah's removal in a communique.

29 August: National Front, under Karim Sanjabi, demanded disbanding of SAVAK, freedom of speech and the trial of those guilty of official killings.

4 September: Peaceful mass demonstration in Tehran celebrating Fetr, the end of Ramadan.

5 September: Fadaiyan attacked and bombed a police command centre in Tehran.

8 September: Black Friday. Imperial regime declared martial law in Tehran and eleven other cities. Troops opened fire on demonstrators in Tehran, killing a number of people.

17 September: First major strike by oil industry workers over pay and political issues.

23 September: As schools opened, high school students joined anti-imperial demonstrations.

APPENDIX: CHRONOLOGY OF EVENTS (1941–83)

27 September: Beginning of a number of working-class strikes in oil, railway and water industries.

5 October: Ayatollah Khomeini left Najaf-Iraq for Paris;. 86 political prisoners released.

7 October: With the start of university terms, students joined demonstrations. Nationwide demonstrations in Tehran, Brujerd, Sari, Dezful, Rasht, Arak, Kerman, Mashhad and Zanjan.

9 October: Nationwide mass demonstrations in major cities, and strikes in key industries.

11 October: Political strike of newspapers. Three killed in Tehran University. Eight Americans injured in bomb blast.

11 October: Government gave in to the journalists' demands and ended censorship in Iran.

15 October: Nationwide strikes in key industries. Hunger strike by political prisoners of Tabriz.

17 October: In response to a call from Ayatollah Khomeini, a nationwide strike was observed in memory of those killed on Black Friday.

20 October: Freedom for a number of political prisoners. Some Tudeh members of the Military Organisation freed after 30 years.

31 October: Strike by 37,000 oil workers over wages and political demands brought the industry to a virtual standstill. Strikers demanded an end to martial law, release of all political prisoners, and the trial of Gen. Nasiri.

1 November: Iranian Airlines employees went on strike, demanding political concessions. Large march in Tehran commemorating the release of Ayatollah Taleqani. In clashes between troops and demonstrators, 23 were killed in Sanandaj and Zarshahr.

3 November: Sanjabi, head of the National Front, met Ayatollah Khomeini in Paris and joined forces with him.

5 November: Riots in Tehran. British Embassy attacked. Civilian cabinet of Sharif-emami's replaced by a military one, headed by Chief of Staff Gen. Gholam Ali Azhari.

6 November: In a nationwide television address, the Shah admitted to past mistakes and told the nation he had heard their demands.

19 November: Government freed 210 political prisoners; Shah renewed his pledge to end martial law and hold free elections.

21 November: Soviet Union warned United States not to interfere in Iran's internal affairs.

2 December: Thousands of demonstrators marched through the streets of Tehran and other cities in defiance of the curfew and clashed with troops. Various accounts put the death-toll between twelve and 70.

3 December: Ayatollah Khomeini called on soldiers to leave their units and for a resumption of strikes by oil workers.

4 December: Fadaiyan attacked a police station in Tehran.

10 December: Millions demonstrated in peaceful processions in Tehran and other cities.

177

REBELS WITH A CAUSE

11 December: 2,000,000 people demonstrated against the regime in Tehran. Demonstrations in other cities were violent. Two Imperial Guard solders attacked and killed a number of officers at the Lavizan garrison, the main base of the Imperial Guard.

2 December: Oil production dropped to 1.2 million barrels a day as workers, heeding Ayatollah Khomeini's appeal, refused to return to work after the religious holidays.

18 December: Oil and other industrial workers staged a general strike, in response to a call by Ayatollah Khomeini and the National Front.

30 December 30: Shapour Bakhtiyar appointed Prime Minister by the Shah.

1979

6 January: Bakhtiyar introduced his new cabinet to the Shah.

8 January: Violent demonstrations in Tabriz. State Department disclosed presence of Gen. Robert E. Huyser in Tehran.

13 January: Formation of a nine-man Regency Council announced by the Government, paving the way for the Shah's departure.

14 January: Iraj Eskandari removed as Tudeh first secretary.

15 January: Fadaiyan assassinated Maj. Majid Majidi, Tabriz police station commander, and his driver. Bakhtiyar's cabinet approved by the Majles.

16 January: Muhammad Reza Pahlavi, last Shah of Iran, and Empress Farah left the country unceremoniously and for the last time.

17 January: In a news conference, Carter expressed support for the Bakhtiyar Government.

21 January: 162 political prisoners released, among them Mas'ud Rajavi and Musa Khiabani, Moslem Mojahedin leaders.

1 February: Ayatollah Khomeini returned to Iran. Over 3,000,000 people greeted him and heard his call for the resignation of the Bakhtiyar Government and suggestion that he would name a new government soon.

5 February: Ayatollah Khomeini asked Mehdi Bazargan to form a government.

9 February: Fadaiyan held its first open commemoration of the Siyahkal operation as tens of thousands of supporters joined the organisation. The demonstration coincided with the beginning of armed clashes with the Imperial Guard.

10 February: As the Tehran airforce base rebelled against the Government, it was attacked by the Imperial Guard. The Fadaiyan, from its base in Tehran University, joined the people in attacking the Imperial Guard in defence of the airforce.

11 February: Battle between the people and the armed forces continued as the army's supreme council ordered the troops back to their barracks and assured Bazargan that the military was ready to recognise his Government; Bakhtiyar Government collapsed in the afternoon; Qasem Siadati, a leadership member of the Fadaiyan, was killed while trying to capture Tehran's main Radio station.

13 February: After its sixteenth plenum, the Tudeh, newly under the leadership of Nur al-Din Kianuri, expressed support for Ayatollah Khomeini's leadership.

14 February: Fadaiyan issued a list of demands to the Provisional Government, including equal rights for women, nationalisation of all industry, the expulsion of foreign military advisors, etc. US Embassy in Tehran attacked and taken over by Fadaiyan. American Ambassador, William H. Sullivan, held hostage for nearly two hours before being released by the Provisional Government.

15 February: The Revolutionary Toiler's Organisation of Kurdistan-Komuleh established.

16 February: Execution of the imperial regime's military and government officials started. The first group of four included Gen. Nasiri, former head of SAVAK, the military governors of Tehran and Isfahan, and the head of Iran's air cavitary units.

18 February: Islamic Republic Party established.

23 February: More than 70,000 people attended a rally by Fadaiyan in Tehran, and demanded the inclusion of Fadaiyan and other leftist groups in the Government.

25 February: The Moslem People's Republican Party established, based in Tabriz.

5 March: Ayatollah Khomeini ordered creation of Islamic Revolutionary Guards Corps. The establishment of The National Democratic Party.

18 March: Thousands of women staged demonstrations in Tehran and other cities, denouncing the Islamic dress code and Government actions against women's rights. Demonstrators were attacked by *hezbollah*.

18 March: Fadaiyan denounced forthcoming referendum for not allowing freedom of choice.

18–21 March: Heavy fighting in Sanandaj between autonomy-seeking Kurds and Government troops.

26–9 March: Fighting between Turkmans and Government forces in Gonbad-e Kavus

31 March: In a referendum, the formation of an Islamic Republic overwhelmingly approved.

2 April: Ceasefire announced in Gonbad-e Kavus.

21–2 April: Fighting broke out between Azari and Kurdish populations of Naqadeh. Government moved troops in to take control of the situation.

May: Ashraf Dehqani split from Fadaiyan.

1 May: Ayatollah Morteza Motahari assassinated in Tehran by an obscure Islamic group called Forqan. First free May Day parades held in different cities.

6 May: Islamic Revolutionary Guards Corps officially formed.

12 May: *Ayandegan*, a leading independent daily, stopped publishing because of a dispute with Ayatollah Khomeini, who had called it depraved.

17 May: US Senate adopted a resolution condemning the summary executions in Iran.

19 May: More than 100,000 people participated in a Tehran demonstration organised by National Democratic Front in support of *Ayandegan*. Demonstrators were attacked by *hezbollah*.

24 May: Hoj. Ali Akbar Hashemi-rafsanjani, an emerging voice in the new Islamic state, shot and wounded in Tehran. Forqan claimed responsibility.

29 May: Bloody clashes in the port city of Khorramshahr between government troops and armed groups affiliated with Arab parties of Khuzestan.

30 May: The daily *Jomhuri-ye Islami*, the official voice of the IRP, first published.

2 June: National Democratic Front accused the Ayatollah Khomeini of abandonning earlier pledges to keep clergy out of the Government's daily activities.

5 June: Ayatollah Khomeini warned lawyers, writers, Western-oriented intellectuals and other secular critics to take heed or be destroyed by the 'same fist that destroyed the Shah'.

6 June: Peace restored to Khorramshahr.

7 June: All private banks, including 14 with appreciable foreign investments, nationalised.

11 June: Ayatollah Khomeini accused Soviet Union of interfering in the internal affairs of Iran and Afghanistan.

14 June: Hemad Sheibani, member of the Fadaiyan, arrested while trying to smuggle in weapons and Muhammad Reza Sa'adati, leading member of the Moslem Mojahedin arrested and charged with spying for the Soviet Union.

22 June 22: Demonstration at Tehran University demanding a popularly elected constituent assembly to draft a new constitution broken up by the hezbollah. The Government had called for a council of experts, made of 75 members, to draft the new constitution.

25 June: All insurance companies were nationalised.

2 July: Muhammad Taqi Shahram, former leading member of the Marxist Mojahedin, arrested.

5 July: Virtually all of Iran's large-scale industries nationalised.

22 July: Fadaiyan announced Mostafa Madani and Roqieh Daneshgari as its candidates for the Assembly of Experts to draft the new constitution.

26 July: Fighting broke out between Kurdish fighters and government troops in Marivan.

3 August: Nationwide balloting held to elect the 73 members of the council of experts to draft the new constitution.

7 August: Revolutionary Guards attacked and occupied the office of daily newspaper *Ayandegan*.

12 August: Hezbollah attacked a demonstration called by the National Democratic Front to protest the new press law and the closing of *Ayandegan*: hundreds injured.

APPENDIX: CHRONOLOGY OF EVENTS (1941–83)

17 August: Heavy fighting between Kurdish fighters and government troops for the control of Paveh.

18 August: Some 400 killed and many more injured as government troops assaulted Paveh to crush rebellion.

19 August: Ayatollah Khomeini ordered general mobilisation of the armed forces to put down the Kurdish rebellion. Kurdish Democratic Party (KDP) banned. Sanandaj captured by KDP.

20 August: Ayatollah Khomeini ordered the closing of 22 publications, including those of the National Democratic Front, Tudeh, Paykar and Fadaiyan. Headquarters of the National Democratic Front, Tudeh and taken over by *hezbollah*.

21 August: Government troops executed a number of people in Paveh, including some affiliated to Fadaiyan, such as Dr Abol Qasem Rashvand-sardari.

23 August: Clashes between government troops and Kurdish rebels near Saqez. Revolutionary Guards captured Saqez as the Kurdish rebels captured regimental headquarters of gendarmerie in Sardasht.

27 August: Informal truce between government troops and Kurdish rebels.

28 August: Ayatollah Khomeini rejected Kurdish truce and ordered troops to crush rebellion.

4 September: Mahabad, the centre of Kurdish rebellion was captured by government troops.

6 September: Sardasht, last urban stronghold of Kurdish rebels, captured.

10 September: Ayatollah Mahmmud Taleqani died.

October: Fadaiyan held its first post-revolution plenum as internal differences brought it closer to a split.

7 October: 72-man troop convoy virtually wiped out by Kurdish rebels near Sardasht.

20 October: Kurdish rebels retook Mahabad.

30 October: Women's demonstrations in Tehran for equal rights attacked by hezbollah.

1 November: Bazargan and aides met Brzezinski in Algiers, and discussed US-Iran relations.

4 November: Bazargan widely criticised for meeting the Americans; US Embassy in Tehran attacked and seized by students followers of the Imam.

5 November: British Embassy in Tehran attacked.

6 November: Bazargan cabinet collapsed, and its duties taken over by the Revolutionary Council.

7 November: Five famous members of the Iranian Writers Association, members of the Tudeh, announced support for hostage taking.

20 November: KDP announced unilateral ceasefire in Kurdestan.

26 November: Office of armed forces' joint chiefs of staff confirmed ceasefire in Kurdestan.

2–3 December: In a nationwide plebiscite, the new Islamic constitution was approved. Referendum widely boycotted in Azarbaijan, Kurdestan and Baluchestan.

5 December: After Grand Ayatollah Kazem Shari'atmadari denounced the new constitution, hezbollah attacked his residence in Qom.

6 December: Fighting broke out in Tabriz as Shari'atmadari's supporters took to the streets to object to his treatment in Qom.

9 December 9: Shari'atmadari's supporters, organised by the Moslem People's Republican Party, battled government troops for control of Tabriz's radio and television stations.

13 December: A huge crowd of 700,000 people demonstrated in Tabriz in support of Shari'atmadari, denounced the new constitution, asked for release of Azari dissidents and removal of the non-Azari militia from East Azarbaijan.

18 December: Forqan gunmen shot and killed Muhammad Mofatteh, an important cleric and dean of the Divinity College of Tehran.

28 December: IRI denounced Soviet occupation of Afghanistan.

1980

4–9 January: Clashes in Tabriz continued.

10 January: Fighting in Tabriz subsided after Shari'atmadari called for calm and the Government imposed a curfew in the province. The leader of Forqan and 15 of his followers arrested.

25 January: In a nationwide election Abol Hasan Bani-sadr was elected as the first president of the IRI.

10 February: Death of four Turkman council leaders and Fadaiyan associates.

20 March: The second round of armed clashes between the IRI and Kurdish rebels started.

25 April: United States failed in its attempt to rescue American hostages in Tehran.

27 April: On the anniversary of the Afghan coup, Soviet Embassy in Tehran attacked.

May: First Majles elected.

June: Majority-Minority split in Fadaiyan. A group of pro-Tudeh members broke away from the Kurdish Democratic Party; A coup attempt against the IRI was uncovered and its participants arrested.

29 July: Muhammad Reza Pahlavi, last Shah of Iran, died in exile.

August: Muhammad Ali Raja'i appointed Premier of the IRI. Muhammad Taqi Shahram executed.

17 September: Saddam Hussein unilaterally abrogated the 1975 Iran-Iraq agreement.

22 September: Iraqi armed forces staged massive attack on Iranian territory, starting the Iran-Iraq War.

1981

20 January: American hostages in Tehran released as Ronald Reagan assumed presidency.

March: Fadaiyan Majority's second plenum and the Tudeh's 17 plenum approved a merger between the two. Fadaiyan Left-Wing Majority broke away from the Majority. Mass rally by Bani-sadr and Mojahedin supporters turned into open confrontation with *hezbollah*.

20 June: In a massive clash between the Moslem Mojahedin and the IRI, open warfare started between the opposition and the Government. In the next few days executions of captive opposition figures, including Sa'id Soltan-pur of the Fadaiyan Minority and Mohsen Fazel of the Paykar, started. Bani-sadr removed as President.

28 June: Massive blast at the headquarters of the IRP killed more than 70 top leaders.

August: Massive blast in the Prime Minister's office in Tehran killed Prime Minister Bahonar and President Raja'i. Split in the Fadaiyan (Dehqani) group.

24 August: Fadaiyan (Liberation Army) started campaign of guerrilla warfare in northern forest areas.

5 October: Death of Siyamak Asadian, head of Fadaiyan Minority's military operations.

December: Fadaiyan Minority's congress in Tehran. Mohsen Shaneh-chi, member of Minority central committee, killed in shoot-out with security forces.

7 December: Split in Fadaiyan Majority.

1982

26 January: Communist League took over the city of Amol.

10 February: Ali Reza Sepasi-ashtiani and Hosein Ruhani, both Paykar central committee members, arrested.

11 February: Musa Khiabani and a number of other Mojahedin activists killed.

4 March: Abdol Karim Sabburi, Fadaiyan (Liberation Army) central committee member, killed.

12 March: A number of Fadaiyan Minority central committee members and other members killed, and the organisation's printing and distribution centres closed down.

24 March: Muhammad Reza Hormati-pur, Fadaiyan (Liberation Army) central committee member killed, signalling the end of this group's operations in the forests of the north.

April: Defection of Velademir Kuzichkin, KGB operative at Soviet Embassy in Tehran.

24 May: Iran won battle of Khorramshahr, liberating the only major city occupied by the invading Iraqi forces.

June: Socialist Revolutionary faction broke away from Fadaiyan Minority.

1983

1 February: The beginning of a series of blows against the Tudeh and the Fadaiyan Majority.

30 April: Second wave of Tudeh arrests in Tehran and other cities.

1 May: First televised confessions of Tudeh leaders, including Kianuri and Muhammad E'temad-zadeh. More Tudeh members arrested in different cities.

3 May: Mohsen Reza'i, commander of the Revolutionary Guards, presented Ayatollah Khomeini with full report on Tudeh arrests. Confessions of five more Tudeh leaders on charges of spying for the Soviet Union.

5 May: 18 Soviet diplomats expelled from Iran on charges of interfering in the country's internal affairs. Ayatollah Khomeini congratulated security forces on Tudeh arrests. Tudeh declared illegal.

June: Mehdi Same', old Fadaiyan member, purged from Minority, along with his supporters.

10 October: IRI started radio broadcasts in the Azari language from Tabriz, and for Soviet Azarbaijani listeners.

7 December: Trial of Bahram Afzali, former commander of IRI navy and Tudeh member. He confessed to passing military secrets to the Tudeh without knowing the party was spying. Kianuri and Partovi acted as prosecution witnesses. Execution of convicted leaders of Communist League.

NOTES ON THE TEXT

NOTES ON INTRODUCTION

1   For a study of the Jangal Movement and the role of the ICP, see Cosroe Chaqueri, *The Soviet Socialist Republic of Iran, 1920–1921: Birth of the Trauma* (Pittsburgh and London: University of Pittsburgh Press, 1995).

2   For more on Sultanzadeh and Amuoghlu, see Cosroe Chaqueri, *Avetis Sultanzadeh: the Forgotten Revolutionary Theoretician* (Tehran: Padzahr, 1985); Rahim Rezazadeh-malek, *Haydar Khan Amuoghli* (Tehran: Donya Publishers, 1973).

3   For more on the group, see the following sources written by two of its participants: Bozorg Alavi, *Panjah va se nafar* (*The Group of Fifty Three*) (Tehran: Javid Publications, 1978); Anvar Khameh'i, *Panjah nafar va se nafar* (*Fifty Persons and Three Persons*) (Saarbruken, Germany: Navid Publications, nd).

4   Ervand Abrahamian has published a document recently which seems to suggest that the group was affiliated by the Comintern. Nevertheless, unless more convincing information is found, the issue remains unresolved. See *Kankash*, no. 7, Winter 1991, 165–72.

5   Hamid Ahmadi, *Tarikhcheh-ye ferqeh-ye Iran va 'grouh-e arani'* (A History of Revolutionary Republican Party of Iran and the 'Arani Group') (Berlin: Society for Social Research of Iran, 1992). Ahmadi has also written follow-up articles arguing and defending his point in *Arash* (Paris) nos 33 (December 1993) and 34 (January 1994).

6   Khosrow Shakeri, *Arash* (Paris) no 32 (November 1993).

7   For more on Alavi's life, see Najmi Alavi, *Sargozasht-e Morteza Alavi* (*Morteza Alavi's Life*) (np: Mard-e Emruz Publications, 1991).

8   Sepehr Zabih, *The Communist Movement in Iran* (Berkeley, Los Angeles: University of California Press, 1966).

9   Ervand Abrahamian, *Iran Between Two Revolutions* (Princeton: Princeton University Press, 1988).

10   Sepehr Zabih, *The Left in Contemporary Iran* (Stanford, California: Hoover Institution Press, 1986).

185

REBELS WITH A CAUSE

NOTES ON CHAPTER 1

1   The Iranian constitution of 1906–7 was disregarded during the rule of Reza Shah (1925–41), except in form. The period 1941–53 represented a relative return to constitutional rule. For a study of this period see Fakhreddin Azimi, *Iran the Crisis of Democracy* (New York: St Martin's Press, 1989). The 1953 coup and the events following it once again undermined the constitution, as the Shah moved to impose his authority. Only in late 1978, in the midst of revolutionary upheaval, did the Shah decree a return to the 1906 constitution, by which time it was too late.

2   James A. Bill, *The Eagle and the Lion* (London, New Haven: Yale University Press, 1988), 98.

3   *Ibid.*, 105–13.

4   Nikki R. Keddie, *Roots of Revolution: an Interpretive History of Modern Iran* (London, New Haven: Yale University Press, 1981), 142.

5   Ervand Abrahamian, *Iran Between Two Revolutions* (Princeton: Princeton University Press, 1982), 422.

6   Some Western newspapers went as far as to call the Tudeh (the principal communist organisation at this point), the only real party in Iran. For example the daily *Kayhan* quoted the *Christian Science Monitor*, in 1950, suggesting that the Tudeh was 'the only organisation which can be called a political party. See *Gozashteh cheragh-e rah-e ayandeh [The Past is the Light to the Future Path]* (np: Jami, nd), 522.

7   *Ibid.*, 135.

8   Bizhan Jazani, *Tarh-e jame'eh shenasi va mabani-ye esteratezhi-ye jonbesh-enqelabi-ye khalq-e Iran (The Sociological Plan and the Strategic Foundation of Iranian People's Revolutionary Movement)* (Tehran: Mizan Publications, 1979), 17–21.

9   Anvar Khameh'i, *Forsat-e bozorg-e az dast rafteh (The Grand Lost Opportunity)* (Saarbrucken, Germany: Navid Publications, nd), 20–1; Iraj Eskandari, *Khaterat-e siyasi (Political Memoirs)* (Saint Cloud Cedex, France: Democratic People's Party of Iran Publications, nd), vol. IV, 54; Ehsanollah Tabari, *Kazh raheh, khaterati az hezbe-e Tudeh (The Diverted Path, Memories of the Tudeh Party)* (Tehran: Amir Kabir Publications, 1987), p43.

10   For the Tudeh history in this period see Abrahamian, *Iran*, 281–325.

11   There is great uncertainty about the Tudeh's role in this attempt on the Shah's life. Much evidence suggests that a faction within the Tudeh was responsible for the attempted assassination, and that the majority of Tudeh leadership had no knowledge of it, or knew but took no action. It must be noted that at this point the Tudeh was a legal party, and for it to be associated with an attempt on the Shah's life was contrary to its policy. It seems that the act was carried out by a faction within the party and headed by Nur al-Din Kianuri, or that Kianuri was aware of it. That the party was taken totally by surprise,

NOTES ON THE TEXT

and failed to protect its leaders from arrest seems to support the argument that only one faction of the party was involved. The issue of factionalism in the Tudeh leadership, and its effects on the party, will be examined later. For arguments that allege Kianuri's involvement, see the memoirs of two Tudeh leaders: Iraj Eskandari, vol. III, 34–40; Fereidun Keshavarz, *Man mottaham mikonam* (*I Condemn*) (Tehran: Ravaq Publications, nd), 118–34. In his memoirs, Kianuri vehemently denied any role in the assassination, but suggested that he was aware of it and reported it to other leading members of the party, who responded that the party should have nothing to do with it. See Nur al-Din Kianuri, *Khaterat-e Nur al-Din Kianuri,* (*Memoirs of Nur al-Din Kianuri*) (Tehran: Didgah Institute, 1992), 183–89. It must be noted that his memoirs were written while he was in captivity in Iran; therefore Kianuri's recollections should be used with care, and only in conjunction with other sources.

12   Abrahamian, *Iran,* 347.
13   *Ibid.,* 353. For more on the party's working-class base and activity see: Habib Ladjevardi, *Labor Unions and Autocracy in Iran* (Syracuse: Syracuse University Press, 1985), 50–76.
14   For more on the Tudeh's class base in this period see Abrahamian, *Iran,* 326–382.
15   *The Past,* 191.
16   Kavtaradze, a Soviet Georgian, had just been released from jail under Stalin after serving a ten-year sentence.
17   *Mosaddeq va nehzat-e melli-ye Iran* (*Mosaddeq and the National Movement of Iran*) (Solon, Ohio: Society of Islamic Students in America and Canada, 1978), 37.
18   *The Past,* 207–8.
19   *Mosaddeq and the National Movement,* 40.
20   *The Past,* 198.
21   *Ibid.,* 201.
22   Javanshir's only reference to this subject is: 'Another important issue that did not allow the southern oil issue to remain hidden was the Iran-Soviet co-operation for the exploration of northern oil fields. There have been, and still are, many non-truths told by anti-communist circles about the northern oil, which is outside our discussion and must be looked at later'. F.M. Javanshir, *Tajrobeh-ye 28 Mordad* (*The Experience of 28th of Mordad*) (Tehran: Tudeh Party Publications, 1980), 35. Kambakhsh's account makes no mention of the party's position on the Soviet sphere of influence and the legitimacy of Soviet demands. Instead, he tries to shift the emphasis to his point that the Soviets, unlike the British and Americans, were not trying to exploit Iran, and were offering a much better deal. He also suggests that were it not for the Soviet offer, the British and the Americans would not have backed down, and Sa'ed would have gone ahead with negotiating new contracts. See Abdol Samad Kambakhsh, *Nazari beh jonbesh-e kargari dar*

Iran (*A Look at the Working Class Movement in Iran*) (np: Golbarg Publications, nd), 86–91.

23   *Mosaddeq and the National Movement*, 76.

24   Bill, 75.

25   Javanshir, reviewing the issue in 1980, suggested that the formation of the society was a necessary step in exposing American imperialism at a time when some National Front leaders viewed the United States as the saviour of exploited people. See Javanshir, 94–95. This book was written by Farajollah (Javad) Mizani, aka F.M. Javanshir, as his dissertation in 1950s. It was revised and published by the party in 1980, and represents the views of the dominant faction of the time. The book is full of distortions, making it worthless as an objective historical study. But it is an important document as a representation of the Tudeh view of the period. Mizani was arrested in the 1983 crackdown on the Tudeh, and was executed in 1988. For the society's attack on Mosaddeq, see Javan, 'Donya chashm beh mobarezeh-ye melal-e sharq darad' ('The World is Watching the Struggle of the People of the East') in *Kabutar-e Solh*, vol. III, no. 1, May 1952. This article was written by Jahangir Behrouz, editor of the publication, and reprinted in Khosrow Shakeri, (ed.), *Asnad-e tarikhi-ye jonbesh-e kargari, sosiyal demokrasi va komonisti-ye Iran* (*Historical Documents: The Workers' Social-Democratic and Communist Movement in Iran*), vol. I, (Florence, Italy: Mazdak, 1974), 348–57.

26   In trying to explain the party's slogan on nationalising the southern oil instead of the oil industry as a whole, Javanshir suggests that the Soviet interest was not a factor at all, and that any suggestions to that effect are by anti-communists and anti-revolutionaries. He states four reasons why the Tudeh picked a slogan which he admits was inaccurate. None of these reasons, such as the Tudeh's lack of understanding of the National Front coalition or the party's infantile communism, explains why the party was against oil nationalisation as a whole (only southern oil had been exploited by this point). On the other hand the southern oil slogan, if successful, would have left the northern oil question open for negotiation at a more opportune time. See Javanshir, 103–5.

27   *The Past*, 523-524.

28   *Ibid.*, 527.

29   *Ibid..*, 530.

30   *Ibid.*, 534–7.

31   See Babak Amir-khosravi, *Nazari az darun beh naqsh-e hezb-e Tudeh-ye Iran* (*A Look From Within at the Role of the Tudeh Party of Iran*) (Tehran: Didgah Institute, 1996), 339–9; *The Past*, 574–8.

32   Javanshir, 276–82.

33   Jazani, *Sociological Plan*, 43.

34   From the publications of the Tudeh's central committee, as quoted in Tabari, 161. Ehsanollah Tabari (1916–89), was the chief ideologue of

NOTES ON THE TEXT

the party from the mid-1960s until 1983. This book was written by him while he was imprisoned in Iran, and so the content of the book should be looked at with care. While Tabari was a Tudeh apologist throughout his life, in this book he portrays the Tudeh negatively. Although it seems that much of what he wrote on the Tudeh is correct, I have used this book only on such occasions as it could be verified by other sources, or when the information was uncontroversial.

35   Ahmad Shamlu, *Kashefan-e forutan-e shokaran* (*The Humble Discoverer of Hemlock*) (Tehran: Ebtekar Publications, nd), 15–16. The poem was also referred to as *Marg-e Nazli*.

36   Olovvi's execution remains a mystery to this day. After his arrest, his letter of regret was published in newspapers alongside other Tudeh leaders. But according to some Tudeh members who were either in prison with him or know of this episode, he never wrote any letters, and this was the cause of his execution in May 1959. According to these sources, the Olovvi letter was written by his brother in his name. See Kianuri, 347–8; interview with Muhammad Baqer Mo'meni, Los Angeles, 10 May 1993; *idem.*, 'Tarhi az yek tasvir' ('A Sketch of a Portrait'), *Seda-ye Mo'aser*, no. 13, June 1979. Mo'meni was in the same prison with Olovvi, and met him daily for a number of years. Another explanation was provided by Qoreishi, who was also kept in the same prison with Olovvi. According to him, Olovvi's execution had more to do with the Shah's two strongmen in charge of repressing the opposition. The two, Gen. Teimur Bakhtiyar and Gen. Hosein Azmudeh are said to have had different policies toward the Tudeh leadership. Bakhtiyar believed that once the Tudeh leaders were co-operative, and full propaganda use was made of them, their lives should be spared. But Azmudeh, the notorious military court prosecutor after the 1953 coup, wanted them dead, regardless of co-operation. Qoreishi believes that Bakhtiyar's policy prevailed eventually, but not before Olovvi's execution. See Interview with Amanollah Qoreishi, London, 20 June 1992.

37   Jazani, *Sociological Plan*, 74.

38   *Defa'iat-e Khosrow Roozbeh qahreman-e melli* (*The Court Defence of Khosrow Roozbeh, the National Hero*) (Washington DC: Asia Books and Periodicals, 1978), 72–3. This document is the censored version of Roozbeh's court defence passed to the party by the Soviets. The party censored those segments of the document which referred to assassinations, and criticised the party leadership for fleeing Iran. See Kianuri, 384.

39   *Seyr-e komonizm dar Iran* (*The Development of Communism in Iran*) (Tehran: Kayhan Publications, 1957). It has been suggested that the book was written by Amanollah Qoreishi, head of the Tudeh's Tehran Organisation and a central committee member. Indeed this has been the popular belief until now. See Jazani, *Sociological Plan*, 75; Kianuri, 353–4. Qoreishi denied writing the book in an interview in London on

7 August 1990. It seems that no matter who wrote this book, it was done by a high-ranking Tudeh member with detailed information on how the party was run. Ali Ziba'i, *Komonizm dar Iran* (*Communism in Iran*) (np: np, 1964). Ziba'i was a colonel in the armed forces and a notorious torturer of the imperial regime's opponents. This book was dedicated to the Shah and, like *Development of Communism*, is a detailed account of communist activities in Iran from the constitutional revolution to the early 1960s. The most interesting section of the book contains some of Roozbeh's written confessions, which shed light on some of the questions regarding the Tudeh and the Military Organisation. Nevertheless, it is highly doubtful that it was written by Ziba'i. Details of the book suggest that one or more of the Tudeh leaders must have been involved in providing information, although Ziba'i may have been the compiler or editor.

40 Ruhollah Abbasi, *Khaterat-e yek afsar-e Tudeh'i 1330–1335* (*The Memoirs of a Tudeh Officer 1951–1956*) (Montreal, Canada: Farhang Publications, 1989), 8.

41 *Communism in Iran*, 628–9. For more on this, see Ahmad Shafaie, *Qiyyam-e afsaran-e Khorasan va si va haftsal sal zendegi dar shoravi* (*The Rebellion of Khorasan Offices and Thirty Seven Years in the Soviet Union*) (Tehran: Ketab Sara, 1986); Abol Hasan Tafreshian, *Qiyyam-e afsaran-e Khorasan* (*The Rebellion of Khorasan Officers*) (Tehran: Atlas, 1988); Muhammad Hosein Khosrow-panah, 'Baznegari-ye yek vaqe'eh: Qiyam-e Afsaran-e Khorasan' ('Revisiting an Incident: The Rebellion of the Khorasan Officers'), *Negah-e No*, no. 32, Spring 1997.

42 See Roozbeh's confessions in *Communism in Iran*, 624–7.

43 'Interview With Fereidun Azarnur', in *Rah-e Azadi*, no. 24, September–October 1992. Azarnur was an active member of the Military Organisation.

44 Jazani gives the highest number while Kianuri gives the lowest number in an article in 1980. Tabari numbered them at 600. See Jazani, *Sociological Plan*, 71; Tabari, 171; Nur al-Din Kianuri, 'The Tudeh Party and Dr Mosaddeq' in *Nameh Mardom*, 4 April 1980. Azar-nur, after considering all accounts and numbers, gives the most realistic estimate of 491: *Rah-e Azadi*, 24.

45 *Rah-e Azadi*, no. 24, 15.

46 Abrahamian, *Iran*, 338.

47 *Ibid.*

48 Jazani, *Sociological Plan*, 71.

49 *Rah-e Azadi*, no. 24, 13–17.

50 Kianuri, 297. One of the most complete volumes on the Military Organisation was provided by the coup organisers, based on the confessions of arrested officers. This volume also includes the names and ranks of all Tudeh officers arrested. See *Ketab-e siyah* (*The Black Book*) (Tehran: Matbu'at Publishers, 1955). Also see Muhammad Hosein Khosrowpanah, 'Tarikhche-ye zohur va soqut-e sazman-e afsaran-e

NOTES ON THE TEXT

hezb-e Tudeh-ye Iran' ('A Brief History of the Rise and Fall of the Offices Organisation of the Tudeh Party of Iran'), *Negah-e No*, no. 33, Summer 1997.

51 Muhammad Ali Amu'i, *Dord-e Zamaneh* (*The Drag of Age*) (Tehran: Anzan Publishers, 1998), 72–3.

52 Keshavarz, 13; Eskandari, vol. III, 40–2.

53 The trials, executions and sentencing of the Tudeh officers made heroes of them. Unlike the Tudeh leaders, the officers showed courage in the face of torture and death. On some occasions, this heroism caused myths. One such myth, which has aroused controversy, was created around a poem written by a National Front supporter. The poet, Dr Haydar Reqabi, pen name Haleh, wrote *mara bebus* (*Kiss Me*), in 1954. This coincided with the sentencing of the first group of Tudeh officers. It became popular belief that the poem was written by a Tudeh officer, supposedly Col. Ezatollah Siyamak, as his last farewell to his daughter. During the following years the poem was made into a popular song which still exists. The poet's efforts to clear up this question remained unsuccessful until he died in 1987. See Haydar Reqabi, *Sha'er-e shahr-e ma* (*Our Town's Poet*) (Berkeley, California: np, 1969), 20.

54 For the plenum's official proceedings, see Khosrow Shakeri, *Historical Documents*, vol. I, 361–401; *Asnad va didgahha* (*Documents and Perspectives*) (Tehran: Tudeh Publications, 1979), 361–83. The complete text of the fourth plenum was never published. The former document was published by an independent researcher, while the latter was published by the party after the revolution. There is a major discrepancy between the two, in that the one published by the Tudeh has a number of paragraphs which support Kianuri's position on his role during the 1953 coup and exonerate him from any major wrong-doing. According to Babak Amir-khosravi, a Tudeh central committee member who was a leading party member until 1983, the paragraphs were added by Kianuri, under whose supervision the proceedings of the fourth plenum were published in 1979. See: *Adineh*, no. 83, September 1993, 19.

55 Keshavarz, 72; Tabari, 165.

56 Shakeri, *Historical Documents*, vol. I, 364.

57 According to one scholar, some of these radical demonstrations, which helped alienate the nationalist Government from the Tudeh, were in fact promoted by CIA operatives. See Mark J. Gasiorowski, *US Policy and the Shah* (Ithaca, N.: Cornell University Press, 1991), 78. Kianuri, who was at the centre of the party's decision-making, denies any such connection. See Kianuri, 270–1.

58 Keshavarz, 42.

59 Ardeshir Avanessian, *Khaterat 1320–1326* (*Memoirs 1941–1946*) (Cologne, Germany: The People's Democratic Party of Iran Publications, 1990), 62. Ardeshir (Ardashes) Avanessian (1904–90)

was a member of the Iranian Communist Party in the 1920s. He spent the 1930s in Reza Shah's prisons, and joined the Tudeh after its establishment. He was a dogmatic thinker, and belonged to the radical wing of the party, being staunchly pro-Soviet and Stalinist. His alias was Ahan (iron), chosen to resemble Stalin.

60   Interview with Amanollah Qoreishi, London, 20 June 1992.

61   Tabari's case should be considered with care. After the coup and the party's move into exile, he gradually became the party's chief ideologue, and after the 1979 revolution its undisputed one. To many, both Tudeh members and otherwise, he was a great thinker and cultured man. Yet some Tudeh leaders who knew him personally, ie Kianuri and Eskandari, have suggested that he was a weak personality and a clear opportunist who usually sided with the radical faction because of its close connection with Soviet intelligence. Here he is depicted as a thinker content to put his talent at the disposal of whoever wielded most power.

62   Anvar Khameh'i, *Panjah nafar va se nafar* (*Fifty Persons and Three Persons*) (Saarbrucken, Germany: Navid Publications, nd), 30–63; Keshavarz, 28–31; Eskandari, vol. I, 35–7; Avanessian, 65–6; Shaker, *Historical Documents*, vol. XV (Tehran: Padzahr Publications, nd), 9–14. Kianuri, Kambakhsh's closest supporter in the party, and his brother-in-law, denied that these claims had any validity. See Kianuri, 56–8.

63   Keshavarz, 28–31; Avanessian, 65.

64   Tabari's account of the members of the two factions is in contrast to all other sources. According to him, the Kianuri-Kambakhsh-Avanessian faction was the moderate faction and the Yazdi-Radmanesh-Eskandari faction was the radical one. His assessment does not match the facts. See Tabari, 170.

65   For more on this see Amir-khosravi, 251–69.

66   Tabari, 160; Keshavarz, 79–80.

67   In his confessions, Roozbeh admitted to taking part in the assassinations of the said five party members (from 1952 on), which included, beside Lankarani, Mohsen Salehi, Dariush Ghafari, Parviz Nava'i and Aqa Barar Fateri. He suggested that the assassinations were ordered by the party leadership and carried out by the intelligence branch of the Military Organisation. See: *Communism in Iran*, 538–54. Kianuri has suggested that the whole party leadership in Iran knew about the assassinations and approved them. This may explain why Keshavarz – Kambakhsh's and Kianuri's most persistent accuser, calling them the masterminds behind the squad, but who was out of the country at this point – did not know about them. During the party's fourth plenum, the issue of the squad was reviewed, and Kianuri and Kambakhsh were exonerated. See Kianuri, 149–64.

68   Keshavarz, 46.

69   Kianuri, 196–9.

NOTES ON THE TEXT

70 Keshavarz, 97–98; Tabari, 31–2.
71 *Communism in Iran*, 430–3; Kianuri, 149–64.
72 Kianuri, 106–7.
73 The correspondence was published in Europe and republished in Kianuri's memoirs. See: Kianuri, 307–35.
74 Tabari, 168.
75 Keshavarz, 72.
76 Tabari, 167–8; Keshavarz, 72–3; Eskandari, vol. III, 43–4.
77 According to a source published by the Islamic Government, Rostam Aliev is in fact Heydar Ali Rezaoqlu Aliev, current President of the republic of Azarbaijan and Soviet Communist Party politburo member between 1982 and 1987. But according to official data, the latter was born to an Iranian emigré family in Nakhjivan on 10 May 1923. This would make Aliev only eighteen years old at the time of his involvement in Iran in 1941. Even if he is slightly older, the above assertion seems highly unlikely. See *Siyasat va sazman-e hezb-e Tudeh az aghaz ta forupashi* (*The Politics and Organisation of the Tudeh Party from the Beginning to its Disintegration*), vol. 1, (Tehran: The Institute for Political Study and Research, 1991), 99–100.
78 Avanessian, 39.
79 *Tarikh-e hezb-e komonist-e shoravi* (*The History of Soviet Communist Party*) (np: The Tudeh Party Publications, 1979), 686–94. The Soviet policy toward the Mosaddeq Government was basically a neutral one, which meant while it did not attack it, it did not offer much help either. This meant an absence of policy, and explains why the Tudeh leadership, which had come to depend on Soviet advice, was able to chart its own course without much consideration of the Soviet view. For a discussion of this see Amir-khosravi, 269–79
80 For a discussion of the CPSU's relation with fraternal parties at the height of Stalin's power, see Fernando Claudin, *The Communist Movement, From Comintern to Cominform*, vol. II (London, New York: Monthly Review Press, 1975).
81 Keshavarz, 79–80.
82 *Ibid.*, 28.
83 *Ibid.*, 45.
84 Eskandari, *Hezb-e Tudeh va shoravi* (*The Tudeh Party and the Soviet Union*), in *Fasli Dar Gol-e Sorkh*, no. 3, Fall 1986, 25–6.
85 *Ibid.*, 29.
86 Eskandari, *Memoirs*, vol. IV, 66–9.
87 Eskandari, *Daru-ye e'teraf* (*Confession Drug*), in *Fasli Dar Gol-e Sorkh*, no.1, Summer 1985, 38–9.
88 Kianuri, 53.
89 Gasiorowski, *Foreign Policy*, 69–70, 78–9; 'The 1953 Coup d'etat in Iran' in *International Journal of Middle East Studies*, vol. 19, no. 3, August 1987, endnote 76. The Lankarani brothers were Sheikh Hosein, Ahmad, Morteza, Mostafa and Hesam. The first one was a

militant cleric, the other four members of the Tudeh. According to Kianuri, the Lankaranis were close associates of Kambakhsh, and were introduced to the party by him; Kianuri, 152–53. Hesam Lankarani, the youngest brother, was assassinated by a Tudeh hit-squad on the orders of the party executive committee. Morteza Lankarani conducted an interview as part of Harvard University's Oral History of Iran. This long interview is restricted until the year 2000, and may shed some light when it becomes available.

90   Interview with Feridun Azarnur, as published in *Rah-e Azadi*, no. 26, February 1993, 20–5; Eskandari, *Memoirs*, vol. IV, 5–11. Both Azarnur and Eskandari imply that Kianuri may have been an agent of MI-6, and leave the question open, but admit the inadequacy of proof.

91   Ervand Abrahamian, 'Communism and Communalism in Iran: The Tudeh Party and the Firqah-I Dimukrat' in *International Journal of Middle East Studies*, no. 1, 1970, 291.

92   For more on Pishehvari, see Shakeri; *Historical Documents*, vol. III (Sweden: Iran's Book Centre, 1985), 129–38.

93   *The Past*, 274.

94   For more on Azarbaijan and the Russo-Iranian wars, see Muriel Atkin, *Russia and Iran 1780–1828* (Minneapolis: University of Minnesota Press, 1980).

95   See *Encyclopedia Iranica*, ed. Ehsan Yarshater, vol. III, (London and New York: Routledge and Kegan Paul, 1989), 205–15; *Encyclopedia of Islam*, editorial committee, new edition, vol. I (Leiden, Netherlands: E.S. Brill, 1960), 188–91.

96   David B. Nissman, *The Soviet Union and Iranian Azarbaijan: The Use of Nationalism for Political Penetration*, (London: Westview Press, 1987), 31–2.

97   Avanessian, 114–16.

98   *Ibid.*, 116–37.

99   Abrahamian, *Communism and Communalism*, 297–306.

100   Keshavarz, 61–2.

101   Abrahamian, *Communism and Communalism*, 311.

102   Keshavarz, 62.

103   For more on the Soviet role in Azarbaijan, see Ladjevardi, 105–17.

104   For more on the ADP and its one-year venture as the autonomous Government of Azarbaijan, see Abrahamian, *Communism and Communalism*, 306–15; Zabih, 95–115; *The Past*, 271–333; Touraj Atabaki, *Azarbaijan: Ethnicity and Autonomy in Twentieth-Century Iran* (London: I.B. Tauris, 1993), 99–179.

105   Pishehvari died in Baku after a car accident. He survived the accident, and was taken to a hospital, where his friends said he was doing well that evening, but he died the next day. According to Keshavarz, Pishehvari had developed deep differences with Baqerov over the reasons for the ADP's defeat. For example, one night at a dinner party in Baku, Baqerov had suggested that the ADP had been defeated

NOTES ON THE TEXT

because the party did not emphasise enough the unity of the two Azarbaijans. Pishehvari had responded that it had been because the ADP did not adequately emphasise the unity of Iranian Azarbaijan with the rest of Iran. This response was characteristic of Pishehvari, who was known for his straight-forwardness, but this opinion enraged Baqerov, and may have contributed to Pishehvari's death. See Keshavarz, 65.

106 Tabari and Eskandari each claimed that the idea of unity was his. See Eskandari, *Memoirs*, vol. III, 68; Tabari, 192–3.

107 For a more detailed description of the union, see Eskandari, *Memoirs*, vol. III, 72–93; Keshavarz, 70–5; Tabari, 192–7; Kianuri, 384–91. For more on the proceedings of the seventh plenum and the unity conference, see *Documents and Perspectives*, 393–410.

108 For Maleki's life see the introduction to his memoirs written by M.A. Homayoun Katouzian, see Khalil Maleki, *Khaterat-e siyasi (Political Memoirs)* (np: Jebheh, 1981), 1–174.

109 For the content of both declarations, see *The Past*, 435–8.

110 Tabari claimed to be the person in charge of meeting Aliev and discussing the declarations. He suggested that Aliev, after long discussions in which he made references to Marxist texts, convinced him that the party should recant some of its positions: see Tabari, 80–1.

111 For the content of the declaration, see *The Past*, 442.

112 Anvar Khameh'i, *Az enshe'ab ta konun (From the Split Till Now)* (Saarbrucken, Germany: Navid Publications, nd), 10.

113 For more on different tendencies in the group, see Abrahamian, *Iran*, 306–12; Khameh'i, *From Split*, 94–100; Zabih, 124–41.

114 For more on the Toilers' Party and Maleki's role, see Katouzian's introduction in Maleki, 92–8; Homa Katouzian, *Musaddiq and the Struggle For Power in Iran* (London, New York: I.B. Tauris, 1990), 95–113.

115 *Ibid.*, 98.

116 *Ibid.*, pp114–20.

117 For more on the Kennedy administration's role in implementing reforms in Iran, see Bill, 131–54; Afsaneh Najmabadi, *Land Reform and Social Change in Iran* (Salt Lake City: University of Utah Press, 1987), 59–99.

118 *Ibid.*, 9–10.

119 The coup was led by Gen. Valiollah Qarahni. He was appointed Chairman of Joint Chiefs of the armed forces after the 1979 revolution and assassinated shortly after. For more on this, see Mark J. Gasiorowski, 'The Qarani Affair and Iranian Politics', in *International Journal of Middle East Studies*, vol. 25, no. 4, November 1993, 625–44.

120 Najmabadi, 76.

121 For more on the opposition in this period, see Keddie, *Roots of Revolution*, 142–60.

122 Eric Hooglund, *Land and Revolution in Iran* (Austin, Texas: University of Texas Press, 1982), ix. For further reading in the causes and

REBELS WITH A CAUSE

results of the land reform programme, see Najmabadi, 3–33 and 99–169.

123 For example, see *US News and World Report*, 27 January 1967, or *Time*, 25 May 1970.

124 Mehdi Bazargan, *Modafe'at dar dadgah-e gheir-e saleh-e tajdid-e nazar-e nezani* (*Defence in the Illegitimate Review Military Tribunal*), quoted in Gholam Reza Nejati, *Tarikh-e bist va panj saleh-ye Iran* (*The Twenty Five Year History of Iran*), vol. I (Tehran: Rasa Cultural Institute, 1992), 373.

125 For more on Radmanesh, his life and party career, see Baqer Mo'meni, 'Mardi tanha' ('a Lonely Man'), in *Alefba*, no. 5, Winter 1983.

126 Aryah Y. Yodfat, *The Soviet Union and Revolutionary Iran* (London, Canberra: Croom Helm, 1984), 44. The above source suggests that the Tudeh broadcasts were against the reform programme and contradicted the Soviet policy, which was more receptive to the Shah's reforms. Jazani suggests that the Tudeh broadcasts were in co-ordination with Soviet policy, which in general viewed the Shah's reforms positively. The explanation for the apparent discrepancy may be found in Tabari's account, which suggests that the competition between the two factions resulted in contradictory broadcasts. He also maintained that the moderate faction viewed the reforms positively, the radical one negatively. See Jazani, *Sociological Plan*, 136; Tabari, 214–15.

127 For more on this, see Eskandari, *Memoirs*, vol. III, 127–37; *Politics and Organisation of the Tudeh*, 152–53; Kianuri, 391–8. For more on the proceedings of the twelfth plenum, see *Documents and Perspectives*, 559–71.

128 Tabari, 188–9.

129 For more on Shahriari and his association with the Tudeh, see Eskandari, *Memoirs*, vol. III, 149–55; *Politics and Organisation of the Tudeh*, 154–56; Tabari, 188–89. Shahriari was assassinated by the Fadaiyan Guerrillas in March 1975. See *E'dam-e enqelabi-ye Abbas Shahriari* (*The Revolutionary Execution of Abbas Shahriari*) (np: OIPFG, 1975).

130 Mehdi Khanbaba-tehrani, *Negahi az darun beh jonbesh-e chap-e Iran* (*A Look From Within at Iran's Left Movement*), ed. Hamid Shokat, vol. I (Saarbrucken, Germany: Baztab Publications, 1989), 133.

131 For more on the criticism of the Tudeh by the departing party, see *Tudeh*, ROTPI Publication, no. 21, August 1971.

132 Kianuri, 440.

133 Jazani, *Sociological Plan*, 146.

134 Fereidun Keshavarz, former Tudeh leader, played an important role in helping the organisation make its first contacts with China and Albania. See *Khanbaba-tehrani*, 133–6.

135 The group's republication of Lenin's selected works, from its Persian edition published in Moscow, censored Lenin's last testament, which attacked Stalin and asked for his removal. The group's explanation

196

NOTES ON THE TEXT

was that the testament was added by revisionists in order to slander Stalin. See: V.I. Lenin, *Selected Works* (np: ROTPI Publications, 1974), i.

136 For more on the group's analysis of the reform programme, see *Tudeh*, ROTPI Publication, no. 16, November 1969.

137 For more on the group's analysis of creating a people's army among the peasantry, see *Tudeh*, ROTPI Publication, no. 24, February 1972.

138 *Tudeh*, ROTPI Publication, no. 21, August 1971.

139 Nikkhah was initially defiant during the trial, condemning the Shah and defending his own views. ROTPI used his case to attack the regime and show revolutionary heroism in practice. But in 1969 Nikkhah suddenly wrote a letter to the Shah asking forgiveness. The embarrassment for ROTPI was increased when he was released and given high positions in the Government. Nikkhah was executed by the Islamic Government after the revolution. His collaboration prompted Jazani, who was in prison, to write essays condemning his actions. See Bizhan Jazani, *Mohre'i bar safhe-ye shatrang* (*A Pawn on the Chess Board*) (np: np, 1969).

140 For more on this, see Jazani, *Sociological Plan*, 159–60.

141 For more on the Kurdish uprising, see Hamid Mo'meni, *Dar bareh-ye mobarezat-e Kurdestan* (*On the Struggles of Kurdestan*) (Tehran: Shabahang, nd), 46–70; Gerard Chaliand (ed.), *People Without a Country* (London: Zed Press, 1978), 124–5. For more on ROTPI history, see *Setareh-ye Sorkh*, ROTPI's theoretical publication, vol. 3, no. 1, February 1979.

142 Tehrani, vol. I, 147–52.

143 For more on the expulsion of the trio, see Eskandari, *Memoirs*, vol. 3, 97–106; *Politics and Organisation of the Tudeh*, vol. 1, 154; Tabari, 234–9. For more on the eleventh plenum proceedings and the Tudeh's position on the Sino-Soviet split, see *Documents and Perspectives*, 482–558.

144 Khanbaba-Tehrani, 141–4. Also see the same source for the miserable treatment of the trio by the younger members.

145 For more on the lack of large-scale peasant rebellion in Iran, see Farhad Kazemi and Ervand Abrahamian, 'The Nonrevolutionary Peasantry of Modern Iran', in *Iranian Studies*, vol. XI, 1978, 259–303.

146 *Tez-e goruh-e Jazani-Zarifi* (*The Jazani-Zarifi Group's Thesis*) (np: 19th of Bahman Publications, 1975). The group's analysis of Iranian society and the effects of the Shah's reforms underwent major revisions in the early 1970s.

147 Takhti was a popular wrestler and medalist known for his anti-regime views. Popularly called the *jahan pahlevan* (world champion), his death sparked a number of anti-regime demonstrations. For more on Takhti, see Morteza Payman, 'Beh monasebat-e bist va panjomin salgard-e marg-e jahan pahlevan Takhti' ('In Commemoration of World Champion Takhti's Twenty-fifth Anniversary'), in *Arash*, no. 12, January 1992; *Qahreman-e melli, jahan pahlevan Takhti* (*The National Hero, World Champion Takhti*) (Sacramento, California: Society of

Iranian Students, 1970); Houchang Chehabi, 'Sport and Politics in Iran: The Legend of Gholamreza Takhti', in *International Journal of the History of Sport*, December 1995, 48.

148 Overall, 14 were arrested: Bizhan Jazani, Hasan Zia'-Zarifi, Abbas Suraki, Sa'id (Mash'uf) Kalantari, Aziz Sarmandi, Ahmad Afshar, Muhammad Chupan-zadeh, Muhammad Kianzad, Muhammad Zahedian, Majid Ahsan, Qasem Rashidi, Kiumars Izadi, Heshmatollah Shahrzad and Farrokh Negahdar. See Jazani, *Sociological Plan*, 165.

149 In his chapter on the Fadaiyan, Ervand Abrahamian suggests that Farahani's team was connected to the Palestinian movement by Radmanesh, the first secretary of the Tudeh. While I have not encountered any evidence of involvement by the Tudeh network abroad, it is a fact that the Farahani team was helped by Shahriari (ie SAVAK) in order to gain the trust of the group and arrest others. The plan worked, as the Jazani Group was compromised. See Abrahamian, *Iran*, 484.

150 For more on the history of the Jazani-Zarifi group, and biographies of some of the individual members, see *Goruh-e Jazani-Zarifi* (*The Jazani-Zarifi Group*) (np: 19th of Bahman Publications, 1976).

151 Ali Reza Nabdel, *Azarbaijan va mas'aleh-ye melli*, (*Azarbaijan and the Problem of Nationality*) (np: OIPFG Publications, 1977).

152 Hamzeh Falahati, 'Qesseh-ye raz-e koshandeh-ye Aras' ('The Story of Aras's Deadly Secret') in *Adineh*, no. 67, January 1992. Falahati was Behrangi's friend, and was swimming nearby when Behrangi drowned.

153 For more on the Ahmadzadeh-Puyan group, and biographies of some of the individual members, see *Goruh-e Ahmadzadeh-Puyan* (*The Ahmadzadeh-Puyan Group*) (np: 19th of Bahman Publications, 1976).

154 Hamid Ashraf, *Jam' bandi-e se saleh* (*The Three Year Summation*) (Tehran: OIPFG, 1979), 8–12.

155 For more on this group, see Jazani, *Sociological Plan*, 169–71.

156 Jazani, *Sociological Plan*, 104–6; interview with Mostafa Madani, Irvine California, 1 February 1992.

157 For some of Shoa'ian's writings in this period, see Mostafa Shoa'ian, *Chand neveshteh* (*Few Writings*) (Florence, Italy: Mazdak Publishers, 1976).

158 For more on the history of the Confederation, see Afshin Matin-asgari, 'The Iranian Student Movement Abroad: The Confederation of Iranian Students, National Union 1960–1978', PhD dissertation, University of California at Los Angeles, Los Angeles, 1993; Hamid Shokat, *Tarikh-e bist saleh-ye konfederasiun-e jahani-ye mohaselin va daneshjuyan-e Irani (etahadieh melli)* (*Twenty Year History of the International Confederation of Iranian Students [National Union]*) (Saarbuecken, Germany: Baztab Publishers, 1993).

NOTES ON THE TEXT

NOTES ON CHAPTER 2

1 Alam makes no mention of any consultation on the part of the Shah when the creation of the new party was announced. See Amir Asadollah Alam, *The Shah and I: The Confidential Diary of Iran's Royal Court*, ed. Alinaghi Alikhani (New York: St Martin's Press, 1992), 409–54.

2 *Ettela'at*, 18 June 1973.

3 M.S. Ivanov, *Tarikh-e novin-e Iran* (*A New History of Iran*), trans. H. Tisabi and H. Ghaempanah (Stockholm, Sweden: Tudeh Publishing Centre, 1977), 237–300.

4 Alam, 146.

5 Hamid Ashraf, *Jam' bandi-e se saleh* (*The Three-Year Summation*) (Tehran: OIPFG Publications, 1979), 6. The section on the Fadaiyan in this chapter and the next is the revised version of a published paper. See Maziar Behrooz, 'Iran's Fadayan 1971–88: A Case Study in Iranian Marxism' in *JUSUR, the UCLA Journal of Middle Eastern Studies*, vol. 6, 1990.

6 The members of the Jangal group who participated in the attack were: Ali Akbar Safa'i-farahani, Eskandar Rahimi-mespehi, Ahmad Farhudi, Muhammad Ali Mohades-qandchi, Muhammad Rahim Sama'i, Sho'a'oldin Mahshidi, Abbas Danesh-behzadi, Hadi Bandeh-khoda-langerudi, Jalil Enferadi, Iraj Nayyeri, Hushang Nayyeri, Mohammad Hadi Fazeli, Naser Saif-dalil-safa'i, Isma'il Mo'in-araqi, Ghafur Hasan-pur-asil and Mehdi Eshaqi. The latter four were arrested before the operation, and the only survivor of the group was Iraj Nayyeri, who received a life sentence.

7 The adjective Fada'i has been incorrectly used by myself and others to refer to the organisation. Its founders used the adjective to identify a movement, not necessarily an organisation. But as we shall see, from 1972 on the guerrillas began to refer to themselves as the Organisation of Fada'i Guerrillas. In later years either the plural Fadaiyan was used as a noun or the term Fada'i Organisation was used. In Persian, the Arabic adjective 'Fada'i' is made plural and pronounced 'Fada'yan' or 'Fadaiyan'. I have chosen the latter as the more proper pronunciation.

8 Amir Parviz Puyan, *Zarurat-e mobarezeh-ye mosalahaneh va rad-e te'ori-ye baqa'* (*The Necessity of Armed struggle and a Refutation of the Theory of Survival*) (np: OIPFG Publications, 1970), 51–2.

9 Mas'ud Ahmadzadeh, *Mobarezeh-ye mosalahaneh ham esteratezhi ham tak-tik* (*Armed Struggle, Both as Strategy and Tactic*) (np: OIPFG, 1970), 78.

10 For a concise English translation of Jazani's writings, see Bizhan Jazani, *Capitalism and Revolution in Iran* (London: Zed Publications, 1976).

11 Bizhan Jazani, *Tarh-e jame'eh shenasi va mabani-ye esteratezhik-e jonbesh-e enqelabi-ye khalq-e Iran* (*The Sociological Plan and the Strategic Foundation of the Iranian People's Revolutionary Movement*) (Tehran: Maziar Publishers, 1979), 144.

199

REBELS WITH A CAUSE

12 For more on Jazani's life and death, see Naser Mohajer, 'Report on a Murder', *Noghteh* (Paris) no. 1, Spring 1995.

13 Ahmadzadeh, 42–57.

14 In their original analysis of the land reform, the Jazani-Zarifi group held similar views to that of Ahmadzadeh. But in later years Jazani changed his view on this subject. See *Tez-e goruh-e Jazani-Zarifi (The Jazani-Zarifi Group's Thesis)* (np: 19th of Bahman Publications), 1–17. Bizhan Jazani, *Jam' bandi-e mobarezat-e si saleh-ye akhir dar Iran (A Summation of the Recent Thirty Years' Struggle in Iran)*, vol. 1, (np: 19th of Bahman Publications, 1975), 96–114.

15 Bizhan Jazani, *Nabard ba diktatori-e shah (War Against the Shah's Dictatorship)* (np: OIPFG Publications, 1978), 26–35.

16 Ali Akbar Safa'i-Farahani, *Ancheh yek enqelabi bayad bedanad (What a Revolutionary Must Know)* (np: Ahang Publications, 1979), 30–1.

17 As late as 1997, Torrab Haqshenas, a former leading member of the Paykar, who presents himself as a reform-minded activist and an expert on the left in Iran, repeated the same accusation. See 'Communist Organisations and Parties in Iran', in *Noghteh* (Paris), no. 7 (Spring 1997).

18 Ahmadzadeh, 39–41.

19 *Ibid.*

20 Hasan Zia'-Zarifi, *Hezb-e Tudeh va kudeta-ye 28 Mordad 32 (The Tudeh Party and the August 19, 1953 Coup)* (np: OIPFG Publications, nd), 18.

21 Jazani, *Summation of Thirty Years*, vol. 1, 58–9.

22 *Ibid.*, 62.

23 Bizhan Jazani, *Cheh kesani beh marxism-leninism khiyanat mikonand, (Which Persons Are Betraying Marxism-Leninism)* (np: 19th of Bahman Publications, nd), 43–5.

24 *Ibid.*, 46–52.

25 Jazani, *Summation of Thirty Years*, 81–2. Here Jazani was referring to the case of Parviz Nik-khah and Kurosh Lasha'i, both of ROTPI, who were arrested and decided to co-operate with the imperial regime.

26 Ahmadzadeh, 73.

27 Bizhan Jazani, *Cheguneh mobarezeh-ye mosalahaneh tudeh'i mishavad (How Armed Struggle Becomes a Mass Movement)* (np: OIPFG Publications, 1978), 16–26, 66–83.

28 *Ibid.*, 40–6.

29 In his thesis, presented to the twenty-second congress of the CPSU, Khrushchev suggested that the road to socialism was passing, mainly, through an economic struggle or competition between the socialist camp, headed by the Soviet Union, and the capitalist camp, headed by the United States. This view was challenged and criticised by Mao and the Chinese Communist Party, and became one of the major point of dispute between the two socialist giants in the 1960s and 1970s. Jazani suggested that the main road to socialism was a revolutionary one based on the struggle of the liberation movements. See Jazani, *Summation of Thirty Years*, vol. II, 189–202.

NOTES ON THE TEXT

30 Bizhan Jazani, *The Sociological Plan*, 19–20; Farahani, 60.

31 Jazani, *Summation of Thirty Years*, vol. 1, 80.

32 Estalinizm (Stalinism) (np: Communist Unity, 1979), 23–135. Ali Reza Nabdel, *Azarbaijan va mas'aleh-ye melli* (*Azarbaijan and the Problem of Nationalism*) (np: OIPFG, 1977). Nabdel was particularly critical of the Soviet Union and its performance during the Azarbaijan crisis of 1945–6.

33 *Tarikh-e jaryan-e kudeta va nazarati dar bareh-ye khat-e mash-ye konuni-ye sazman-e Mojahedin-e khalq-e Iran* (*A History of the Process of the Coup and Views on the Current Political Line of the Organisation of People's Mojahedin of Iran*) (Tehran: Abuzar Publications, 1979), 14.

34 *Barrasi-e sakht-e eqtesadi-e rustaha-ye fars* (*A Study of the Economic Structure of the Villages of Fars*), Rural Studies Series, no. 3 (np: OIPFG, 1973); *Barrasi-e sakht-e eqtesadi-e rustaha-ye Kerman* (*A Study of the Economic Structure of the Villages of Kerman*), Rural Studies Series, no. 4 (np: OIPFG, 1978); *Barrasi-e sherkatha-ye sahami-e zera'i* (*A Study of the Agricultural Corporations*), Rural Studies Series, no. 2, (np: OIPFG, 1973); *Eslahat-e arzi va nataej-e mostaqim-e an* (*Land Reform and its Direct Results*), Rural Studies Series, no. 1, (np: Tondar Publications, 1978).

35 *San Francisco Chronicle*, 12 April 1971.

36 *Nabard-e Khalq*, OIPFG publication, no. 5, November 1974, 1–23.

37 *E'dam-e enqelabi-ye Abbas Shahriari* (*The Revolutionary Execution of Abbas Shahriari*) (np: OIPFG, 1975).

38 *E'lamiaha-ye tozihi* (*Explanatory Communique*) (np: OIPFG, nd), 26–9, 33–8.

39 The Fadaiyan emblem went through a process of evolution. Originally, it did not carry the term 'organisation'. This was added in the later version. The latest version consists of the red star (vanguard), the planet earth (internationalism), Iran's map (national liberation), a fist holding a machine-gun (armed struggle), the hammer and sickle (workers and peasants), and the organisation's full name.

40 Jazani, *Who is Betraying?*, 70–86.

41 Mehdi Khanbaba-Tehrani, *Negahi az darun beh jonbesh-e chap-e Iran* (*A Look from Within at Iran's Left Movement*), ed. Hamid Sholat, vol. I, (Saarbrücken, Germany: Baztab Publications, 1989), 133.

42 Osku'i became an active member of the Fadaiyan and a poet in her own right. She was killed in a street battle in April 1974. See Marzieh Ahmadi-osku'i, *Khaterati az yek rafiq* (*Memoirs of a Comrade*) (np: OIPFG, nd).

43 Mostafa Shoa'ian, *Pasokhha-ye nasanjideh beh 'qadamha-ye sanjideh'* (*Injudicious Replies Against 'Judicious Steps'*) (Florence, Italy: Mazdak Publications, 1976).

44 For more on the history of the People's Democratic Front and Shoa'ian's ordeal, see Mostafa Shoa'ian, *Panj nameh-ye sar-goshadeh beh sazman-e cherikha-ye Fada'i khalq* (*Five Open Letters to the OIPFG*) (np: Mazdak Publications, 1979); *Sheshomin nameh-ye sar-goshadeh beh*

REBELS WITH A CAUSE

sazman-e cherikha-ye Fada'i khalq (*The Sixth Open Letter to the OIPFG*) (Florence, Italy: Mazdak Publications, 1976).

45 *Nabard-e Khalq*, OIPFG publication, no. 7, May 1976. This publication was the Fadaiyan's official voice in this period (1971–9), and in all seven issues were published.

46 *Iran Times*, 9 July 1976. For more on Ashraf's death, see *Etehad-e Kar*, the central publication of the Organisation of Fadaiyan Unity, no. 52 (August 1998).

47 For the Fadaiyan's admiration of Maoism during this period, see *Nabard-e Khalq*, OIPFG publication, no. 3, March 1974, 38–47.

48 Interview with Mostafa Madani, Irvine California, 1 February 1992. Madani, an active member of the Fadaiyan in the 1970s and a central committee member between 1979 and 1980, confirmed the bloody purges without providing details, noting that he was in prison at the time.

49 For an account of Dehqani's arrest and escape, see Ashraf Dehqani, *Hamaseh-ye moqavemat* (*Epic of Resistance*) (Middle East: National Front Publications, 1974).

50 *Ettela'at*, 19 May 1976.

51 Hasan Masali, 'Ta'sir-e binesh va manesh dar mobarezeh-ye ejtema'i' ('Influence of Insight and Conduct on Social Struggle') in *The Results of Wiesbaden Conference on the Crisis of Iran's Left Movement* (Frankfurt: np, 1985), 55.

52 Ashraf, *Three Years Summation*, 68–9. Here, Ashraf clearly writes about his disagreement with Ahmadzadeh on this issue.

53 Masali, 51–4.

54 *Siyasat va sazman-e hezb-e Tudeh az aqaz ta forupashi* (*Politics and Organisation of the Tudeh Party From Beginning to Disintegration*), vol. I, (Tehran: The Institute for Political Study and Research, 1991), 217.

55 For more on the Splinter Group, see *E'lamiyeh tozihi-ye mavaze'-e ide-ologik-e goruh-e monsha'eb* (*The Explanatory Communique of Ideological Stands of the Splinter Group*) (1978); *Turaj Haydari-bigvand, Te'ori-ye tabliq-e mosalahaneh enheraf az Marxism-Leninism* (*The Theory of Armed Propaganda, a Deviation from Marxism-Leninism*) (np: OIPFG Splinter Group, 1978); *Zendeh bad hezb-e Tudeh-ye Iran* (*Long Live the Tudeh Party of Iran*) (np: OIPFG Splinter Group, 1978).

56 Interview with Ali Reza Mahfuzi, Iranian Oral History Collection, Harvard University, 1987. Other members of the leadership at this point were: Hasan Farjudi (alias Rahim), Simin Bizhanzadeh (alias Saba), Reza Ghebraie (alias Mansur).

57 *Cherik* (*Guerrilla*) (np: OIPFG, 1978).

58 Ali Reza Mahfuzi, Iranian Oral History Collection.

59 The members of the group, 10 men and two women, were: Khosrow Golesorkhi, Karamatollah Daneshian, Mohammad Reza Allameh-zadeh, Teifur Batha'i, Abbas Ali Samakar, Manuchehr Moqadam-salimi, Iraj Jamshidi, Morteza Siyahpush, Farhad Qeysari, Ebrahim

NOTES ON THE TEXT

Farhang-razi, Shokuh Farhang-razi (Mirzadegi) and Mariam Ettehadieh.

60 Mohammed Reza Allamehzadeh, letter to the author, 11 November 1997.

61 For scholarly research on the history of the Moslem Mojahedin, see Ervand Abrahamian, *Radical Islam, the Iranian Mojahedin* (London: I.B. Tauris, 1989); for the organisation's version of its history, see *Sharh-e ta'-sis va tarikhcheh-ye vaqaye'-e sazman-e Mojahedin-e khalq-e Iran az sal-e 1344 ta sal-e 1350 (The History of Establishment and Development of the Organisation of Iranian People's Mojahedin from 1965 to 1971)* (Tehran: Mojahedin Publications, 1979); *Tarikh-e jaryan-e kudeta va nazarati dar bareh-ye khat-e mash-ye konuni-ye sazman-e Mojahedin-e khalq-e Iran (A History of the Process of the Coup and Views on the Current Political Line of the Organisation of Iranian People's Mojahedin)* (Tehran: Abuzar Publications, 1979).

62 Abrahamian, *Mojahedin*, 105–45.

63 For Ayatollah Khomeini's version of this event, see *Ettela'at*, 26 June 1980.

64 For their version of the event, see *Paykar*, nos 67-9, August 11-25, 1980; nos 70–84, 1 September to 23 November 1980.

65 For more on Sharif-vaqefi and Labbaf purges and deaths, see *Ettela'at*, 5 May 1979, 11 January 1982.

66 The differences between the Moslem and Marxist Mojahedin emblems was that the Marxists initially dropped the Qur'anic quotation on the top, and later replaced the gun with an AK-47 and dropped the reference to the year the Mojahedin was established.

67 Nejati, *Political History of Iran*, vol. I, 423; for the Moslem Mojahedin's version, see *A History of Current Political Line*, 20–1.

68 *Bayanieh-e e'elam-e mavaze'-e ideolozhik-e sazman-e Mojahedin-e khalq-e Iran (Manifesto Declaring the Ideological Position of the Organisation of Iranian People's Mojahedin)*, vol. I (np: Mojahedin Organisation, 1976), henceforth the *Manifesto*.

69 *Taghier va tahavvolat darun-e sazman-e Mojahedin-e khalq-e Iran (Change and Transition Within the Organisation of Iranian People's Mojahedin)* (np: Organisation of Paykar, 1979), 1–10.

70 For example, see *Eqtesad beh zaban-e sadeh (Economics in Simple Language)* (np: Mojahedin Publications, 1972).

71 Abrahamian, *Mojahedin*, 146.

72 *Piramun-e taqier-e mavaze'-e ideolozhik-e sazman-e Mojahedin-e khalq-e Iran (On the Ideological Conversion of the Organisation of Iranian People's Mojahedin)* (np: Iranian National Front Publications Abroad, 1976), 2–5.

73 Masali, 59.

74 *Manifesto*, 108–31.

75 *Ibid.*, 47–58.

76 *Nashrieh-ye vizheh-ye bahs-e darun-e du sazman (Special Bulletin for Intra-Discussions of the Two Organisations)*, no. 1, (np: OIPFG Publications, 1976).

REBELS WITH A CAUSE

77 *Masa'el-e had-e jonbesh-e ma* (*The Critical Problems of Our Movement*) (np: Mojahedin Publications, 1976).

78 *Se bayaniyeh az sazman-e Mojahedin-e khalq* (*Three Manifestos by the Organisation of People's Mojahedin*) (np: Mojahedin Publications, 1975). This is a collection of three military-political communiques regarding each operation. For more on the assassinations, see *Ettela'at*, 25 January 1976; *Kayhan*, 11 August 1975.

79 *Etela'iyeh-ye mehr 57* (*The September 1978 Communique*); *Etela'iyeh-ye tozihi-ye zemestan-e 57* (*The Explanatory Communique of Winter of 1979*), both published by the Marxist Mojahedin; *Paykar*, no. 11, 10 July, 1979.

80 *Paykar*, no. 93, 9 February 1981, 17.

81 Official Tudeh documents suggest that Radmanesh was removed during the thirteenth plenum, but Eskandari's memoirs suggest that he was removed after the plenum. The discrepancy here is probably because the executive committee did not have the authority to remove Radmanesh and the official documents try to hide it. See *Asnad va didgah-ha* (*Documents and Perspectives*) (Tehran: Tudeh Publications, nd), 572–8; Iraj Eskandari, *Khaterat-e siyasi* (*Political Memoirs*), ed. Babak Amir-khosravi and Fereidun Azar-nur, vol. III, (Saint Cloud Cedex, France: Democratic People's Party of Iran, nd), 158.

82 Eskandari, *Memoirs*, vol. III, 162–78.

83 *Ibid.*, p163, 178–82.

84 For more on the fourteenth plenum, see *Politics and Organisation*, vol. I, 182; *Documents and Perspectives*, 579–84.

85 Eskandari, *Memoirs*, vol. III, 176.

86 For more on Eskandari's life, see Cosroe Chaqueri, 'Iradj Eskandary and the Tudeh Party of Iran', in *Central Asian Survey*, vol. 7, no. 4, 1988, 101–33.

87 *Documents and Perspectives*, 905.

88 *Politics and Organisation of the Tudeh*, 209–24.

89 For a history of Navid, see *Documents and Perspectives*, 901–22.

90 *Documents and Perspectives*, 913.

91 *Mardom-e Mahaneh*, vol. VI, no. 17, July 1966.

92 *Documents and Perspectives*, 699–705.

93 For a discussion of Tudeh position on this issue, see Mehdi Kayhan, *Dah sal komak eqtesadi va fani-ye etehad-e shoravi beh Iran 1344–1354* (*Ten Years of Economic and Technical Aid by the Soviet Union to Iran 1965–1975*) (Stockholm, Sweden: Tudeh Publishing Centre, 1976). Kayhan was a member of the moderate faction.

94 *Ibid.*, 32.

95 Nur al-Din Kianuri, *Khaterat-e Nur al-Din Kianuri* (*The Memoirs of Nur al-Din Kianuri*) (Tehran: Didgah Institute, 1992), 478.

96 Ehsanollah Tabari, *Kazh raheh, khaterati az hezb-e Tudeh* (*The Diverted Path, Memories From the Tudeh Party*) (Tehran: Amir Kabir Publications, 1987), 262.

NOTES ON THE TEXT

97 Eskandari, *Memoirs*, vol. III, 200.

98 *Ibid.*, 201.

99 Eskandari, *Memoirs*, vol. IV, 18–19.

100 For the proceedings of the fifteenth plenum and the Tudeh's party programme, see *Documents and Perspectives*, 651–98.

101 *Ibid.*, 691.

102 *Ibid.*, 678.

103 *Donya*, Tudeh central committee political and theoretical journal, vol. III, no. 7, September 1975, 15–21.

104 *Donya*, vol. III, no. 11, February 1976, 14.

105 Interview with Jahangir Behrouz, London, 13 July 1991; *Ruzegar-e Now*, no. 138, July–August 1993, 66–75; no. 139, September 1993, 69–70. Behrouz delivered the sealed envelope to Prime Minister Hoveyda.

106 Eskandari, *Memoirs*, vol. IV, 20–1.

107 Kianuri, *Memoirs*, 483–4.

108 For Alam's account of the imperial court's events in 1975, see Alam, 409–54.

109 Perhaps an additional explanation for the Soviet Union's inability to comprehend the Iranian revolution lay in a decline in the KGB's performance in Iran. According to Vladimir Kuzichkin, at the time a KGB operative in Iran, starting in 1977 there was a marked decline in the KGB's standards in Iran, due to 'the replacement of many officers, including the heads in the Residency'. See Vladimir Kuzichkin, *Inside the KGB: My Life in the Soviet Espionage*, trans. Thomas B. Beattie (New York: Pantheon Books, 1990), 148–9.

110 Iraj Eskandari, *Yadmandeh-ha va yaddashtha-ye parakandeh* (*Memoirs and Scattered Notes*) (np: Mard-e Emruz Publications, 1986), 135–6.

111 For example, see the party's communique in support of the movement in September 1978 in *Asnad va e'lamiyeha-ye hezb-e Tudeh-ye Iran* (*Documents and Communiques of the Tudeh Party of Iran*) (Tehran: Tudeh Publications, 1980), 21–4.

112 Kianuri, 488–9.

113 Kianuri identified executive committee members supporting Eskandari's platform as follows: Hamid Saffari (ADP member, which meant this faction stood with the moderates), Mohammed Purhormozan, Malektaj (Malekeh) Mohammadi, Fatollah Nazer, Gholam Hosein Qa'em-panah, Ali Gelavizh, Mehdi Kayhan and Ashut Shahbazian, with Hosein Joudat, a long-time moderate, swinging between the two. Those supporting Kianuri's platform were: Ehsanollah Tabari, Farajollah Mizani, Manuchehr Behzadi, Raf'at Mohammed-zadeh, Bahram Danesh, Hushang Nazemi, Babak Amirkhosravi. *Ibid.*, 489–90.

114 Eskandari, *Memoirs*, vol. III, 202–3.

115 Kianuri, 497.

116 Eskandari, *Memoirs*, vol. III, 207–9.

205

117 Kianuri, 497–8.
118 *Donya*, vol. III, no. 11, February 1976, 46–50; vol. III, no. 5, August 1978, 38–44.
119 *Donya*, vol. III, no. 8, October 1975, 34–8.
120 Kayhan, 48–54.
121 *Zaman-e No*, no. 6, October 1984, 102–8.
122 *Ibid.*, p110. Members present at the meetings discussing this issue were Kianuri, Forutan, Sagha'i, Shafabakhsh, Joudat and Hasan Nazari.
123 *Ibid.* 116.
124 *Ibid.* 118–19.
125 *Donya*, vol. III, no. 12, February 1976, 18.
126 *Documents and Perspectives*, 748.
127 F.M. Javan, *Cherikha-ye khalq cheh miguyand (What Do the People's Guerrillas Say?)* (Stassfurt: Tudeh Publishing Centre, 1972), 8–9.
128 *Donya*, vol. III, no. 6, August 1975, 7–17.
129 For a brief history of the group see the appendix to the following pamphlet: Bizhan Jazani, *Who is Betraying*, 1-7; *Asrar-e fa'aliyatha-ye zed-e Irani dar kharej az keshvar (The Secrets Behind Anti-Iranian Activities Abroad)* (np: np, 1976), 19. This pamphlet was published by SAVAK.
130 *Tudeh*, ROTPI publication, no. 23, April 1973. For ROTPI's defence of Nahavandi, see *Setareh-ye Sorkh*, ROTPI publication, no. 33, January 1974.
131 *Tehrani*, vol. I, 216. Among these can be named Parviz Va'ez-vadeh, his wife, Ma'sumeh Tavachian, and Mahvash Jasemi. The first died in a shoot-out, the other two under torture.
132 For Lasha'i's views after his arrest, see *Kayhan*, 30 December 1972.
133 *The Secrets Behind*, 23.
134 *Tehrani*, vol. I, 271–2.
135 For ROTPI's defence of Maoism, see *Tudeh*, ROTPI publication, no. 10, September 1968; no. 12, March 1969. For the group's view on the Soviet Union, see *Tudeh*, no. 20, August, 1970.
136 *Tudeh*, ROTPI publication, no. 17, January 1970.
137 For example, see *Setareh-ye Sorkh*, ROTPI publication, no. 7, October 1970; no. 18, February,1971; no. 40, October–November 1974.
138 *Setareh-ye Sorkh*, ROTPI publication, no. 1, February 1979.
139 *Tudeh*, ROTPI publication, no. 22, February 1972.
140 *Ibid.*, 28–32.
141 *The Secrets Behind*, 27–8. According to this SAVAK document, 60 were arrested in this connection.
142 *Tufan*, Marxist-Leninist Organisation of The Tufan publication, no. 21, July 1971, 24–8; no. 27, July 1972, 54–8.
143 *Tufan*, Marxist-Leninist Organisation of The Tufan publication, no. 44, July 1975, pp84-95.
144 *Tufan*, Marxist-Leninist Organisation of The Tufan publication, no. 21, 36–8; 41–2.

NOTES ON THE TEXT

145 *Roshanfekran, hezb, mobarezeh-ye mosalahaneh, (Intellectuals, Party, Armed Struggle),* Tufan Organisation publication, no. 34.
146 Interview with Ali Shakeri, Los Angeles, 10 April 1993.
147 Because of its insistance on depicting itself as the party of two classes, namely workers and peasants, the party's critics dubbed it the 'double-decker party' ('hezb-e du tabaqeh').
148 *Andisheh-ye Mao Tse-dun va siyasat-e khareji-ye chin (Mao Zedong's Thought and China's Foreign Policy)* (np: The Communist Unity Group, 1977).
149 *Moshkelat va masa'el-e jonbesh (The Movement's Obstacles and Problems)* (np: The Communist Unity Group, 1977).
150 *Enqelab-e sosialisti ya demokratik? (Socialist or Democratic Revolution?)* (np: The Communist Unity Group, nd).
151 Interview with Mohammed Amini, Los Angeles, 19 April 1993.
152 *Ibid,* and Parviz Shokat, interview with author, Berkeley, 18 September 1997
153 Interview with Hozhabr Khosravi-arzarbaijani, London, 8 August 1990.
154 *Karnameh-ye hezb-e karganran-e sosiyalist (History of the Socialist Workers Party)* (unpublished manuscript), 3.
155 *Ibid,* 4–5.
156 For example, it is clear that in the late 1960s and early 1970s the atmosphere of prisons changed with the arrival of the new generation of Maxists associated with the guerrilla movement. It became more combative, and the morale of prisoners became much higher. See Muhammad Ali Amu'i, *Dord-e Zamaneh (The Drag of Age)* (Tehran: Anzan Publishers, 1998), 258–337.

NOTES ON CHAPTER 3

1 Marvin Zonis, *Majestic Failure: The Fall of the Shah* (Chicago and London: The University of Chicago Press, 1991), 209.
2 Mehdi Bazargan, *Enqelab-e Iran dar du harekat (Iran's Revolution in Two Motions)* (Tehran: np, 1984), 26.
3 Jimmy Carter, *Keeping Faith: Memoirs of a President* (Toronto, New York, London, Sidney: Bantam Books, 1982), 433–58.
4 Gary Sick, *All Fall Down: America's Tragic Encounter With Iran* (London: Penguin Books, 1986), 50–1.
5 William H. Sullivan, *Mission to Iran* (London, New York: W.W. Norton and Company, 1981), 167.
6 For an interesting study of many educated Iranians' subscription to this theory, see Ervand Abrahamian, 'Paranoid Style in Iranian Politics', in *Khomeinism* (Berkeley, Los Angeles: University of California Press, 1993), 111–32. Here, Abrahamian argues that the fact that Iran was never a direct colony of European powers meant that

foreign influence was always exerted through indirect, yet obvious, methods. This fact, he argues, has been an important element in giving legitimacy and popularising conspiracy theories among Iranians.

7   Sick, 102–3.
8   Mohammad Reza Pahlavi, *Answer to History* (New York: Stein and Day Publishers, 1980), 145–75.
9   Sick, 104–6.
10   Zbigniew Brzezinski, *Power and Principle*, (New York: Straus, Giroux, 1983), 358.
11   *Ibid.*, 354–5.
12   *Ibid.*, 379.
13   For example, see Henry Kissinger's remarks. He wrongly assumed that the well-organised nation-wide strikes that were crippling the imperial regime in the autumn of 1978 were organised by communist elements connected to the Soviet Union: *Time*, 15 January 1978.
14   Muriel Atkin, 'Soviet Attitudes Toward Shi'ism and Social Protest' in Nikki R. Keddie and Juan R.I. Cole (eds), *Shi'ism and Social Protest* (New Haven: Yale University Press, 1986), 275–301.
15   *Ibid.*, 283.
16   Vladimir Kuzichkin, *Inside the KGB: My Life in the Soviet Espionage*, trans. Thomas B. Beattie (New York: Pantheon Books, 1990), 148–9.
17   *Current Digest of Soviet Press (CDSP)*, no. 36, 14 October 1978. The author, as a nineteen-year-old student, had the rare opportunity to be present at this mass demonstration, his first. As he stood on what was then called Pahlavi Avenue (now Vali-e Asr), masses of people to the north and south were calling for Ayatollah Khomeini's return and the creation of an Islamic republic. How the Soviet media could interpret this as a call for a return to Iran's 1906 constitution is simply inexplicable.
18   *CDSP*, no. 46, 13 December 1978.
19   *CDSP*, no. 1, 31 January 1979.
20   *CDSP*, no.3, February 14, 1979.
21   *CDSP*, no. 6, 14 March 1979.
22. For more on factionalism in the IRI, see Maziar Behrooz, 'Factionalism in Iran Under Khomeini', in *Middle Eastern Studies*, vol. 27, no. 4, October 1991, 597–614.
23   For a discussion of the IRI's foreign policy during the 1980s and how it was effected by factional conflicts, see Maziar Behrooz, 'Trends in the Foreign Policy of the Islamic Republic of Iran, 1979–1988', in Nikki R. Keddie and Mark J. Gasiorowski (eds), *Neither East Nor West: Iran, the Soviet Union and the United States* (New Haven and London: Yale University Press, 1990), 13–36.
24   *KAR*, Publication of the OIPFG (Supreme Council), no. 203, September 1986.
25   *KAR*, Publication of the OIPFG, no. 4, 29 March 1979.
26   Interview with Mostafa Madani, Irvin, California, 2 January 1992. Madani was among those Fadaiyan members in prison at this time.

NOTES ON THE TEXT

27 *Ibid.*

28 As far as is known, the Fadaiyan leadership before the revolution, six in all, were: Ahmad Gholamian-Langerudi (alias Hadi), Qorbanali Rahim-pur (alias Majid), Qasem Siyadati, Farrokh Negahdar, Reza Ghebra'i (alias Mansur). After the revolution, with Siyadati killed during the revolution and Langerudi dropped, the leadership, now called the central committee, was increased to eleven, and included: Negahdar, Qorbanali Rahimpur (alias Majid), Reza Ghebra'i, Mehdi Fattapur, Mostafa Madani, Kazem Mobini, Asghar Soltanabadi (alias Kiumars), Ali Tavasoli, Haydar and Akbar, both aliases. Negahdar, Madani and Mobini acted as executive committee members and Haydar, never participated in leadership meetings.

29 Farah Azari, 'The Post Revolutionary Women's Movement in Iran' in Farah Azari (ed.), *Women of Iran: The Conflict With Fundamentalism* (London: Ithaca Press, 1983), pp195–6.

30 *KAR*, Publication of OIPFG, no. 4, 29 March 1979.

31 For more on the Fadaiyan's attitude on the women's issue, see Eliz Sanasarian, *An Analysis of Fida'i and Mojahedin Positions on Women's Rights*, in Guity Nashat (ed.), *Women and Revolution in Iran* (Boulder, Colorado: Westview Press, 1983), 97–108.

32 Sorayya Afshar, 'The Attitude of the Iranian Left to the Women's Question' in Azari (ed.), *Women of Iran*, 157–69.

33 For more on the history and activity of the Turkman Councils, see *Zende-gani va mobarezat-e khalq-e torkman* (*The Life and Struggle of the Turkman People*) (np: The Central Office of the Turkman Sahra's Councils, 1980).

34 *KAR*, OIPFG publication, no. 5, 5 April 1979; *Sosialism va Enqelab*, no. 4, September 1983, 29–9.

35 For the group's initial views, see *Mosahebeh ba rafiq Ashraf Dehqani* (*Interview with Comrade Ashraf Dehqani*) (np: np, 1979).

36 *KAR*, Publication of OIPFG, no. 2, March, 1979

37 For more on the first post-revolution plenum, see *Pasokh-e aqaliyyat beh nameh-ye 'markaziyyat'* (*Minority's Answer to the Letter of the 'Central Committee'*) (np: OIPFG Publications, 1980).

38 The four Turkman leaders were Shir Mohammad Derakhshandeh-Tumaj, Abdol Karim Makhtum, Tovvaq Mohammad Vahedi and Hosein Jorjani. See *KAR*, OIPF (Majority) publication, no. 92, 7 January 1981.

39 At this point, both factions claimed to be supporters of the Jazani theses, but the Minority claimed that the Majority did not believe in the theses, and that in fact it had accepted the Tudeh analyses both on the anti-imperial regime period and on the nature of the IRI. The Minority grievances showed that many of Dehqani's claims were true. See *Diktatori va tabligh-e mosalahaneh (qahr)* (*Dictatorship and Armed Propaganda (Violence)*) (np: OIPFG Publications, 1983).

40 For more on the two factions' views immediately after the split, see *KAR*, the publication of both factions, nos 61–3.

209

REBELS WITH A CAUSE

41 KAR, Publication of OIPF (Majority), no. 62, June 1980.

42 Of the two, the Minority remained with Fadaiyan traditions: struggle against a non-socialist dictatorship, defence of the people's rights as it perceived it, and a militant stand on social issues. See *Nabard-e Khalq*, theoretical journal of the OIPFG (Minority), no. 1, June 1980; no. 2, December 1980.

43 *KAR*, Publication of OIPF (Majority), no. 90, 23 December 1980.

44 *KAR*, Publication of OIPF (Majority), no. 73, 27 August 1980.

45 The OIPFG (Left-Wing Majority) also accused the Majority of bureaucratism and undemocratic methods in confronting its opponents. See *Nokati piramun-e mas'aleh-ye anternasionalizim-e proleteri* (*A Few Points on the Problem of Proletarian Internationalism*) (Tehran: OIPFG (Left-Wing Majority), 1981); *Naqdi bar binesh-e hakem bar jenah-e rast-e aksariyyat* (*A Critique of the Majority-Right Wing's Perspective*) (Tehran: OIPFG (Left-Wing Majority), 1981); *Bahsi piramun-e bohran dar sazman-e ma* (*A Discussion on Crisis in Our Organisation*) (Tehran: OIPFG (Left-Wing Majority), 1981).

46 *KAR*, OIPF (Majority) publication, no. 120, August 1981.

47 This document was first published by the Kurdish Democratic Party of Iran, and was reprinted by the Mojahedin, see *Mojahed*, publication of the Organisation of People's Mojahedin of Iran, no. 257, August 1985.

48 *KAR*, Publication of OIPF (Majority), no. 127, February 1982.

49 For more on the planned attack on the Majority and the Tudeh, see *KAR*, OIPFG (Minority) publication, no. 112, May 1981.

50 For more on developments of the Keshtgar faction, see the resolutions of the organisation's sixth and seventh plenums in *Fada'i*, OIPF publication, no. 11, 1985; no. 30, 1986. For more on the developments of the Negahdar faction, see *KAR*, OIPF (Majority) publication, no. 29, 1986.

51 *KAR*, OIPFG publication, no. 122, 12 August 1981.

52 *Sosialism va Enqelab*, no. 3, January 1983, 35. For an evaluation of the Minority's military wing, and how its back was broken after Asadian's death, see *Zaman-e Now*, no. 1, October 1983, 28–30.

53 For more on developments of this faction, see *KAR*, its official publication and *KAR*, Theoretical-Political Journal, nos 1–2, 1983; no. 3, 1984.

54 For more on the Minority congress, see *KAR*, OIPFG (Minority) publication, nos 140–141, December 1981; *Sosialism va Enqelab*, no. 3, January 1983; no. 4, September 1983.

55 The minority members of the new central committee were Mohammad Reza Behkish (alias Kazem), and Abbas Hashemi (alias Hashem). The majority members were Mohsen Modir-Shanehchi, Akbar Kamiabi, Ahmad Gholamian-Langerudi and Mehdi Same'.

56 *Barnameh-ye amal* (*Programme of Action*) (OIPFG [Minority]).

57 For more on the Socialist Revolutionary faction, see *Nazm-e Kargar*, five issues of which were published clandestinely in Iran; *Sosialism va*

210

NOTES ON THE TEXT

Enqelab, only the first three issues of which were published with the participation of the Socialist Revolutionary faction; *Nataej va Cheshmandaz* (*Results and Perspectives*) (np: OIPFG [Minority], 1982).

58 For more on Same' and his views, see *Nabard-e Khalq*, his group's publication, and: *Mojahed*, Publication of OPMI, nos 160–1, August 1983; no. 165, September 1983; no. 185, November 1983; no. 221, September 1984. Mehdi Khanbaba-tehrani has suggested that Same' was initially accepted in the National Council of Resistance as an individual, but that after seven months he suddenly claimed to be representing an organisation. See *Mehdi Khanbaba-Tehrani, Negahi az darun beh jonbesh-e chap-e Iran* (*A Look From Within at Iran's Left Movement*), ed. Hamid Shokat, vol. 2, (Saarbrücken, Germany: Baztab Publications, 1989), 527.

59 For more on Hormati-pur and Sabburi's life and the faction's activities in this period, see Mokhtar Niknezhad, *Khaterat-e jangal* (*Memories of Jungle*) (np: OIPF Publications, nd); *Bayaniyyehha-ye amaliyyat-e Jangal* (*Communiques of the Jungle Operations*) (Sweden: IPFG (Liberation Army), nd); *Beh yad-e A.R. Sabburi* (*In Memory of A.R. Sabburi*) (Europe: IPFG (Liberation Army), nd).

60 *Pasokh beh enhelal talaban* (*Answer to the Abolitionists*) (np: IPFG [Liberation Army], nd).

61 *Paykar*, no. 15, 6 August 1979.

62 For example, see *Eqtesad-e shoravi kamelan va qat'an sarmaiehdari* (*The Soviet Economy Completely and Definitely Capitalistic*) (Berkeley CA: Paykar Organisation, nd).

63 *Paykar*, no. 93, 9 February 1981.

64 For the Paykar's position on Shahram's arrest, trail and execution, see *Paykar*, no. 62, 7 July 1980; no. 65, 28 July 1979.

65 *Paykar*, no. 11, 9 July 1979.

66 *Paykar*, no. 22, 13 August 1979.

67 See, for example, *Paykar*, no. 13, 23 July 1979; no. 26, 17 September 1979.

68 *Jonbesh-e novin-e komonisti va sazman-e cherikha-ye fada'i khalq* (*The New Communist Movement and the OIPFG*) (np: Organisation of Paykar, 1980), 21.

69 *Paykar*, no. 35, 24 December 1979; no. 57, 2 June 1980.

70 *Paykar*, no. 110, 15 June 1981.

71 For more on this faction's views, see *Nabard-e Marxism ba opurtunism* (*The War of Marxism Against Opportunism*) (np: np, nd).

72 For a vivid description of Ruhani and his role, see *Bazandeh* (*The Loser*) (Minneapolis: Paykar Cell, 1984). This is in fact the story of the arrest and execution of Qasem Abedini, a Paykar member, in whose demise Ruhani played an important role.

73 For the plenum's documents, see *Asnad va didgah-ha* (*Documents and Perspectives*) (Tehran: Tudeh Publications, nd), 940–77.

74 For a list of the Tudeh's leadership, see Nur al-Din Kianuri, *Khaterat-e Nur al-Din Kianuri* (*The Memoirs of Nur al-Din Kianuri*) (Tehran: Didgah Institute, 1992), 518–21.

75 *Ibid.*, 499.

76 *Ibid.*, 540–1.

77 For example, see *Nameh-ye Mardom*, Tudeh publication, no. 94, 17 November 1979; no. 95, 18 November 1979. Articles in both issues attempt to show the failure of the Fadaiyan to support the US Embassy takeover, and thus to support the revolution. For the party's support for the Majority faction immediately after the split, see *Nameh-ye Mardom*, no. 253, 8 June 1979. According to a new document, the party had a clear policy of infiltrating other organisations for the purpose of promoting division and gathering information. The information on opposition groups was passed to the IRI in order to buy favour for the party. This document was published in Tehran under uncertain circumstances. Clearly, it was written by well-informed former Tudeh members, but it is unclear what role was played by IRI intelligence. Nevertheless, the information it provides simply confirms already existing data on Tudeh activities after the revolution. See *Ketabcheh-ye Haqiqat (The Booklet of Truth)* (Tehran: np, 1998) 8–13.

78 See *Nemeh-ye Mardom*, Tudeh publication, no. 273, 26 June 1980; no. 298, 3 July 1980.

79 *Nameh-ye Mardom*, Tudeh publication, no. 243, 25 May 1980.

80 *Kudeta-ye nozheh (The Nozheh Coup d'etat)* (Tehran: The Institute for Political Studies and Research, 1986), 185–6. The coup was named after Nozheh air-base, Iran's largest fighter station located in Hamadan, because the coup was to start from there.

81 For example, see *Nameh-ye Mardom*, Tudeh publication, no. 241, 22 May 1980; no. 250, 3 June 1979; *Chehre-ye goruhak-e zed-e enqelabi-ye Kumoleh (The Portrait of Anti-Revolutionary Group Kumoleh)* (np: Tudeh Publications, nd).

82 Kuzichkin, 291. See also *The Booklet of Truth*, 5–13.

83 For example, see V. Solodovnikov and V. Bogoslovky, *Non-Capitalist Development: An Historical Outline* (Moscow: Progress Publishers, 1975).

84 Shahrough Akhavi, 'Soviet Perceptions of the Iranian Revolution' in *Iranian Studies*, vol. XIX, no. 1, Winter 1986, 4.

85 Nur al-Din Kianuri, *Hokm-e tarikh beh pish miravad (The Judgment of History Goes Forward)* (Tehran: OIPF [Majority] Publications, 1982), 22.

86 Nur al-Din Kianuri, *Porseh va pasokh (Questions and Answers)*, nos 2–3 (Tehran: Tudeh Publications, 1980), 30–4.

87 Kuzichkin, 288.

88 Rostislav Ulyanovsky, 'The Iranian Revolution and its Peculiar Features' in *Socialism Theory and Practice*, no. 2, February 1983, 104. This article was originally published in the journal *Komunist*, no. 10, 1982, a few months before the arrest of the Tudeh leadership.

89 Rostislav Ulyanovsky, *Sarnevesht-e Enqelab-e Iran (The Fate of Iranian Revolution)*, trans. Tudeh Party, (np: Tudeh Publishers, 1985), 11. This article was originally published in *Komunist*, no. 8, 1985.

NOTES ON THE TEXT

90 Kuzichkin, 290–3. The Tudeh's first secretary has denied most allegations directed at him by Kuzichkin. See Kianuri, 552–3.

91 *KAR*, OIPFG publication, no. 112, May 1981.

92 Kuzichkin, 358.

93 *New York Times*, 20 November 1986.

94 For a concise version of Tudeh leaders' confessions, see *Confessions of the Central Cadres of the Tudeh Party* (Tehran: Islamic Propaganda Organisation, 1983).

95 Before the assault on the Majority and Tudeh, when members and leaders of other groups were paraded on television, confessing to their misdeeds, the Tudeh and Majority propaganda depicted these confessions as signs of ideological bankruptcy and proof of guilt. But when Majority and Tudeh leaders' turn came, the remnant of the party abroad claimed that the IRI had received and was using special drugs. Obviously, no explanation was given as to why – even if such drugs had been developed by Western powers – they worked on Tudeh members and not necessarily on other groups.

96 Rinaldo Galindo, *Report on the Human Rights in the Islamic Republic of Iran* (New York: UN Economic and Social Council, 1990), 33–42.

97 Ehsanollah Tabari, *Shenakht va sanjesh-e marxism* (*Understanding and Evaluation of Marxism*) (Tehran: Amir Kabir Publishers, 1989); *Bazgasht az marxism* (*Return From Marxism*) (Rome: Islamic Cultural Centre in Europe, 1984).

98 For Kianuri's views on Gorbachev's reforms, see *Kayhan Hava'i*, nos 953–4, 23 and 30 October 1991.

99 Kianuri, 544–5. See also *The Booklet of Truth*, 5–8.

100 For a background on the Mahabad republic, see Gerard Chaliand (ed.), *People Without a Country* (London: Zed Press, 1980), 118–22.

101 For a brief history of the KDP before the revolution, see Mehrdad R. Izady, *The Kurds: A Concise Handbook* (Washington, London: Taylor & Francis, 1992), 209–11.

102 *Payam*, Iran's Voice of Revolution publication, no. 38, February 1989.

103 For more on this arrangement, see *The Programme of the Communist Party* (np: Kumoleh Publications, 1982).

104 For more on the history of this group, see *Organisation of Revolutionary Workers of Iran: A Short Introduction* (Cedex, France: Organisation of Revolutionary Workers of Iran Publications, nd).

105 *Ibid.*, 7–8.

106 For more on the policies and programmes of this Organisation, see *Marzha-ye hoviyat-e ma* (*The Borders of Our Identity*) (Berlin: The Revolutionary Workers Organisation of Iran, 1984); *Tarh-e barnameh* (Programme Draft) (np: The Revolutionary Workers Organisation of Iran, 1987).

107 Ramin Safizadeh, interview with author, Berkeley, 5 January 1998.

108 For an account of the operation, see the League's military communiques of the time and *Bayaniyyeh-ye qiyyam-e panjom-e Bahman* (*The Manifesto of January 25 Uprising*).

REBELS WITH A CAUSE

109 See the communique of the league of January 1983.
110 For the trial and confessions of the league leadership, see *Ettela'at*, 29 January 1983.
111 *Declaration of the Revolutionary Internationalist Movement*, March 1984.

NOTES ON CHAPTRER 4

1 Said Amir-Arjomand, *The Turban for the Crown: The Islamic Revolution in Iran* (New York, Oxford: Oxford University Press, 1988), 91–3.
2 Mehrdad Mashayekhi, 'The Politics of Nationalism and Political Culture' in Samih K. Farsoun and Mehrdad Mashayekhi (eds), *Iran: Political Culture in the Islamic Republic* (London and New York: Routledge, 1992), 82–115; Ali Mirsepassi-Ashtiani and Valentine M. Moghadam, 'The Left and Islam in Iran: A Retrospective and Prospects' in *Radical History Review*, no. 51, 1991, 27–62.
3 Mashayekhi, 87.
4 Ervand Abrahamian, *Khomeinism* (Berkeley, Los Angeles: University of California Press, 1993), 111–32.
5 For a discussion and analysis of the urban-based nature of recent revolts in Iran, see Nikki R. Keddie, *Iran and the Muslim World* (New York: University Press of New York, 1995), 60–95.
6 Nikki Keddie, 'Stratification, Social Control, and Capitalism in Iranian Villages' in Richard Antoun and Iliya Harik (eds), *Rural Politics and Social Change in the Middle East* (Bloomington: Indiana University Press, 1972), 365–72.
7 Carlos Marigla, *Jozveh-ye rahnama-ye jang-e cheriki* (*Manual on Guerrilla Warfare*) (np: Bakhtar-e Emrouz Publications, 1970).
8 The letters were first published in Europe and republished in Kianuri's memoirs. See Kianuri, 307–35; *Rah-e Azadi*, nos 22–3, June, August 1992.
9 For the text of the letters, see Nur al-Din Kianuri, *Katerat-e Nur al-Din Kianuri* (*Memoirs of Nur al-Din Kianuri*) (Tehran: Didgah Institute, 1992), 309–34. For the fourth plenum, see Khosrow Shakeri (ed.), *Asnad-e Tarikhi* (*Historical Documents*) (Florence, Italy: Mazdak, 1974), vol. I, 367.
10 Baqer Mo'meni, 'Mardi tanha' ('A Lonely Man') in *Alefba*, no. 5, Winter 1983.
11 Mehdi Khanbaba-tehrani, *Negahi az darun beh jonbesh-e chap-e Iran* (*A Look From Within at Iran's Left*), ed. Hamid Shokat, vol. I (Saarbruken, Germany: Baztab Publications, 1989), 142–3.
12 Mostafa Shoa'ian, *Panj nameh-ye sar-goshadeh beh sazman-e cherikha-ye Fada'i-ye khalq* (*Five Open Letters to the OIPFG*) (np: Mazdak Publications, 1979).
13 Iraj Eskandari, *Khaterat-e siyasi* (*Political Memoirs*), Babak Amir-khosravi and Fereidun Azar-nur, (eds), vol. III, (Saint Cloud, France: Democratic People's Party of Iran, 1985), 121–2.

NOTES ON THE TEXT

14 Interview with Iraj Nayyeri, in Sa'id Rahnama (ed.), *Tajdid-e hayat-e social demokrasi dar Iran? (The Rebirth of Social Democracy In Iran?)* (Spanga, Sweden: Baran Publishers, 1996), 126.

15 *Ibid.,* 375.

16 *Ibid.,* 377.

17 Ali Reza Mahfuzi, *Oral History of Iran,* Harvard University.

18 Assef Bayat, *Workers and Revolution in Iran* (London and New Jersey: Zed Books, 1987), 25.

19 *Ibid.,* 77.

20 Habib Ladjevardi, *Labor Unions and Autocracy in Iran* (Syracuse: Syracuse University Press, 1985), 239.

21 Bayat, 100.

22 *Ibid.,* 92.

23 Ladjevardi, 48–9.

24 See the party's platform, drafted after its fifteenth plenum in 1975, in: *Asnad va didgahha (Documents and Perspectives)* (Tehran: Tudeh Publications, 1979), 667–98; *Nameh-ye Mardom,* nos 107 and 109, May and June 1986.

25 In many cases, the Tudeh opposed workers' strikes and suggested the creation of bodies designed to protect workers' rights while keeping anti-revolutionary elements, ie the IRI opposition, out of the factories. See *Etehad-e Mardom,* 2 December 1981.

26. *Nameh-ye Mardom,* March 1981.

27 *Chehel sal dar sangar-e mobarezeh (Forty Years in the Trench of Struggle)* (np: Tudeh Publications, 1981).

28 *Nameh-ye Mardom,* no. 109, June 1986.

29 *KAR,* OIPF (Majority) publication, no. 64, July 1980.

30 *KAR,* OIPF (Majority) publication, nos 101–2, March–April 1981.

31 *KAR,* OIPF (Majority) publication, no. 121, July 1981.

32 For the organisation's views on this subject, see the results of its first congress, especially the resolution on the stage of revolution, in *KAR,* OIPFG publication, no. 142, January 1982.

33 *KAR* (Special Issue for International Workers' Day), May 1981.

34 For example, see the article 'Du rah bishtar vojud nadarad' ('There are Only Two Paths') known to have been written by the organisation's chief ideologue of the period, Akbar Kamiyabi in *KAR,* OIPFG publication, no. 166, April 1983.

35 *Paykar,* no. 3, May 1980.

36 *Paykar,* no. 71, August 1980.

37 *KAR,* OIPFG publication, no. 99, March 1980.

38 *Paykar,* no. 16, August 1979.

39 Ervand Abrahamian, *Iran Between Two Revolutions* (Princeton, New Jersey: Princeton University Press, 1982), 328.

40 Azadeh Kian-Thie'baut, *Secularisation of Iran: A Doomed Failure?* (Paris: Peetersand Institute d'etudes iraniennes, 1998), 108–12.

41 *Ibid.,* 481.

215

42 Information on the Tudeh is from Mirsepassi, 45.

43 Information on the post-revolution Fadaiyan and Paykar is extracted from *Shohada-ye javidan-e azadi, parchamdaran-enqelab-e novin-e khalq-e qahreman-e Iran* (*The Immortal Martyrs of Liberty, the Standard Bearers of the Heroic People of Iran's New Revolution*) (np: Mojahedin publications, 1984); this source contains 12,028 names and identities of activists killed while opposing the IRI. The Mojahedin, as well as many other opposition groups, did not consider the Majority factions as part of the revolutionary movement, and did not include their fallen members in their publications.

44 Asef Bayat, *Street Politics: The Poor People's Movement in Iran* (New York: Columbia University Press, 1997).

45 Ibid., 133–53.

46 Ibid., 92–5.

47 Stephen F. Cohen, Rethinking the Soviet Experience: Politics and History Since 1917 (New York, Oxford: Oxford University Press, 1985), 48.

48 J.V. Stalin, *Works*, vol. 10, (Moscow: Foreign Languages Publishing House, 1954), 368–9.

49 *History of the Communist Party of the Soviet Union (Bolsheviks)* (San Francisco: Proletarian Publishers, 1976).

50 *Estalinism* (*Stalinism*) (np: The Communist Unity Group, 1977), 113.

51 Kianuri, 409–10.

52 According to Moghissi this attitude is partially rooted in Marxism internationally, see Haideh Moghissi, *Populism and Feminism in Iran* (New York: St Martin's Press, 1994),88–97.

53 'Sazmandehi-ye mobarezat-e zanan' ('Organising Women's Struggle') in *Jahan-e No*, nos 2–3, February 1987, 30.

54 Moghissi, 139–59.

55 Azadeh Kian, 'The Tudeh Party of Iran: Political Violence or Political Legalism? (1941–1953)' in *Jusur*, vol. 8, 1992, 69–90.

56 See interview with Hemad Shaybani, *Rahnama*, 172–82.

57 See Baba Ali's interview, *ibid.*, 203–16.

58 See interview with Naser Pakdaman, *ibid.*, 191.

BIBLIOGRAPHY

PERSIAN

Abbasi, Ruhollah, *Khaterat-e yek afsar-e Tudeh'i 1330–1335* (*The Memoirs of a Tudeh Officer 1951–1956*) (Montreal, Canada: Farhang Publications, 1989).

Ahmadi, Hamid, *Tarikhcheh-ye feqeh-ye jomhuri-ye enqelabi-ye Iran va 'goruh-e Arani'* (*A History of the Revolutionary Republican Party of Iran and the 'Arani Group'*) (Berlin: Society for Social Research of Iran, 1992).

Ahmadi-osku'i, Marzieh, *Khaterati az yek rafiq* (*Memoirs of a Comrade*) (np: OIPFG, nd)

Ahmadzadeh, Mas'ud, *Mobarezeh-ye mosalahaneh ham esteratezhi ham taktik* (*Armed Struggle, Both as Strategy and Tactic*) (np: OIPFG, 1970).

Alamuti, Zia'oddin, *Fosuli az tarikh-e mobarezat-e siyasi va ejtema'i-ye Iran* (*A Look at the Socio-Political History of Iran*) (Tehran: Chapbakhsh Publications, 1991).

Alavi, Bozorg, *Khaterat-e Bozorg-e Alavi* (*The Memoirs of Bozorg Alavi*) ed. Hamid Ahmadi (Spanga, Sweden: Baran Publishers, 1997).

Alavi, Bozorg, *Panjah va se nafar* (*The Group of Fifty-three*) (Tehran: Javid Publications, 1978).

Alavi, Najmi, *Sargozasht-e Morteza Alavi* (*Morteza Alavi's Life*) (np: Mard-e Emrouz Publications, 1991).

Al-e Ahmad, Jalal, *Dar khedmat va khianat-e roshanfekran* (*On the Intellectual's Serving and Betrayal*), 2 vols (Tehran: Kharazmi Publications, 1978).

Amir-khosravi, Babak, *Nazar az darun beh naqsh-e hezbe-e Tude-ye Iran* (*A Look From Within at the Role of the Tudeh Party of Iran*) (Tehran: Didgah Institute, 1996).

Amu'i, Muhammad Ali, *Dord-e Zamaneh* (*The Drag of Age*) (Tehran: Anzan Publishers, 1998).

Andisheh-ye Mao Tse-dun va siyasat-e khareji-ye chin (*Mao Zedong's Thought and China's Foreign Policy*) (np: The Communist Unity, 1977).

Ashraf, Hamid, *Jam' bandi-e se saleh* (*The Three Year Summation*) (Tehran: OIPFG, 1979).

Idem, Tahlili az yek sal jang-e cheriki dar shahr va kuh (*An Analysis of One Year Guerrilla War in City and Countryside*) (np: np, nd).

REBELS WITH A CAUSE

Asnad-e jonbesh-e Terotekisti-ye Iran (*Iran's Trotskyite Movement Documents*) (New York: Barrasi-e Sosiyalisti, nd).

Asnad va didgahha (*Documents and Perspectives*) (Tehran: Tudeh Publications, 1979).

Asnad va e'lamiyeha-ye hezb-e Tudeh-ye Iran (*Documents and Communiques of the Tudeh Party of Iran*) (Tehran: Tudeh Publications, 1980).

Asrar-e fa'aliyatha-ye zed-e Irani dar kharej az keshvar (*The Secrets Behind Anti-Iranian Activities Abroad*) (np: np, 1976).

Avanessian, Ardeshir (Ardashes), *Khaterat 1320–1326* (*Memoirs 1941–1946*) (Koln, Germany: The People's Democratic Party Publications, 1990).

Bahsi piramun-e bohran dar sazman-e ma (*A Discussion on Crisis in Our Organization*) (Tehran: OIPFG [Left-Wing Majority], 1981).

Barrasi-e sakht-e eqtesadi-e rustaha-ye Fars (*A Study of the Economic Structure of the Villages of Fars*), Rural Studies Series, no. 3 (np: OIPFG, 1973).

Barrasi-e sakht-e eqtesadi-e rustaha-ye Kerman (*A Study of the Economic Structure of the Villages of Kerman*), Rural Studies Series, no. 4 (np: OIPFG, 1978).

Barrasi-e sherkatha-ye sahami-e zera'i (*A Study of the Agricultural Corporations*), Rural Studies Series, no. 2 (np: OIPFG, 1978).

Bayaniyeh-e e'lam-e mavaze'-e ideologik-e sazman-e Mojahedin khalq-e Iran (*Manifesto Declaring the Ideological Position of the Organization of Iranian People's Mojahedin*), vol. 1 (np: Mojahedin Organisation, 1976).

Bayaniyehha-ye amaliyyat-e Jangal (*Communiques of the Jungle Operations*) (Sweden: IPFG [Liberation Army], nd).

Bayat, Kaveh and Tafreshi, Majid (eds), *Khaterat-e doran-e separi shodeh* (*Memoirs of the Bygone Epoch*) (Tehran: Ferdos Publications, 1991).

Bazandeh (*The Loser*) (Minneapolis: Paykar Cell, 1984).

Bazargan, Mehdi, *Enqelab-e Iran dar du harekat* (*Iran's Revolution in Two Motions*) (Tehran: np, 1984).

Beh-azin, A.M. (E'temadzadeh, Mahmud), *Zendegi-ye siyasi-ejtema'i* (*The Socio-political Life*) vol. 2 (Tehran: Jami Publications, 1993).

Beh yad-e A. R. Sabburi (*In Memory of A.R. Sabburi*) (Europe: IPFG [Liberation Army], nd).

Chehre-ye goruhak-e zed-e enqelabi-ye Kumoleh (*Portrait of Anti-Revolutionary Group Kumoleh*) (np: Tudeh Publications, nd).

Cheh nabayad kard (*What is Not to be Done*) (np: Communist Unity Group, 1978).

Chehel sal dar sangar-e mobarezeh (*Forty Years in the Trench of Struggle*) (np: Tudeh Publications, 1981).

Cherik (*Guerrilla*) (np: OIPFG, 1978).

Defa'iat-e Khosrow Roozbeh qahreman-e melli (*The Court Defence of Khosrow Roozbeh, the National Hero*) (Washington DC: Asia Books and Periodicals, 1978).

Dehqani, Ashraf, *Hamaseh-ye moqavemat* (*Epic of Resistance*) (Middle East: National Front Publications, 1974).

218

BIBLIOGRAPHY

Diktatori va tabligh mosalahaneh (qahr) (Dictatorship and Armed Propaganda [Violence]) (np: OIPFG, 1983).

E'lamiyeh tozihi (Explanatory Communique) (np: OIPFG, nd).

E'lamiyeh tozihi-ye mavaze'-e ideolozhik-e goruh-e monsha'eb (The Explanatory Communique of the Ideological Stands of the Splinter Group) (1978).

E'dam-e enqelabi-ye Abbas Shahriari (The Revolutionary Execution of Abbas Shahriari) (np: OIPFG, 1975).

Enqelab-e sosialisti ya demokratik (Socialist or Democratic Revolution) (np: The Communist Unity Group, nd).

Eqtesad beh zaban-e sadeh (Economics in Simple Language) (np: Mojahedin Publications, 1972).

Eqtesad-e shoravi kamelan va qat'an sarmaiehdari (The Soviet Economy Completely and Definitely Capitalistic) (Berkeley, CA: Paykar Organisation, nd).

Eskandari, Iraj, *Khaterat-e siyasi (Political Memoirs)*, ed. Babak Amir-khosravi and Fereidun Azar-nur, 3 vols (Saint Cloud, France: Democratic People's Party of Iran Publications, nd).

Idem, Yadnameh-ha va yaddashtha-ye parakandeh (Memoirs and Scattered Notes) (np: Mard-e Emruz Publications, 1986).

Eslahat-e arzi va nataej-e mostaqim-e an (Land Reform and its Direct Results), Rural Studies Series, no. 1 (np: Tondar Publications, 1978).

Estalinism (Stalinism) (np: Communist Unity, 1979).

Etela'iyeh-ye mehr 57 (The September 1978 Communique) (Marxist Mojahedin, 1978).

Etelaiyeh-ye tozihi-ye zemestan-e 57 (The Explanatory Communique of Winter of 1979) (Marxist Mojahedin, 1979).

E'terafat-e saran-e hezb-e Tudeh-ye Iran (The Confessions of the Leaders of the Tudeh Party of Iran) (Tehran: Negareh Publishers, 1996).

Farzaneh, Hosein, *Parvandeh-ye Panjah va se nafar (The File of the Fifty Three)* (Tehran: Agah Publishers, 1993).

Firouz, Maryam, *Khaterat-e Maryam Firouz (Framan Framaian) (Memoirs of Maryam Firouz Farman Farmaian)* (Tehran: Didgah, 1994).

Goruh-e Ahmadzadeh-Puyan (The Ahmadzadeh-Puyan Group) (np: 19th of Bahman Publications, 1976).

Goruh-e Jazani-Zarifi (The Jazani-Zarifi Group) (np: 19th of Bahman Publications, 1979).

Gozashteh cheragh rah-e ayandeh (The Past is the Light to the Future Path) (np: Jami, nd).

Haydari-bigvand, Turaj, *Te'ori-ye tabliq-e mosalahaneh enheraf az Marxism-Leninism (The Theory of Armed Propaganda, a Deviation from Marxism-Leninism)* (np: OIPFG Splinter Group, 1978).

Ivanov, M.S., *Tarikh-e novin-e Iran (The Modern History of Iran)*, trans. H. Tisabi and H. Ghaempanah, (Stockholm, Sweden: Tudeh Publishing Center, 1977).

Kambakhsh, Abdol Samad, *Nazari beh jonbesh-e kargari dar Iran (A Look at the Working Class Movement in Iran)* (np: Golbarg Publications, nd).

Karnameh-ye hezb-e kargaran-e sosialist (*The History of the Socialist Workers' Party*) (unpublished manuscript).

Kayhan, Mehdi, *Dah sal komak eqtesadi va fani-ye etehad-e shoravi beh Iran 1344–1354* (*Ten Years of Economic and Technical Aid by the Soviet Union to Iran 1965–1975*) (Stockholm, Sweden: Tudeh Publishing Center, 1976).

Kay-maram, Manuchehr, *Rofaqa-ye bala* (*Comrades Above*) (Tehran: Sabaviz, 1995).

Keshavarz, Fereidun, *Man mottaham mikonam* (*I Condemn*) (Tehran: Ravaq Publications, nd).

Ketabche-ye Haqiqat (*The Booklet of Truth*) (Tehran: np, 1998).

Ketab-e siyah (*The Black Book*) (Tehran: Matbu'at Publications, 1955).

Khal'atbari, Farideh, *Kianuri va ede'ahayash* (*Kianuri and His Claims*) (Tehran: Shabaviz, 1994).

Khameh'i, Anvar, *Az enshe'ab ta konun* (*From Split Till Now*) (Saarbrucken, Germany: Navid Publications, nd).

Idem, Forsat-e bozorg-e az dast rafteh (*The Grand Lost Opportunity*) (Saarbrucken, Germany: Navid Publications, nd)

Idem, Panjah nafar va se nafar (*Fifty Persons and Three Persons*) (Saarbrucken, Germany: Navid Publications, nd).

Khanbaba-tehrani, Mehdi, *Negahi az darun beh jonbesh-e chap-e Iran* (*A look From Within at Iran's Left Movement*), ed. Hamid Shokat, 2 vols, (Saarbrucken, Germany: Baztab Publications, 1989).

Kianuri, Nur al-Din, *Goft-o-gu ba Tarikh* (*Diologue With History*) (Tehran: Negareh Publishing and Cultural Institute, 1997).

Idem, Hokm-e tarikh beh pish miravad (*The Judgment of History Goes Forward*) (Tehran: OIPF [Majority] Publications, 1982).

Idem, Khaterat-e Nur al-Din Kianuri (*Memoirs of Nur al-Din Kianuri*) (Tehran: Didgah Institute, 1992).

Kudeta-ye nozheh (*The Nozheh Coup d'etat*) (Tehran: The Institute for Political Studies and Research, 1986).

Javan, F.M., *Cherikha-ye khalq cheh miguyand* (*What Do the People's Guerrillas Say*) (Stassfurt: Tudeh Publishing Center, 1972).

Javanshir, F.M. (Mizani, Farajollah), *Tajrobeh-ye 28 Mordad* (*The Experience of 28 Mordad*) (Tehran: Tudeh Party Publications, 1980).

Jazani, Bizhan, *Cheguneh mobarezeh-ye mosalahaneh tudeh'i mishavad* (*How Armed Struggle Becomes a Mass Movement*) (np: OIPFG, 1978).

Idem, Cheh kesani beh marxism-leninism khiyanat mikonand (*Which Persons Are Betraying Marxism-Leninism*) (np: 19th of Bahman Publications, nd).

Idem, Jam' bandi-e mobarezat-e si saleh-ye akhir dar Iran (*A Summation of the Recent Thirty Year Struggle in Iran*), 2 vols (np: 19th of Bahman Publications, 1975).

Idem, Marxism-e eslami ya eslam-e marxisiti (*Marxist Islam or Islamic Marxism*) (np: Pishro Students, nd).

Idem, Mohre'i bar safhe-ye shatranj (*A Pawn on the Chess Board*) (np: np, 1969).

Idem, Nabard ba diktatori-e shah (*War Against the Shah's Dictatorship*) (np: OIPFG, 1978).

BIBLIOGRAPHY

Idem, Tarh-e jame'eh shenasi va mabani-ye esteratezhi-ye jonbesh-e enqelabi-ye khalq-e Iran (*The Sociological Plan and the Strategic Foundation of Iranian People's Revolutionary Movement*) (Tehran: Mizan Publications, 1979).

Jonbesh-e novin-e komonisti va sazman-e cherikha-ye fada'i khalq (*The New Communist Movement and the OIPFG*) (np: Paykar Organisation, 1980).

Maleki, Khalil, *Khaterat-e siyasi* (*Political Memoirs*) (np: Jebheh, 1981).

Marigla, Carlso, *Jozveh-ye rahnama-ye jang-e cheriki* (*Manual on Guerrilla Warfare*) (np: Bakhtar-e Emrouz Publications, 1970).

Marzha-ye hovyyat-e ma (*Borders of Our Identity*) (Berlin: The Revolutionary Workers Organisation of Iran, 1984).

Masa'el-e had-e jonbesh-e ma (*The Critical Problems of Our Movement*) (np: Mojahedin Publications, 1976).

Mehraban, Rasul, *Gushehha'i az tarikh mo'aser-e Iran* (*Aspects of Iran's Contemperory History*) (np: Atarod Publisjers, 1982).

Mesah, Jalal, *Khosrow Roozbeh ra beshenasid* (*Know Khosrow Roozbeh*) (Tehran: Chaman Publisjers, nd).

Mesl-e barf ab khahim shod: mozakerat-e shora-ye farmandehan-e artesh (*We will Melt Like Snow: Deliberations of the Armed Forces High Command*) (Tehran: Ney Publishers, 1987).

Mobasser, Mohsen, *Pazhuhesh* (*Research*) (London: np, 1996).

Mo'meni, Hamid, *Dar bareh-ye mobarezat-e Kurdestan* (*On the Struggles of Kurdestan*) (Tehran: Shabahang Publications, nd).

Mosaddeq va nehzat-e melli-ye Iran (*Mosaddeq and the National Movement of Iran*) (Solon, Ohio: Society of Islamic Students in America and Canada, 1978).

Mosahebeh ba rafiq Ashraf Dehqani (*Interview With Comrade Ashraf Dehqani*) (np: np, 1979).

Moshkelat va masa'el-e jonbesh (*The Movement's Obstacles and Problems*) (np: The Communist Unity, nd).

Nabard-e Marxism ba opurtunism (*The War of Marxism Against Opportunism*) (np: np, nd).

Nabdel, Ali Reza, *Azarbaijan va mas'aleh-ye melli* (*Azarbaijan and the Problem of Nationalism*) (np: OIPFG, 1977).

Naqdi bar binesh-e hakem bar jenah-e rast-e aksariyyat (*A Critique of the Majority-Right Wing's Perspective*) (Tehran: OIPFG [Left-Wing Majority], 1981).

Nashrieh-ye vizhe-ye bahs-e darun-e du sazman (*Special Bulletin for Intra-Discussions of the Two Organizations*), no. 1 (np: OIPFG, 1976).

Nejati, Gholam Reza, *Tarikh-e bist va panj saleh-ye Iran* (*The Twenty Five Year History of Iran*), 2 vols (Tehran: Rasa Cultural Institute, 1992).

Niknezhad, Mokhtar, *Khaterat-e Jangal* (*Memoirs of Jungle*) (np: OIPF Publications, nd).

Nokati piramun-e mas'aleh-ye anternasionalism-e proleteri (*Few Points on the Problems of Proletarian Internationalism*) (Tehran: OIPFG [Left-Wing Majority], 1981).

Pasokh beh enhelal talaban (*Answer to the Abolitionists*) (np: IPFG [Liberation Army], nd).

Pasokh-e aqaliyyat beh nameh-ye 'Markaziyyat' (*Minority's Answer to the Letter of the 'Central Committee'*) (np: OIPFG, 1980).

Pesiyan, Najafali, *Vaqe'eh-ye 'edam-e Jahansuz* (*The Case of Jahansuz's Execution*) (Tehran: Modabber Publishers, 1991).

Piramun-e taqier-e mavaze'-e ideologik-e Mojahedin-e khalq-e Iran (*On the Ideological Conversion of the People's Mojahedin of Iran*) (np: Iranian National Front Publications Abroad, 1976).

Puyan, Amir Parviz. *Zarurat-e mobarezeh-ye mosalahaneh va rad-e te'ory-ye baqa'* (*The Necessity of Armed Struggle and a Refutation of the Theory of Survival*) (np: OIPFG, 1970).

Qahreman-e melli, jahan pahlevan Takhti (*The National Hero, World Champion Takhti*) (Sacramento, California: Society of Iranian Students, 1970).

Rahnama, Sa'id, *Tajdid hayat-e social demokrasi dar Iran?* (*The Rebirth of Social Democracy in Iran?*) (Spanga, Sweden: Baran Publishers, 1996).

Reqabi, Haydar, *Sah'er-e shar-e ma* (*Our Town's Poet*) (Berkeley CA: np, 1969).

Roozbeh, Khosrow, *Eta'at-e kourkouraneh* (*Blind Obedience*) (Arlington VA: Asia Books, 1978).

Rezazadeh-malek, Rahim, *Haydar Khan Amoughli* (Tehran: Donya Publishers, 1973).

Safa'i-farahani, Ali Akbar, *Ancheh yek enqelabi bayad bedanad* (*What a Revolutionary Must Know*) (np: Ahang Publications, 1979).

Sazmandehi va taktikha (*Organisation and Tactics*) (np: Mojahedin Publications, 1974).

Se bayaniyeh az sazman-e Mojahedin-e khalq (*Three Manifestos by the Organization of People's Mojahedin*) (np: Mojahedin Publications, 1975).

Seyr-e komonizm dar Iran (*The Development of Communism in Iran*) (Tehran: Kayhan Publications, 1957).

Shafaie, Ahmad, *Qiyam-e afsaran-e Khorasan va si va haft sal zendegi dar shoravi* (*The Khorasan Officers Rebellion and Thirty Seven Years Living in the Soviet Union*) (Tehran: Ketab Sara, 1986).

Shakeri, Khosrow (ed.), *Asnad-e tarikhi-ye jonbesh-e kargari, sosial demokrasi va komonisti-ye Iran* (*Historical Documents: The Workers', Social-Democratic and Communist Movement in Iran*), 20 vols (Florence, Italy: Mazdak, 1974).

Shamlu, Ahmad, *Kashefan-e forutan-e shokaran* (*The Humble Discoverer of Hemlock*) (Tehran: Ebtekar Publications, nd).

Sharh-e ta'sis va tarikhcheh-ye vaqaye'-e sazman-e Mojahedin-e khalq-e Iran az sal-e 1344 ta sal-e 1350 (*The History of Establishment and Development of the Organization of People's Mojahedin from 1965 to 1971*) (Tehran: Mojahedin Publications, 1979).

Shoa'ian, Mostafa, *Chand neveshteh* (*Few Writings*) (Florence, Italy: Mazdak Publishers, 1976).

Idem, *Panj nameh-ye sar-goshadeh beh sazman-e cherikha-ye Fada'i khalq* (*Five Open Letters to the OIPFG*) (np: Mazdak Publications, 1979).

Idem, *Pasokha-ye nasanjideh beh 'qadamha-ye sanjideh'* (*Injudicious Replies Against 'Judicious Steps'*) (Florence, Italy: Mazdak Publications, 1976).

BIBLIOGRAPHY

Idem, Sheshomin nameh-ye sar-goshadeh beh sazman-e cherikha-ye Fada'i khalq (*The Sixth Open Letter to the OIPFG*) (Florence, Italy: Mazdak Publications, 1976).

Shohada-ye javidan-e azadi, parchamdaran-e enqelab-e novin-e khalq-e qahreman-e Iran (*The Immortal Martyrs of Liberty, the Standard Bearers of the Heroic People of Iran's New Revolution*) (np: Mojahedin Organisation, 1984).

Shokat, Hamid, *Tarikh-e bist saleh-ye konfederasiun-e jahani-ye mohaselin va daneshjuyan-e Irani (ettehadiyeh melli)* (*A Twenty Year History of the Confederation of Iranian Students [National Union]*) (Saarbruecken, Germany: Baztab Publishers, 1993).

Siyasat va sazman-e hezb-e Tudeh az aqaz ta forupashi (*The Politics and Organization of the Tudeh Party from Beginning to its Disintegration*), vol. 1 (Tehran: The Institute for Political Study and Research, 1991).

Tabari, Ehsanollah, *Bazgasht az marxism* (*Return From Marxism*) (Rome: Islamic Cultural Center in Europe, 1984).

Idem, Kazh raheh, khaterati az hezb-e Tudeh (*The Diverted Path, Memories of the Tudeh Party*) (Tehran: Amir Kabir Publications, 1987).

Idem, Shenakht va sanjesh-e marxism (*Understanding and Evaluation of Marxism*) (Tehran: Amir Kabir Publishers, 1989).

Tafreshian, Abol Hasan, *Qiyam-e afsaran-e Khorasan* (*The Rebellion of Khorasan Officers*) (Tehran: Atlas, 1988).

Taghier va tahavvolat darun-e sazman-e Mojahedin-e khalq-e Iran (*Change and Transition Within the Organisation of Iranian People's Mojahedin*) (np: Organisation of Paykar, 1979).

Tarikh-e hezbe-e komonist-e shoravi (*The History of Soviet Communist Party*) trans. Tudeh Party (np: Tudeh Party Publications, 1979).

Tarikh-e jaryan-e kudetah va nazarati dar bareh-ye khat-e mash-ye konuni-ye saz-man-e Mojahedin-e khalq-e Iran (*A History of the Process of the Coup and Views on the Current Political Line of the Organisation of People's Mojahedin*) (Tehran: Abuzar Publications, 1979).

Tez-e goruh-e Jazani-Zarifi (*The Jazani-Zarifi Group's Thesis*) (np: 19th of Bahman Publications, 1975).

Yazdi, Ebrahim, *Akharin talashha dar akhrin ruzha* (*The Last Efforts During the Last Days*) (Tehran: Qalam Publications, 1984).

Zendegani va mobarezat-e khalq-e torkman (*The Life and Struggle of the Turkman People*) (np: The Central Office of the Turkman Sahra's Councils, 1980).

Zendeh bad hezb-e Tudeh-ye Iran (*Long Live the Tudeh Party of Iran*) (np: OIPFG Splinter Group, 1978).

Zia'-zarifi, Hasan, *Hezb-e Tudeh va kudeta-ye 28 mordad 32* (*The Tudeh Party and the August 19, 1953 Coup*) (np: OIPFG, nd).

Ziba'i, Ali, *Komonizm dar Iran* (*Communism in Iran*) (np: np, 1964).

Articles

Abrahamian, Ervand, 'Fekr-e tute'eh chini 'dar farhang-e Iranian' ('The Thought of "Conspiracy in Iranians" Culture'), *Kankash*, no. 7, Winter 1991, 95–107.

Eskandari, Iraj.,'Daru-ye E'teraf' ('Confession Drug'), *Fasli Dar Gol-e Sorkh*, no. 1, Summer 1985, 30–44.

Idem, 'Hezb-e Tudeh va shoravi' ('The Tudeh Party and the Soviet Union'), *Fasli Dar Gol-e Sorkh*, no. 3, Fall 1986, 11–33.

Falahati, Hamzeh, 'Qesseh-ye raz-e koshandeh-ye Aras' ('The Story of Aras's Deadly Secret'), *Adineh*, no. 67, January 1992, 11–12.

Kianuri, Nur al-Din, 'Az khateratam defa' mikonam' ('I Defend My Memoirs'), *Adineh*, no. 23, September 1993, 12–17.

Khosrow-panah, Mohammad Hosein, 'Baznegari-ye yek vaqe'eh: Qiyam-e Afsaran-e Khorasan' ('Revisiting an Incident: The Rebellion of Khorasan Officers'), *Negah-e No*, no. 32, Spring 1997.

Idem, 'Tarikhche-ye zohur va soqut-e sazman-e afsaran-e hezb-e Tudeh-ye Iran' ('A Brief History of the Rise and Fall of the Officers Organisation of the Tudeh Party of Iran'), *Negah-e No*, no. 33, Summer 1997.

Mo'meni, Baqer M., 'Anban-e mard-e jahandideh' ('The Learnings of an Experienced Man'), *Rah-e Azadi*, no. 27, March 1993, 31–2.

'Mardi tanha' (A Lonely Man) (Alefba, no. 5, Winter 1983, 164-175.

Idem, 'Tarhi az yek tasvir' ('A Sketch of a Portrait'), *Seda-ye Mo'aser*, no. 13, June 1979.

Masali, Hasan, 'Ta'sir-e binesh va manesh dar mobarezeh-ye ejtema'i' ('Influence of Insight and Conduct on Social Struggle') in *The Results of the Wiesbaden Confrence on the Crisis of Iran's Left Movement* (Frankfurt: np, 1985), 40–84.

Mohajer, Naser, 'Gozaresh-e yek jenayat' ('Report on a Murder'), *Noqteh*, no. 1, Spring 1995.

Payman, Morteza, 'Beh Monasebat-e bist va panjomin salgard-e marg-e jahan pahlevan Takhti' ('In Commemoration of World Champion Takhti's Twenty Fifth Anniversary'), *Arash*, no. 12, January 1992, 38–9.

'Sazmandehi-ye mobarezat-e zanan', *Jahan-e No*, nos 2–3, February 1987, 29–34.

Tohidi, Nayereh, 'Mas'aleh-ye zan va roshanfekran tei-ye tahvvolate-e daheha-ye akhir' ('The Issue of Women and Intellectuals During Changes in Recent Decades') *Nimeh-ye Digar*, no. 10, Winter 1990, 50–95.

Ulyanovsky, Rostislav, 'Sarnevesht-e enqelab-e Iran' ('The Fate of Iranian Revolution), trans. Tudeh Party (np: Tudeh Publishers, 1985).

BIBLIOGRAPHY

Newspapers and Journals

Donya, The Political and Theoretical Journal of the Central Committee of the Tudeh Party of Iran, vol. III, no. 6, August 1975; no. 7, September 1975; no. 8, October 1975; no. 11, February 1976; no. 12, February 1976.

Etehad-e Mardom (2 December 1981).

Etehad-e Kar, the central publication of the Organisation of Fadaiyan Unity, no. 52, August 1998.

Ettela'at, 18 June 1973; (25 January 1976; 19 May 1976; 5 May 1979; 26 June 1980; 11 January 1982; 29 January 1983.

Fada'i, OIPF publication, no. 11, 1985.

Iran Times, 9 July 1979.

Jahah-e No, nos 2–3, February 1987.

KAR, OIPF (Majority) publication, no. 62 , June 1980; no. 64, July 1980; no. 73, 27 August 1980; no. 90, 23 December 1980; no. 92, 7 January 1981; no. 101, March 1981; no. 102, April 1981; no. 120, August 1981; no. 121, July 1981; no. 127, February 1982.

KAR, Organisation of Iranian People's Fada'i Guerrillas publication, no. 4, 29 March 1979; no. 5, 5 April 1979; no. 99, March 1980; no. 112, May 1981; no. 122, 12 August 1981; no. 140, December 1981; no. 141, December 1981; no. 142, January 1982; no. 166, April 1983.

KAR, OIPFG (Supreme Council) publication, no. 203, September 1986.

KAR, Theoretical and Political Journal, no. 1, 1983; no. 2, 1983; no. 3, 1984.

Kayhan Hava'i, 31 January 1990; 23 October 1991; 30 October 1991.

Kayhan, 30 December 1972; 11 August 1975.

Mardom-e Mahaneh, Tudeh Party of Iran publication, vol. VI, no. 17 (July 1966).

Mojahed, Organisation of People's Mojahedin of Iran publication, no. 257, August 1985; no. 160, August 1983; no. 161, August 1983; no. 165, September 1983; no. 185, Novemebr 1983; no. 221, September 1984.

Nabard-e Khalq, OIPFG publication, no. 3, March 1974; no. 5, November 1974; no. 7, May 1976.

Nabar-e Khalq, OIPFG (Minority) theoretical journal, no. 1, June 1980; no. 2, December 1980.

Nameh Mardom, Tudeh Party of Iran publication, 4 April 1980; no. 94, 17 November 1979; no. 95, 18 Novemebr 1980; no. 243 , 25 May 1980; no. 241, 22 May 1980; no. 250, 3 June 1979; no. 253, 8 June 1979; no. 273, 26 June 1980; no. 298, 3 July 1980; March 1981.

Noghteh (Paris), no. 1, Spring 1995; no. 7, Spring 1997.

Payam, Iran's Voice of Revolution publication, no. 38, February 1989.

Paykar, Organisation of Paykar publication, no. 3, May 1980; no. 11, 9 July 1979; no. 13, 23 July 1979; no. 15, 6 August 1979; no. 16, August 1979; no. 22, 13 August 1979; no. 26, 17 September 1979; no. 35, 24 December 1979; no. 57, 2 June 1980; no. 62, 7 July 1980; no. 65, 28 July 1980; nos 67–9, 11–25 August 1980; nos 70–84, 1 September to 23 November 1980; no. 93, 9 February 1981; no. 110, 15 June 1981.

225

Rah-e Azadi, no. 24, September–October 1992; no. 26, February 1993.

Ruzegar-e Now (Paris), vol. VI, no. 138, July–August 1993; no. 139, August–September 1993.

Setareh-ye Sorkh, Revolutionary Organisation of the Tudeh Party of Iran political-theoretical publication, no. 1, February 1979.

Setareh-ye Sorkh, Revolutionary Organisation of the Tudeh Party of Iran publication, no. 7, October 1970; no. 18, February 1971; no. 33, January 1974; no. 40, October–November 1974.

Sosialism va Enqelab, no. 3, January 1983; no. 4, September 1983.

Tudeh, Revolutionary Organisation of the Tudeh Party of Iran publication, no. 10, September 1968; no. 12, March 1969; no. 17, January 1970; no. 20, August 1970; no. 21, August 1971; no. 22, February 1972; no. 23, April 1973; no. 24, February 1972.

Tufan, Tufan Organisation Marxist-Leninist publication, no. 21, July 1971; no. 27, July 1972; no. 44, July 1975.

Zaman-e Now, no. 1, October 1983; no. 6, October 1984.

ENGLISH

Abrahamian, Ervand, *Iran Between Two Revolutions* (Princeton: Princeton University Press, 1988).

Idem, Khomeinism (Berkeley, London: University of California Press, 1993).

Idem, Radical Islam: Iranian Mojahedin (London: I.B. Tauris, 1989).

Afshar, Haleh (ed.), *Iran a Revolution in Turmoil* (New York: State University of New York Press).

Alam, Amir Asadollah, *The Shah and I: The Confidential Diary of Iran's Royal Court*, ed. Alinaqi Alikhani (New York: St Martin's Press, 1992).

Akhavi, Shahrough, *Religion and Politics in Contemporary Iran* (Albany: State University of New York Press, 1980).

Altstadt, Audrey L., *The Azerbaijani Turks: Power and Identity under Russian Rule* (Stanford, California: Hoover Institution Press, 1992).

Amir Arjomand, Said, *The Turban for the Crown* (New York, Oxford: Oxford University Press, 1988).

Antoun, Richard and Iliya Harik (eds), *Rural Politics and Social Change in the Middle East* (Bloomington: Indiana University Press, 1972).

Atabaki, Touraj, *Azerbaijan: Ethnicity and Autonomy in the Twentieth-Century Iran* (London: I.B. Tauris, 1993).

Atkin, Muriel, *Russia and Iran 1780–1828* (Minneapolis: University of Minnesota Press, 1980).

Azari, Farah (ed.), *Women of Iran: The Conflict With Fundamentalist Islam* (London: Ithaca Press, 1983).

Azimi, Fakhreddin, *Iran the Crisis of Democracy* (New York: St Martin's Press, 1989).

BIBLIOGRAPHY

Bakhash, Shaul, *The Reign of the Ayatollahs* (New York: Basic Books, 1984).
Bayat, Assef, *Street Politics: Poor People's Movement in Iran* (New York: Columbia University Press, 1997).
Idem, Workers and Revolution in Iran (London: Zed Books Ltd., 1987).
Bill, James A., *The Eagle and the Lion* (London, New Haven: Yale University Press, 1988).
Brzezinski, Zbigniew, *Power and Principle* (New York: Strauss Giroux, 1983).
Carter, Jimmy, *Keeping Faith: Memoirs of a President* (Toronto, New York: Bantam Books, 1982).
Chaliand, Gerard (ed.), *People Without a Country* (London: Zed Press 1978).
Chaqueri, Cosroe, *Avetis Sultanzade: the Forgotten Revolutionary Theoretician* (Tehran: Padzahr, 1985).
Idem, The Soviet Socialist Republic of Iran, 1920–1921: Birth of a Trauma (Pittsburgh and London: University of Pittsburgh Press, 1995).
Chehabi, Hushang H., *Iranian Politics and Religion Modernism: the Liberation Movement Under the Shah and Khomeini* (Ithaca: Cornell University Press, 1990).
Claudin, Fernando, *The Communist Movement: From Comintern to Cominform*, vol. II (London, New York: Monthly Review Press, 1975).
Cohen Stephen F., *Rethinking the Soviet Experience, Politics and History Since 1917* (New York, Oxford: Oxford University Press, 1985).
Confessions of the Central Cadres of the Tudeh Party (Tehran: Islamic Propaganda Organisation, 1983).
Dabashi, Hamid, *Theology of Discontent: The Ideological Foundation of the Islamic Revolution in Iran* (New York, London: New York University Press, 1993).
Farsoun, Samith K. and Mehrdad Mashayekhi (eds), *Iran: Political Culture in the Islamic Republic* (New York: Routledge, 1992).
Galdino, Rinaldo, *Report on the Human Rights in the Islamic Republic of Iran* (New York: UN Economic and Social Council, 1990).
Gasiorowski, Mark J., *US Policy and the Shah: Building A Client State in Iran* (Ithaca, NY: Cornell University Press, 1991).
Hooglund, Eric, *Land and Revolution in Iran* (Austin, Texas: University of Texas Press, 1982).
History of the Communist Party of the Soviet Union (Bolsheviks) (San Francisco: Proletarian Publishers, 1976).
Izady, Mehrdad R., *The Kurds: A Concise Handbook* (Washington, London: Taylor & Francis, 1992).
Jazani, Bizhan, *Capitalism and Revolution in Iran* (London, Zed Press, 1976).
Jordan, Hamilton, *Crisis: The Last Year of Carter Presidency* (New York: Putam, 1982).
Katouzian, Homa, *Musaddiq and the Struggle For Power in Iran* (London, New York: I.B. Tauris, 1990).
Keddie, Nikki R., *Iran and the Muslim World* (New York: New York University Press, 1995).

227

Keddie, Nikki R. and Eric Hoogland (eds), *The Iranian Revolution and the Islamic Republic* (Syracuse: Syracuse University Press, 1986).

Keddie, Nikki R. (ed.), *Religion and Rebellion in Iran* (New Haven: Yale University Press, 1983).

Keddie, Nikki R., *Roots of Revolution: An Interpretive History of Modern Iran* (London, New Haven: Yale University Press, 1981).

Keddie, Nikki R. and Mark J. Gasiorowski (eds), *Neither East Nor West: Iran, The Soviet Union, And The United States* (New Haven, London: Yale University Press, 1990).

Keddie, Nikki R. and Juan R.I. Cole (eds), *Shi'ism and Social Protest* (New Haven: Yale University Press, 1986).

Kian-Thiebaut, Azadeh, *Secularisation of Iran: a Doomed Failure?* (Paris: Peeters and Institute d'etudes iraniennes, 1998).

Kuzichkin, Vladimir, *Inside the KGB: My Life in Soviet Espionage*, trans. Thomas B. Beattie (New York: Pantheon Books, 1990).

Ladjevardi, Habib, *Labor Unions and Autocracy in Iran* (Syracuse: Syracuse University Press, 1985).

Idem, Reference Guide to the Iranian Oral History Collection (Harvard University, 1987).

Matin-asgari, Afshin, 'The Iranian Student Movement Abroad: The Confederation of Iranian Students, National Union 1960–1978', PhD dissertation, University of California at Los Angeles, 1993.

McDowall, David, *A Modern History of the Kurds* (London, New York: I.B. Tauris, 1997).

Milani, Mohsen M., *The Making of Iran's Islamic Revolution: From Monarchy to Islamic Republic* (London, Boulder: Westview Press, 1988).

Moghissi, Haideh, *Populism and Feminism in Iran* (London: St Martin's Press, 1994).

Najmabadi, Afsaneh, *Land and Social Change in Iran* (Salt Lake City: University of Utah Press, 1987).

Nashat, Guity (ed.), *Women and Revolution in Iran* (Boulder CO: Westview Press, 1983).

Nissman, David B., *The Soviet Union and Iranian Azerbaijan: The Use of Nationalism for Political Penetration* (London: Westview Press, 1980).

Organisation of Revolutionary Workers of Iran: A Short Introduction (France: Organisation of Revolutionary Workers of Iran Publication, nd).

Pahlavi, Mohammad Reza, *Answer to History* (New York: Stein and Day Publishers, 1980).

Parsons, Anthony, *The Pride and the Fall: Iran 1974–1979* (London: Jonathan Cape, 1984).

Sanasarian, Eliz, *The Women's Rights Movement in Iran: Mutiny, Appeasement and Repression from 1900 to Khomeini* (New York: Praeger Publishers, 1982).

Shawcross, William, *The Shah'e Last Ride: The Fate of an Ally* (New York: Simon and Schuster, 1988).

BIBLIOGRAPHY

Sick, Gary, *All Fall Down: America's Tragic Encounter With Iran* (London: Penguin Books, 1986).

Sicker, Martin, *The Bear and the Lion: Soviet Imperialism and Iran* (New York: Praeger, 1988).

Sullivan, William H., *Mission to Iran* (London, New York: W.W. Norton, 1981).

Solodovnikov, V. and V. Bogoslovsky, *Non-Capitalist Development: An Historical Outline* (Moscow: Progress Publishers, 1975).

Stalin, J.V., *Works*, vol. X (Moscow: Foreign Languages Publishing House, 1954).

Tabari, Azar (Najmabadi, Afsaneh) and Nahid Yeganeh (eds), *In the Shadow of Islam: The Women's Movement in Iran* (London: Zed Press, 1982).

Tulsiram, *The History of Communist Movement in Iran* (Bopal, India: Grafix, 1981).

Yodfat, Aryah Y., *The Soviet Union and Revolutionary Iran* (London, Canberra: Croom Helm, 1984).

Zabih, Sepehr, *Ci* (Berkeley, Los Angeles: University of California Press, 1966).

Idem, The Left in Contemporary Iran (Stanford, California: Hoover Institution Press, 1986).

Zonis, Marvin, *Majestic Failure: The Fall of the Shah* (Chicago and London: The University of Chicago Press, 1991).

Articles

Abrahamian, Ervand, 'Communism and Communalism in Iran: The Tudeh Party and the Firqah-i Dimukrat', *International Journal of Middle East Studies*, no. 1, 1970, 291–316.

Abrahamian, Ervand and Farhad Kazemi, 'The Nonrevolutionary Peasantry of Modern Iran', *Iranian Studies*, vol. XI, 1978, 259–303.

Akhavi, Shahrough, 'Soviet Perceptions of Iranian Revolution', *Iranian Studies*, vol. XIX, no. 1, Winter 1986, 3–29.

Alaolmolki, Nozar, 'The New Iranian Left', *Middle East Journal*, vol. 41, no. 2, Spring 1987, 218–33.

Bakhash, Shaul. 'Iran', *American Historical Review*, vol. 96, no. 5, December 1991, 1479–96.

Behrooz, Maziar, 'Factionalism in Iran Under Khomeini', *Middle East Studies*, vol. 27, no. 4, October 1991, 597–614.

Idem, 'Iran's Fadayan 1971–1988: A Case Study in Iranian Marxism', *Jusur*, vol. 6, 1990, 1–39.

Chaqueri, Cosroe, 'Iradj Eskandary and the Tudeh Party of Iran', *Central Asian Survey*, vol. 7, no. 4, 1988, 101–33.

Chehabi, Houchang, 'Sport and Politics in Iran: The Legend of Gholamreza Takhti', *International Journal of the History of Sport*, December 1995, 48–60.

229

Dailami, Pezhman, 'The Bolshevik Revolution and the Genesis of Communism in Iran, 1917–1920', *Central Asian Survey*, vol. 11, no. 3, 1992, 51–82.

Gasiorowski, Mark J., 'The 1953 Coup d'etat in Iran', *International Journal of Middle East Studies*, vol. 19, no. 3, August 1987.

Idem, 'The Qarani Affair and Iranian Politics', *International Journal of Middle East Studies*, vol. 25, no. 4, November 1993, 625–44.

Hottinger, Arnold, 'The Shah and Iran's Constitution', *Swiss Review of World Affairs*, no. 28, July 1978.

Kian, Azadeh, 'The Tudeh Party of Iran: Political Violence or Political Legalism', *Jusur*, vol. 8, 1992, 69–89.

Milani, Mohsen, 'Harvest of Shame: Tudeh and the Bazargan Government', *Middle Eastern Studies*, vol. 29, no. 2, April 1993, 305–20.

Mirsepassi-Ashtiani, Ali and M. Moghadam, Valentine, 'The Left and Political Islam in Iran: A Retrospect and Prospects', *Radical History Review*, no. 51, 1991, 27–62.

Nikazmerad, Nicholas M., 'A Chronological Survey of the Iranian Revolution', *Iranian Studies*, vol. XIII. no. 1-4, 1980, 327–68.

Ulyanovsky, Rostislav, 'The Iranian Revolution and its Peculiar Features', *Socialism Theory and Practice*, no. 2, February 1983, 97–104.

Newspapers and Journals

Current Digest of Soviet Press, no. 36, 14 October 1978; no. 46, 13 December 1978; no. 1, 31 January 1979; no. 3, 14 February 1979; no. 6, 14 March 1979.

New York Times, 20 November 1986.

San Francisco Chronicle, 12 April 1971.

Time, 25 May 1970.

US News and World Report, 27 January 1967.

INTERVIEWS AND CORRESPONDENCE

Allamehzadeh, Reza, letter to author, 11 November 1997.

Amini, Mohammad, telephone conversation with author, Los Angeles, California, 19 April 1993.

Behrouz, Jahangir, interview with author, London 13 July 1991.

Khosravi-azarbaijani, Hozhabr, interview with author, London, 18 August 1990.

Madani, Mostafa, interview with author, Irvin, California, 2 January 1992.

Mahfuzi, Ali Reza, Iranian Oral History Collection, Harvard University, 1987.

Mo'meni, Mohammad Baqer, interview with author, Los Angeles, California, 10 May 1993.

Oney, Ernest R., letter to author, 2 September 1993.
Qoreishi, Amanollah, interview with author, London, 7 August 1990; 20 July 1992.
Safizadeh, Ramin, interview with author, Berkeley, 5 January, 1998.
Shakeri, Ali, telephone conversation with author, Los Angeles, California, 10 April 1993.
Shokat, Parviz, interview with author, Berkeley, 18 September 1997.

INDEX

Abbasi, Cap. Abol Hasan 20
Abedini, Qasem 121
Abrahamian, Ervand xvii, 139, 155
Acheson, Dean 8
Afzali, Capt. Bahram 129
Ahmadi, Afkham 121
Ahmadi-osku'i, Marzieh 64
Ahmadzadeh-heravi, Mastureh
   (A'zam) 119
Ahmadzadeh-heravi, Mas'ud
   43–45, 51–57, 59–60, 62–63,
   65–66, 86–87, 106, 108–109, 120,
   139
AJAX 3
Akhavi, Shahrough 127
Aladpush, Morteza 121
Alam, Amir Asadollah 35, 41, 82
Alavi, Morteza xv
Ali-abadi, Fereidun 92
Aliev, Haydar 84
Aliev, Rostam 22
Allamehzadeh, Muhammad Reza
   70
Amini, Ali 8, 35
Amini, Muhammad 92
Amir-Arjomand, Said 136
Amirkhizi, Ali 27–28
Amuoghlu, Haydar Khan xv
Aqazi-No (publication) 118
Aram, Bahram 71–73
Arani, Taqi xv
Arman-e Khalq 46

Asadian, Siyamak (Eskandar)
   116–117
Ashraf, Hamid 44, 52, 54, 60,
   62–68, 73, 91, 106, 117, 144, 146
Avanessian, Ardeshir(Ardashes)
   xv, 16–17, 22, 28,
Avareh, Mollah 41
Azar, Col. Muhammad Ali 13
Azarbaijan Democratic Party
   (ADP) 3–4, 24, 26–29, 31, 37, 42,
   74–75, 78, 80, 83, 84, 125,
   130–131, 145
Azarbaijan Province Committee
   (APC) 27–28
Azarbaijan Toiler's Organisation 27
Azmaiesh, Abdol Rahman 133

Bahonar, Muhammad Javad
   (Hojjat al-Islam) 102
Bahrami, Muhammad 11, 12, 21,
   143
Bakhtiar, Shapour 99
Bani-sadr, Abol Hasan 102, 112,
   114–115
Baqa'i, Mozaffar 8, 32–33,
Baqerov, Ja'far 22, 24, 26, 29
Barzani, Molla Mostafa 49
Batha'i, Teifur 70
Bayat, Asef 148–149, 155, 158
Bazargan, Mehdi 37, 102, 112
Beheshti, Muhammad Hosein
   (Ayatollah) 102

Behkish, Muhammad Reza 118
Behmanesh, Sima, 67
Behrangi, Samad 45
Behrouz, Jahangir 81–82
Behrouzi, Zhaleh 92
Beria, Lavrenti, P. 22, 24–25
Besui-ye Ayandeh (publi-cation) 9
Blurian, Ghani 115, 130–131
Bolshevik xiv, 37, 141, 159, 160
Borujerdi, Muhammad Hosein
   (Grand Ayatollah) 8
Bozorg, Abbas 92
Brezhnev, Leonid I. 49, 160
Brzezinski, Zbigniew 99

Carter, Jimmy 96–99,
CENTO 2
CIA 1, 3, 25, 126, 129
Cheshm-azar, Qasem 28–30
Comintern xiv, 3, 22,
Communists for Unity and
   Struggle 131
Communist Party of Iran
   (Sarbedaran) 93, 120, 122, 133
Communist Party of Iran (CPI)
   120, 124, 131
Communist Unity 66, 73, 91–92,
   132, 159–160
Confederation of Iranian Students
   Abroad 46, 90–94, 97,
Cohen, Stephen 159
CPSU (Communist Party of the
   Soviet Union) 23, 25, 28, 30, 84,
   126–128, 144, 159–161

Dadgar, Farzad 67
Daneshian, Gholam Yahya 28, 30,
   75, 125

Daneshian, Karamatollah 69–70
Davar, Ali Akbar xiv
Debray, Regis 53
Dehqan, Ahmad 20
Dehqani, Ashraf 66, 68, 108–109
Dehqani, Behrouz 45, 66
Deutscher, Issac 160
Donya (publication) xv, 81
Dubchek, Alexander 130

Elm va Zendegi (publi-cation) 33
Eprime, Eshaq 32
Equality (publication) 107
Eskandani, Maj. Ali Akbar 13–15, 21
Eskandari, Iraj 16, 18, 20, 24, 38–39,
   74–76, 70–80, 82–84, 125, 145, 162
Eskandari, Soleiman Mirza 4

Fada'i (publication) 116
Fada'i's Path 69
Fadaiyan (ADP) 28
Fadaiayn (Ashraf Dehqani) 109, 120
Fadaiyan (In Search of Identity) 120
Fadaiyan (Islamic) xiv, 8
Fadaiyan (Left Wing-Majority) 112,
   114, 118
Fadaiyan (Liberation Army) 120
Fadaiyan (Majority) 111–117, 123,
   125–129, 137, 145–146, 151–152,
   154, 159, 161
Fadaiyan (Minority) 111–112, 114,
   117–120, 123, 128, 132, 134, 138,
   152–154
Fadaiyan (Guerrillas) 45–46, 51–55,
   59–69, 73, 79, 86–92, 95,
   104–109, 111, 114–117, 123, 125,
   132, 138, 140, 144–148, 151,
   154–157, 160–162

INDEX

Fadaiyan (Socialist Revolutionaries) 119–120, 134
Farah, Empress (Diba) 96
Farkhondeh, Muhammad Ali (Ali Keshtgar) 109, 116
Farsiu, Gen. Zeinolabedin 62
Fateh-yazdi, Muhammad Sadeq 63
Fazel, Mohsen 121, 123
Firouz, Maryam 24, 143
Ford, Gerald 96
Forutan, Gholam Hosein 17, 19, 143

Gas-Golsha'ian 7, 9
Gasiorowski, Mark 25
Gholamian-langerudi, Ahmad (Hadi) 68, 118
Glostnost 134
Golesorkhi, Khosrow 69–70
Golestan (treaty) 26
Gorbachev, Mikhail S. xvi, 134
GPU 22, 24
Group of Fifty Three xv, 3, 17, 75

Haqiqat (publication) 93, 133
Haqshenas, Torrab 70, 72–73, 121
Harriman, Averell 9
Hashemi, Abbas 108, 118–119
Hashemi-rafsanjani, Ali Akbar (Hojjat al-Islam) 102
Hatefi, Rahman 77, 125
Haydar 112, 117
Haydari-bigvand, Turaj 67
Hekmat, Bizhan 40
Hekmatju, Parviz 39
Hesabi, Abdol Hosein xv,
Hezbollah 107
Hormati-pur, Muhammad 66–68, 109, 120

Hoveida, Amir Abbas 81
Hussein, Saddam 49
Huyser, Robert 99

Iran Labour Party 133
Iranian Communist Party (ICP) xiv, xv, 3, 26
Islamic Republic Party (IRP) 102, 122, 150, 163

Ja'fari, Ali Akbar 66
Ja'fari, Hadi 89
Jazani, Bizhan 43, 45, 48, 51–63, 65, 67–69, 87, 106, 109, 138, 140, 147, 161–162
Joudat, Hosein 12, 18, 21, 80, 143

Kadrha 41
Kalantari, Khosrow 91
Kambakhsh, Abdol Samad xv, 13, 17, 19–21, 23–24, 38, 41, 74–75
Kamenev, Lev B. 160
Kamiabi, Akbar (Abbas Tavakkol) 117–120
Kand va Kav (publication) 93–94
Kar (publication) 109–111, 116–117, 119, 153
Karimi, Naser 46
Karimi, Rahman 115
Kashani, Abol Qasem (Ayatollah) xiv, 8,
Kasravi, Ahmad 92
Katira'i, Homayoun 46
Kavtaradze, Sergei 5,
Kayhan (publication) 77
Keddie, Nikki R. 139
Kennedy (administration) 34–35

Keshavarz, Fereidun 18–21, 23–24,
KGB 22–23, 25, 75, 100, 126–127,
129, 162
Khaksar, Naser 46
Khameh'i, Anvar 32
Khameneh'i, Ali (Hojjat al-Islam)
102
Khanbaba-tehrani, Mehdi 40–41,
144
Khavari, Ali 39
Khomeini, Ruhollah al-Musavi
(Grand Ayatollah) xiv, 35–36,
80, 83, 95–98, 100–103, 109,
112–115, 124, 163
Khonji, Ali 32
Khosravi-azarbaijani, Hozhabr 93,
134
Khrushchev, Nikita S. 25, 60, 160
Kian, Azadeh 155
Kianuri, Nur al-Din 12, 14, 16–21,
23, 25, 41, 74–77, 79–80, 82–85,
124–125, 127–130, 142–143, 162
Kissinger, Henry 49
Komonist (publication) 92–93, 131
Kosari, Hamid 92
Kuchak-shushtari, Mahmud 11
Kumoleh (Revolutionary Toiler's
Organisation of Iranian
Kurdestan) 122–123, 131–132
Kurdestan (publication) 131
Kurdestan Democratic Party
(KDP) 122–123, 126, 130–132, 146
Kuzichkin, Vlademir 100, 128–129

Lahroudi, Amir Ali 28, 125
Ladjevardi, Habib 149
Lankarani (brothers) 25
Lankarani, Hesam 20, 143

Lasha'i, Kurosh 40–41, 88
Lenin, Vlademir I. 59, 87, 127,
160–161
Liberation Movement xiv, 102,
Liberation of Women (publication)
107
Louis, XVI (King) 96

Madani, Mostafa 46, 112, 118
Mahfuzi, Ali Reza 118
Majles (Iranian parliament) 2, 5–8,
23, 29, 49
Maktabi 102–104, 112–115, 126,
132–133, 146, 151, 163
Maleki, Khalil 4, 17, 31, 32–33
Malenkov, Greorgy, M. 25
Mansur, Hasan Ali 49
Mansur, Parviz 145
Mao Zedong 19, 41–42, 45, 58, 60,
72, 84, 89–91, 121, 141
Mard-e Emrooz (publication) 20
Mardom (publication) 9,
Mardom Barai–e Roshanfekran
(publi-cation) 6
Marigla, Carlos 140
Masali, Hasan 66–67, 72, 91
Mashayekhi, Mehrdad 138
Mas'ud, Muhammad 20
Ma'sumzadeh, Muhammad
Hosein 39
Mazandarani, Hashem 92
Meftahi, Abbas 44–45, 62
Menshevik 19
MI6 1, 25, 129
Militant Workers 91
Military Governor of Tehran 11, 12,
Military Organisation 12–13, 16,
19, 20, 84, 106

INDEX

Modarres, Hasan (Ayatollah) xiv
Modir-shaneh-chi, Mohsen 118
Mo'ini, Abdollah 41
Mojahedin (Marxist) 70–73, 92,
  121, 132, 155, 157, 161
Mojahedin (Moslem) 61–61, 65,
  70–73, 91–92, 95, 103, 113–115,
  118–121, 158, 162–163
Mo'meni, Baqer 143
Mo'meni, Hamid 52, 61, 64, 91, 160
Montaqemi, Fereidun 91
Montazeri, Hasan Ali (Ayatollah)
  102
MOSAD 1,
Mosaddeq, Muhammad
  xiv, 1, 5–10, 15–16,
  18–19, 23, 32, 33, 35, 104
Mosavat 26
Muhammad Reza Shah (Pahlavi) 1,

Nabard-e Khalq (publication) 65, 120
Nabdel, Ali Reza 45, 61
Naderpour, Nader 32
Nahavandi, Cyrus 88
Najmabadi, Afsaneh (Azar Tabari)
  34, 94
Nasiri, Lt Gen. Ne'matollah 49
National Council of Resistance 120
National Front 5, 7–11, 15, 18, 91
National Front (Second) 33, 83
National League of Women 107
Navid (publication) 67, 77, 125
Nazari, Ebrahim 121
Nazari, Hasan 84–85
Nayyeri, Iraj 145
Nazm-e Kargar (publi-cation) 119
Negahdar, Farrokh 106, 109, 116
Nikkhah, Parviz 40

Niktab', Maj. Alinaqi 63
Niru-ye Sevom
  (publication) 32
Nixon, Richard (doctrine) 48–49,
  84, 96
Noruzi, Davoud 80, 82
Nozheh (coup)126

Olovvi, Ali 11–12, 21,
Organisation for the Liberation of
  the Iranian People 87
Organisation of Com-munist Unity
  92, 132
Organisation of Freedom of
  Labour 117
Organisation of Revolutionary
  Communists 92–93, 133

Padegan, Ali 28
Pak-nezhad, Shokrollah 46
Pakravan, Gen. Hasan 49
Palestine Group 46
Panjeh-shahi, Abdollah 68
Partovi, Muhammad Mehdi 77,
  125, 129
Party of Labour 91
Paykar 72, 104, 121–123, 133, 138,
  148, 153–154, 156–158
People's Democratic Front 64, 66
Pishehvari, Ja'far (Javadzadeh) xv,
  26–27
Pishmargeh 131
Pishrow (publication) 131
Pravda (publication) 100–101
Perestroika 134
Proseh 46
Puyan, Amir Parviz 43–45, 51–52,
  54, 56, 59, 62, 65, 86

237

Qajar xiv, 4, 26, 75, 104
Qalambar, Hosein 67
Qashqa'i, Bahman 41
Qasemi, Ahmad 16, 19, 90, 143
Qasemlu, Abdol Rahman 130
Qavam, Ahmad 5, 29
Qoreishi, Amanollah 11, 12, 17, 143

Rad, Behrouz 46
Radmanesh, Reza 16, 18, 21, 38, 41, 74–75, 76–77, 125, 143
Raha'i (publication) 132
Rah-e Kargar (publication); 132
Rahimi, Hormoz 93, 134
Rahim-pur, Qorban Ali (Majid) 68
Rahnama, Sa'id 164
Ramzi, Hasan 39
Ranjbar (publication) 133
Ranjbaran 133–134
Rastakhiz (party) 49
Revolutionary Organisation of the Tudeh Party Of Iran (ROTPI) 40–42, 56–58, 74, 4, 87–90, 93, 133, 140, 143–144
Reza Shah (Pahlavi) xiv, xv, 3, 7, 13, 17, 27, 104
Reza'i, Reza 71
Rezvani, Mohsen 40
Roozbeh, Khosrow 1, 11–14, 20
Ruhani, Hosein 70, 72–73, 121, 123

Sa'adati, Ali (Sanjar) 90–91
Sabburi, Abdol Rahim 109, 120
Sa'ed (Premier) 5–7, 23
Safa'i-farahani, Ali Aakbar 44, 51–52, 54, 60–62
Saffari, Hamid 80
Saffari-ashtiani, Muhammad 44, 62

Sagha'i, Hasan 41–42, 143
Salakhanian, Vartan (Balakhian) 11
Salehi, Fariborz 67
Samadieh-labbaf, Morteza 71
Samakar, Abbas Ali 70
Same', Mehdi 118–120
Sari'olqalam, Farid 133
Sari'olqalam, Vahid 133
SAVAK 1, 11, 38–39, 41, 44–46, 49–50, 62–63, 66, 70–71, 73–74, 77, 82, 84, 88, 98
Sayyad-shirazi, Brig. Gen. Ali 115
Semnani, Faramarz 92
Sepasi-ashtiani, Ali Reza 72–73, 121, 123
Setareh-ye Sorkh (publication) 40, 88
Shabestari, Ali 28
Shahed (publication) 32
Shahram, Muhammad Taqi 71–73, 121–122
Shamlu, Ahmad 11–12
Shahriarinezhad (Shahriari) Abbas Ali 39, 44, 63, 74
Shari'atmadari, Kezem (Grand Ayatollah) 83
Sharif-vaqefi, Majid 71, 122
Sharifzadeh 41
Sharmini, Nader 11, 12, 16, 18, 143
Shaygan-shamasbi, Nader 64
Shoa'ian, Mostafa 46, 63–64, 109, 144, 161
Shokat, Hamid 92
Shokat, Parviz 92
Showra 149–151
Siyadati, Qasem 68
Siyahkal 51–52, 54, 61–62, 68, 70, 86, 91, 145
Siyamak, Col. Ezatollah xv, 12–13

INDEX

Socialist Worker's Party 119, 134

Stalin, Josef, V. 19, 22–23, 25, 29, 41, 91, 148, 158, 160–161

Sullivan, William 99

Sultan-pur, Sa'id 116

Sultanzadeh, Avetis xv

Tabari, Ehsanollah 17, 19–21, 24–25, 31, 39, 80, 130, 161–162

Tajir-riahi, Hosein (Puya) 46, 93, 133

Takhti, Gholam Reza 44, 46

Taqizadeh, Hasan xiv, 7,

Taqva'i, Ahmad 92

Tarreh-gol, Hushang 46

Third Force 3, 17, 32, 33

Tito (Marshal) 33

Toilers Party 32–33

Trotsky, Leon D. 93, 158

Truman (administration) 8,

Tudeh (party) xv, xvi, 3–6, 8–9, 11–12, 14–20, 22–24, 26–31, 37–42, 46, 50, 55–58, 60, 62, 67, 73–75, 76–83, 85–90, 94, 97, 104, 106, 110–116, 121, 123–133, 136–137, 142–152, 154–157, 159–163

Tudeh (publication) 40, 88

Tufan 42, 74, 84, 87, 89, 90, 93, 133

Tufan (publication) 90–91, 133

Turkman People's Councils 108

Turkmanchai (treaty) 26, 145

Ulyanovsky, Rostislav 127–128

Vosuqi, Naser 32

Women and Struggle (publication) 107

Women's Emancipation 107

Worker's Path 69, 132

Yazdi, Fereidun 38

Yazdi, Hosein 38

Yazdi, Morteza 11, 12, 18, 21, 38, 41, 143

Zabih, Sepehr xvi, xvii

Zahedi, Gen. Fazlollah 8, 14

Zahra'i, Babak 94, 134

Za'im, Siyamak 92, 133

Zia'-Zarifi, Hasan 43, 45, 51–52, 57, 62, 65

Zohari, Hosein (Bahram) 119

Zolanvar, Kazem 71

Zomorrodi, Leila 71

239

Printed in the USA
CPSIA information can be obtained
at www.ICGtesting.com
LVHW021631050424
776549LV00001B/145